Retranslation

Bloomsbury Advances in Translation Series

Series Editor:
Jeremy Munday, Centre for Translation Studies, University of Leeds, UK

Bloomsbury Advances in Translation Studies publishes cutting-edge research in the field of translation studies. This field has grown in importance in the modern, globalized world, with international translation between languages a daily occurrence. Research into the practices, processes and theory of translation is essential and this series aims to showcase the best in international academic and professional output.

Other titles in the series:

Corpus-Based Translation Studies
Edited by Alet Kruger, Kim Wallmach & Jeremy Munday

Global Trends in Translator and Interpreter Training
Edited by Séverine Hubscher-Davidson & Michał Borodo

Music, Text and Translation
Edited by Helen Julia Minors

Quality In Professional Translation
Joanna Drugan

The Pragmatic Translator
Massimiliano Morini

Translation, Adaptation and Transformation
Edited by Laurence Raw

Translation and Translation Studies in the Japanese Context
Edited by Nana Sato-Rossberg & Judy Wakabayashi

Translation as Cognitive Activity
Fabio Alves & Amparo Hurtado Albir

Translating For Singing
Mark Herman & Ronnie Apter

Translation, Humour and Literature
Edited by Delia Chiaro

Translation, Humour and the Media
Edited by Delia Chiaro

Translating the Poetry of the Holocaust
Jean Boase-Beier

Retranslation

Translation, Literature and Reinterpretation

Sharon Deane-Cox

Bloomsbury Advances in Translation

Bloomsbury Academic
An imprint of Bloomsbury Publishing Plc

B L O O M S B U R Y
LONDON • OXFORD • NEW YORK • NEW DELHI • SYDNEY

Bloomsbury Academic
An imprint of Bloomsbury Publishing Plc

50 Bedford Square
London
WC1B 3DP
UK

1385 Broadway
New York
NY 10018
USA

www.bloomsbury.com

BLOOMSBURY and the Diana logo are trademarks of Bloomsbury Publishing Plc

First published 2014
Paperback edition first published 2016

British Library Cataloguing-in-Publication Data
A catalogue record for this book is available from the British Library.

ISBN: HB: 978-1-4411-4734-9
PB: 978-1-4742-7547-7
ePDF: 978-1-4411-5466-8
ePub: 978-1-4725-8508-0

Library of Congress Cataloging-in-Publication Data
Deane-Cox, Sharon.
Retranslation : translation, literature and reinterpretation / Sharon Deane-Cox.
pages cm
ISBN 978–1–4411–4734–9 (hardback) – ISBN 978–1–4411–5466–8 (epdf) –
ISBN 978–1–4725–8508–0 (epub) 1. Translating and interpreting–Methodology. 2. Translating and interpreting–Evaluation. 3. Literature–Translations–History and criticism. I. Title.
P306.2.D43 2014
418'.04 – dc23
2014003415

Series: Bloomsbury Advances in Translation

Typeset by Integra Software Services Pvt. Ltd.

For Simon

Contents

List of Tables

Series Editor's Preface

This series provides an outlet for advanced research in the broad interdisciplinary field of translation studies. Consisting of monographs and edited themed collections of the latest work, it is of particular interest to academics and postgraduate students researching in translation studies and related fields, and also to advanced students studying translation and interpreting modules

Translation studies has enjoyed huge international growth over recent decades in tandem with the expansion in both the practice of translation globally and in related academic programmes. The understanding of the concept of translation itself has broadened to include not only interlingual but also various forms of intralingual translation. Specialized branches or subdisciplines have developed for the study of interpreting, audio-visual translation and sign language, amongst others. Translation studies has also come to embrace a wide range of types of intercultural encounter and transfer, interfacing with disciplines as varied as applied linguistics, comparative literature, computational linguistics, creative writing, cultural studies, gender studies, philosophy, postcolonial studies, sociology and so on. Each provides a different and valid perspective on translation, and each has its place in this series.

This is an exciting time for translation studies, and the Bloomsbury Advances in Translation Studies series is an important plank in the development of the discipline. As General Editor, I look forward to overseeing the publication of more important new work that will provide insights into all aspects of the field.

Jeremy Munday
General Editor
University of Leeds, UK

Acknowledgements

Or, how this book came to be. For this book is not the result of an individual effort; instead, it has grown out of the guidance, support, advice and patience of many inspiring people, to whom I owe a huge debt of gratitude. My unreserved thanks goes first to those who have supervised, examined, read and commented on my doctoral thesis which is at the origin of this book: Peter Dayan, Charlotte Bosseaux, Ian Mason and Marion Schmid. Also, none of this would have been possible without the assistance of the Arts and Humanities Research Council, whose Doctoral Award allowed me to pursue this work. I am further grateful to the publishers of *Essays in French Literature and Culture*, who have kindly granted me permission to reprint an article I wrote in 2012. I would particularly like to express how appreciative I am of the editorial guidance so generously and insightfully given to me by Jeremy Munday and by the rest of the team at Bloomsbury.

Above all, my wholehearted thanks go to my family for their unwavering encouragement over the years, and for all the much-needed distractions in the forms of travel, food and laughter. And a very special thanks to my husband, Simon, whose love and support never changes, and is never daunted.

List of Abbreviations

General

CF	Character Focalizer
CV	Character Vocalizer
EF	External Focalizer
EV	External Vocalizer
FIS	Free Indirect Style
RH	Retranslation Hypothesis
SFG	Systemic Functional Grammar
SL	Source Language
ST	Source Text
TL	Target Language
TT	Target Text

Texts in Case Study

MB	Gustave Flaubert *Madame Bovary* ST
TT1 Marx-Aveling	Gustave Flaubert *Madame Bovary* TT Marx-Aveling
TT2 Blanchamp	Gustave Flaubert *Madame Bovary* TT Blanchamp
TT3 May	Gustave Flaubert *Madame Bovary* TT May
TT4 Hopkins	Gustave Flaubert *Madame Bovary* TT Hopkins
TT5 Russell	Gustave Flaubert *Madame Bovary* TT Russell
TT6 Wall	Gustave Flaubert *Madame Bovary* TT Wall
TT7 Mauldon	Gustave Flaubert *Madame Bovary* TT Mauldon
TT8 Thorpe	Gustave Flaubert *Madame Bovary* TT Thorpe
MD	George Sand *La Mare au diable* ST
TT1 Anon	George Sand *Marie* TT Anon
TT2 Anon	George Sand *The Haunted Marsh* TT Anon
TT3 Shaw	George Sand *The Devil's Pool* TT Shaw
TT4 Sedgwick	George Sand *The Devil's Pool* TT Sedgwick
TT5 Miles	George Sand *The Devil's Pool* TT Miles
TT6 Cowan	George Sand *The Devil's Pool* TT Cowan
TT7 Brown	George Sand *The Devil's Pool* TT Brown

List of Abbreviations

General

Introduction: A Return to Retranslation

Retranslation is very much a temporal phenomenon in the sense that its status as translation 'done again' is determined by the prior existence of an initial translation of a given work into a given language.[1] By dint of originating after this point, retranslation is generally understood as a reiterative and a multiplicative event which gives rise to a second, third, ad infinitum target language instantiation of a source text. But in another sense, retranslation resists easy delineation, marked as it is by a mercurial inconstancy with regard to frequency, behaviour and motivations. There is usually no discernible rhythm to retranslation, with intervals between the appearance of new target texts ranging from the sporadic to the periodic and the simultaneous. Nor are the unique dynamics of retranslation straightforward to unravel, for the practice yields multiples of one which relate not only to the source text but also to each other. To this already complex configuration can be added those socio-cultural factors which facilitate or obstruct retranslation in particular contexts and at particular moments.

It is against this differentiated backdrop that the paradox of retranslation as an object of enquiry emerges. Susam-Sarajeva notes in 2003 that 'although the practice itself is common, theoretical discussions on the subject are rather rare' (2003: 2), while Brisset registers her surprise 'that such a common translation phenomenon has brought about critical thinking which is, all told, rather scant' (2004: 41, my translation). Almost a decade later these appraisals still hold true, and a cogent empirical and conceptual understanding of retranslation remains elusive. However, two recent edited volumes in France, entitled *La retraduction* [*Retranslation*] (eds Kahn and Seth 2010) and *Autour de la retraduction: Perspectives littéraires européennes* [*On Retranslation: European Literary Perspectives*] (eds Monti and Schnyder 2011), have reopened the debate on retranslation behaviour, while presenting a wealth of illuminating case studies. The latter, in particular, acknowledges the enduring research lacuna as well as the established precedent for further inquiry:

> the widespread practice of retranslation within the European literary context remains a little explored area in terms of its multiple stakes. […] However, a renewed interest in the question has come to light in recent years, in particular as a response to the call of several translation studies scholars who have engaged with the subject and who have denounced the lack of studies in this area. (Monti 2011: 10–1, my translation)

This book hopes to sustain and build on that momentum in a number of respects. First, by undertaking its own contextual and textual analyses of selected (re)translations of Flaubert's *Madame Bovary* and Sand's *La Mare au diable*, this study aims to reveal how these literary works have been successively (re) interpreted from the outside in terms of their role in the target literary system (i.e. which socio-cultural factors have influenced their temporal and physical appearance?), and from the inside in terms of their form and content (i.e. how 'close' are they to the original?). The empirical findings derived from the case studies can then be aligned with or contrasted against existing assumptions on how, why and when retranslation operates. At the same time, these findings will also shed new light on the extent to which the fate of these two authors in Britain was contingent on retranslation. In addition, this book sets out a flexible, multi-methodological approach that draws on a diverse, but complementary, array of paradigms from narrative theory, narratology, Systemic Functional Grammar and sociology; this has been designed with future investigations in mind, and should facilitate an exploration of the capricious contours of retranslation in any number of linguistic and contextual settings. Finally, a new way of looking at the phenomenon of retranslation will be proposed which frees the researcher from the sometimes restrictive horizon offered by previous approaches, and which offers a more useful, dynamic and illuminating model for the study of retranslation in all its unpredictable permutations.

The rest of this chapter will distinguish among existing textual and contextual avenues of enquiry into retranslation, thereby establishing the conceptual background against which the case studies in this book are set. It will then finish with an overview of the main structure of the book and a brief introduction to the source and target texts at the centre of those case studies.

Time and (a)gain

While retranslation can certainly be understood as a reiterative act, it does not necessarily follow that the repetition is tautological. To say the same thing twice (or multiple times) would appear to be a redundant enterprise, unless motivated by an alternative logic. According to Goethe, that logic is one of producing different types of translation for different phases in a target culture's reception of the source culture:

> There are three kinds of translation. The first acquaints us with the foreign country on our own terms […]. A second epoch follows, in which the translator endeavors to transport himself into the foreign situation but actually only appropriates the foreign idea and represents it as his own […]. The third epoch of translation […] is the final and highest of the three. In such periods, the goal of the translation is to achieve perfect identity with the original, so that the one does not exist instead of the other but in the other's place […]. We are led, yes, compelled as it were, back to the source text. (1992: 64–6)

These three epochs of (re)translation represent a gradual move from an initial rejection of the foreign, via a tentative but nevertheless appropriating foray into the source culture, culminating in an idealized move which privileges the source text and all its alterity. Behind these three steps is the notion of time as progress, its passage 'compelling' us to great achievements, to what is 'perfect'. And it is precisely this momentum which, in Goethe's estimation, invests retranslation with the power to reveal the true identity of the source text within a given receiving culture, thereby constituting advancement – a gain.

After Goethe, intellectual enquiry into retranslation, its motivations and machinations seems to stall until 1990 when the French journal *Palimpsestes* issues a volume dedicated to the phenomenon. One of the most pervasive (and ostensibly persuasive) theoretical approaches to retranslation is encapsulated in the writing of Antoine Berman who mirrors Goethe's rationale, claiming that 'the accomplishment of any human action demands repetition' (1990: 4). Following this claim to its conclusion, Berman argues that 'The whole path of experience must be travelled to arrive at a translation which is self-aware. Every initial translation is clumsy. It is in the wake of this blind and faltering initial translation that the possibility of an accomplished translation arises' (1990: 3–4, my translation). Such ineptitude, unawareness and incertitude are, as far as Berman is concerned, symptomatic of 'la défaillance', that is 'the shortcomings' (1990: 5) which characterize initial acts of translation and which can only be counteracted by the restorative, corrective and illuminating properties of retranslation. Or, as Bensimon puts it in his introduction to the *Palimpsestes* issue:

> After some or much time has passed since the appearance of the initial translation, the reader finds themselves capable of receiving and of perceiving

> the indomitable foreignness, the 'exoticism', of the original. A retranslation is generally more alert than a preliminary translation to the letter of the source text, to its linguistic and stylistic contours, to its singularity. (1990: ix–x, my translation)

As was the case with Goethe, Berman's 'path of experience' appears destined to lead us back towards the specificities of the source text, accompanied by the resounding conviction that retranslation alone has the power to reveal its foreign identity and that time is the necessary ally of this revelatory process.

In addition, Berman maps out the end of this path at a particular pinnacle of accomplishment: the 'grande traduction' or 'great translation'. In keeping with Goethe's teleological reasoning, the great translation 'brings the original, previously concealed by initial translations, back to light and restores its meaning' (1990: 7, my translation), while 'setting an inimitable precedent for contemporary or subsequent translation activity' (1990: 3). At this lofty point, all great translations have one thing in common in that 'they are all retranslations' (1990: 3), since only the passage of time and the accumulation of experience can supposedly pave the way to such a feat of illumination and restoration in the service of the source text.

The rationale of Goethe, and then of Berman, has since found itself condensed into the laconic Retranslation Hypothesis (RH) that 'later translations tend to be closer to the source text' (Chesterman 2004: 8). In other words, the hypothesis implicitly presupposes that the reiterative (and therefore progressively accomplished) force of retranslation will bring about a recovery of the source text and its specificities, be they linguistic or cultural. However, it should be noted that the coinage of the Retranslation Hypothesis does not have its roots in detailed, empirical analyses of retranslation behaviour, nor was it formulated as a deliberate endorsement of Goethe or Berman's idealized logic. Rather, Chesterman simply uses it as a means of illustrating different types of hypotheses and potential translation universals, accompanying it with the caveat that 'the jury is still out' (Chesterman 2004: 7) as far as its validity is concerned. It is perhaps this caveat which has stimulated further interest in the phenomenon, allowing the Retranslation Hypothesis to move beyond its humble origins in the service of illustrating descriptive research methods and become a concrete heuristic tool in its own right.

Before considering the findings of the various case studies presented next, it would be useful to first outline in broad terms to what extent the reasoning behind the Retranslation Hypothesis is flawed. If we map its trajectory of increased closeness on to Berman's path towards the great and restorative translation, then Brisset's criticism of the latter holds in both contexts: 'This finalist stance epitomizes critical assumptions which, since the eighteenth century, have worked history into a temporal pattern characterized by *perfection*: translation, like history, is deemed to be marching towards progress' (2004: 42, original emphasis, my translation). This march is at once mechanistic and anonymous, and should therefore be regarded with some degree of suspicion. To reprise Berman's own cutting lexicon, there is a certain irony in the fact that this approach is 'blind' to the material conditions of translation production, namely to the external influences which exist beyond the confines of the text. Moreover, the idea that one (re)translation will beget a closer retranslation presumes the presence of a symbiotic link between successive versions and precludes the possibility of a move backwards. There is always the chance that a given retranslation has been carried out without a priori knowledge of an antecedent, or that actual translation choices will contradict this theoretical blueprint for advancement at any given moment; both scenarios will create a chink in the deterministic and linear chain of the Retranslation Hypothesis.

Signs of ageing

Berman also introduces an argument of ageing into his account of retranslation behaviour, one which diametrically opposes the longevity of a source text against that of a target text: 'Whereas the originals remain eternally young (whatever the degree of interest we have in them, and however near or far they are in cultural terms), translations "age"' (1990: 4, my translation). In line with the teleology of perfection, the act of retranslation is then deemed a necessary, albeit temporary, antidote to the (imperfect) impermanence of the previous translation. That is until such time as a 'grande traduction' appears, because great translations 'do not age' (1990: 2), and are therefore imbued with the power to put an indefinite halt to future reiterations. Granted, there is a brief allusion to the fact that each (re)translation 'correspond[s] to a particular linguistic, literary or cultural phase' (1990: 2) and therefore runs the risk of becoming quickly outdated. But any attempt to understand retranslation as updating from an extratextual perspective is clearly subordinate to the idea that retranslation happens because of the inherent flaws of translation itself. The notion of ageing is another way of holding a mirror up to these flaws, of emphasizing the 'caducity and incompleteness' (1990: 2) of translation, and, consequently, of reinscribing retranslation into a paradigm of progress.

However, where Berman proposes that the original will remain untouched by the passage of time and that any translation will grow old, Topia argues in the same volume of *Palimpsestes* that such a comparison is unfair since the original and the translation 'exist in two parallel and disparate time spectrums' (Topia 1990: 46, my translation). Basing his observations on the French (re)translations of James Joyce, Topia draws attention to the fact that the original language of *Ulysses* will never be open to accusations of ageing as the source text is integrated into a literary canon which continually reframes the work in accordance with its time and space of production, and in light of new interpretations. Since a translation is generally denied any such re-evaluation, it becomes 'frozen in a relationship of dependency with the original work' (Topia 1990: 48). It is this static, derivative position which prevents the translation from evolving and which thus attracts criticism for ageing. Put succinctly, 'it is the original which changes, and the translation which does not change' (Topia 1990: 46).

From the perspective of both Berman and Topia, the lifeblood of the original is its dynamism; its enduring prestige in the face of time according to the former, and its constant re-contextualization over time according to the latter. And the fatal flaw of the translation is its dependency, on target language norms and on the original, respectively. The incongruity between the two modes of writing is further highlighted in the work of Monti, with the striking imagery that '"originals" get wrinkles which makes them all the more charming, [whereas] the age-related imperfections of translations have a definite propensity to render them grotesque' (Monti 2011: 16, my translation). But all these approaches to the question of ageing are marked by oppositional textual thinking which risks diverting attention away from any number of source and/or target culture configurations which might increase or diminish the lifespan of a given work and its (re)translations.

Retranslation on trial

The extent to which Berman's alignment of progress and retranslation has suffused even the most recent studies is apparent in the two French volumes on retranslation. In *La retraduction*, for example, Kahn's work on the German (re) translations of Proust shows that, although later versions have not necessarily brought with them any particular gain, there is nevertheless evidence of hope in 'the arrival of a translator of genius' (2010: 216, my translation) who can produce Berman's great translation in terms of literary integrity. In the same collection of essays, Arnoux-Farnoux explores the French (re)translations of the Greek poet Kavafis; here, the initial collection of poems translated by Yourcenar is aligned with Goethe's introductory (and unsatisfactory) phase, while the retranslation by Grandmont with its 'obstinate efforts to remain as close as possible to the prosodic and syntactic structure of the original' (2010: 317, my translation) is deemed to lead us near to the third phase, the return to the identity of the source text. Likewise, in *Autour de la retraduction*, Jakubowska-Cichoń identifies the impoverishment of narrative voice in the Polish initial translation and retranslation of Duras's *L'Amant*, but the potential for a great translation to arrive is nevertheless hailed: '*L'Amant* is still waiting for its time to come, for its translator, and for its third translation' (2011: 210, my translation). Elsewhere in the volume, Béghain justifies her own retranslation into French of Charlotte Brontë's *Villette* since it 'allows for an accurate restitution of the plurilingual and polyphonic dimensions of the text' (Béghain 2011: 85, my translation), an accuracy which was deemed to be missing from Baccara's previous attempt. What unites these studies is thus a singular focus on the textual dynamics of retranslation and a more or less explicit acceptance of Berman's rationale of cumulative improvement in respect of the source text's portrayal.

In contrast, the following case studies choose to look outwards from the text, placing frequent and illuminating emphasis on the socio-cultural factors as the driving force behind the shape and substance of retranslation. They all engage with the textual and extratextual dynamics of retranslations, and in so doing, instigate evidence-based examinations of the phenomenon which then underscore the capacity and the limitations of the Retranslation Hypothesis as a descriptive model in particular or of the history-as-progress model in general.

A question of where, when and who

Placing themselves clearly and necessarily beyond the confines of the translated text, Finnish researchers Paloposki and Koskinen (2004) set out to correct the fact that 'there seems to be no substantial body of evidence in support of or against the retranslation hypothesis' (2004: 27). While their point of departure is that the reasons behind the Retranslation Hypothesis 'seem plausible' (2004: 28), their investigation into a number of Finnish initial translations and retranslations serves to nuance this stance.

Returning to an earlier exploration of Finnish fiction translations in the first half of the nineteenth century, Paloposki finds evidence that 'seems to confirm the claims in RH, at least partially' (2004: 29). However, she also makes the forceful argument that this textual behaviour is wholly dependent on the time period under investigation; in this instance, a time when the translation of fiction was in its infancy in Finland and exhibited domesticating tendencies. The Retranslation Hypothesis thus holds within the parameters of a specific phase in the history of a specific national literature. But by changing the start and end points of the investigation, and the national context, it is highly feasible that a different pattern will emerge.

Paloposki's argument is further reinforced by her study of the Finnish (re) translations of Goldsmith's *The Vicar of Wakefield* and *The Thousand and One Nights* which appeared from the latter half of the nineteenth century and into the early twentieth. From this new temporal perspective, a reversal of the Retranslation Hypothesis comes to light, with initial literal translations giving way to later adaptations. This pattern is mapped on to an evolution in the receiving system which is now deemed to be open to the introduction of translations with a less assimilated feel. But another valid reason for the reversal is proposed, one which speaks to the fundamental unpredictability of the phenomenon and against the mechanistic leanings of the Retranslation Hypothesis: 'Idiosyncratic constraints – the translator's own preferences, or even difficulties in interpreting the text – may have a role to play' (2004: 31).

In turn, Koskinen also shows the logic of the Retranslation Hypothesis to be transient in its applicability by focusing on a later Finnish version of Lewis Carroll's *Alice's Adventures in Wonderland* which 'complicates the picture' (2004: 33). Although the previous (re)translations fit with the trend of a return to the ST, the most recent attempt, published in 2000, adopts a noticeably domesticating strategy. In addition, its appearance a mere five years after its predecessor cannot be explained by the need to update target language usage for a new audience. Recognizing the inadequacy of the Retranslation Hypothesis to account for either anomalous behaviour or synchronic versions, Koskinen concludes that 'retranslations are affected by a multitude of factors, relating to publishers, intended readers, accompanying illustrations and – not least – the translators themselves' (2004: 34). This outward looking stance again underscores the agency of the translator, while indicating that no exploration of retranslation can or should be divorced from the wider socio-cultural context.

A normative approach

There has been a tendency elsewhere to collapse socio-cultural explorations into a study of target language norms, no doubt stemming from Gambier's claim that, since translations are 'frozen in the norms of a given era' (Gambier 1994: 416, my translation), retranslation will update in accordance with the target reader's evolving needs and expectations. Take for example Du-Nour's (1995) study of the translation of children's literature from English, German, Italian and Swedish into Hebrew over a span of seventy years, where the focal point is the change in the target culture's 'linguistic and translational norms' (1995: 331). Here, shifts in the latter are shown to emulate shifts in the former; the almost Biblical tone of translated children's literature in the 1920s reflects the promotion of Hebrew as a classical language, while the more 'recent retranslations tend to lower the high literary style customary in previous translations and comply with up-to-date linguistic norms' (1995: 327). Similarly, Desmidt (2009) explores the (re) translations (and adaptations) into German and Dutch of the Swedish children's classic *Nils Holgersson*, identifying a tendency 'to prioritise target culture norms' (Desmidt 2009: 678) of readability above and beyond any considerations of the source text's form and content.

A broader approach to the influence of norms can be found in Kujamäki's exploration of eight German (re)translations of Kivi's Finnish work, *Seitsemän veljestä*. This study raises the interesting issue of stalled translation whereby the initial translation is published in 1921, fifty years after its completion, due to the fact that the ST was until then 'simply far too removed from the [German] poetic ideal of the period' (2001: 54). Its appearance is also aligned to a key political event in the shape of Finland's independence from Russia. Against this backdrop, the translation and translator become integrated into a particular agenda, namely the promotion of Finish national identity abroad. On one hand, this example demonstrates that the reasons for translation may be located in the source culture; on the other, the lack of demand from Germany attests to the power asserted by the target culture to accept or reject a particular translation attempt. Nevertheless, the following two retranslations of 1935 and 1942 are inextricably tied to the target system and to the ideologies of the National Socialist party. The heavily abridged version of 1935 effectively appropriates the work as a 'valuable poetic model' (2001: 57) for the rebuilding of German national identity in line with the supposed racial and cultural supremacy of the Nordic people. The growing alliance between Germany and Finland facilitates a retranslation in 1942 which is 'more open to foreign cultural-specific elements' (2001: 60), that is one in which Finnish identity becomes less an archetype of Nordic culture, and more valuable in its own right.

Towards a more elaborate model

Questions of poetological and ideological norms, as well as the idiosyncratic input of the translator, are reprised once more in Brownlie's investigation into the five British (re)translations of Zola's *Nana*. In concordance with the above studies, Brownlie shows how retranslation can be used to map changing ideologies in the target culture. In particular, the crudeness and sensuality inherent in Zola's writing 'were not acceptable to the British Victorian middle class ideology of moral uprightness and "delicacy"' (2006: 157), an ideology which then manifests itself in the first translation of 1884 as self-censorship, that is in omission and substitution. Brownlie also sees 'a clear overlap between social ideologies and literary norms, in that what is acceptable in literary texts is affected by current social mores' (2006: 161). Again, the notion of delicacy serves as a basis for normative comparison, and Brownlie outlines how the treatment of sensual material progressed towards the explicit pole over time.

But what sets this work apart from those norm-oriented studies that have come before is its alertness to the issue of heterogeneity. Brownlie acknowledges the heuristic power of investigating norms and ideologies, but cautions that this approach may paint in broad brush strokes and therefore overlook more complex workings in the surrounding context (2006: 155). As with Paloposki and Koskinen (2004), Brownlie highlights the potential agency of the translator and/or translation commissioner, who may chose at any moment to go against the normative or ideological grain, but she also stresses the fact that different norms and ideologies may coexist within a given timeframe (Brownlie 2006: 156). This coevality is illustrated by the contrast between the initial translation of 1884 and first retranslation of *Nana*, published in 1895; although they share the same Victorian setting, the retranslation 'does not shy away from sexual topics or unflattering religious references' (Brownlie 2006: 164). The reason behind this disparity can be found in the publishing context, in that the retranslation was commissioned by the secret, elite and private Lutetian society who were at liberty to provide their members with unexpurgated works which subverted the prevailing norms of decency.

Challenging thus the supposed 'neat and homologous relationship between time period and norms/ideology' (Brownlie 2006: 157), Brownlie proposes instead a more fluid, post-structuralist approach to the study of retranslation. Such an approach reframes retranslation within a 'rhizomatic' space (Brownlie 2006: 155), an intricate, entangled network of influences and agents, which then allows for a more finely tuned, sensitive and illuminating window on to the multitude of factors which shape retranslation.

In a comparable move away from the straight-line teleology of Berman's model, Susam-Sarajeva brings into view 'the spiral-like and vertiginous "evolution" pattern of the indigenous literary critical discourse' (2003: 6) which serves to explain the significant concentration of (re)translations of Barthes into Turkish from 1975 to 1990. In this instance, the high number of (re)translations within a short space of time is indicative of the state of the receiving system which had no pre-established discourse into which to place the terminology of semiotics, structuralism, linguistics, Marxism and psychoanalysis in Barthes's works. The resultant helical behaviour of the system and of the (re)translations points to a 'a synchronous struggle in the receiving system to create the target discourse into which translations will be incorporated' (2003: 5). Whereas the coexistence of (re)translations in Brownlie's (2006) study highlights diverging norms, the coexistence of (re)translations in this context attests to the very absence of norms. But both Susam-Sarajeva and Brownlie place necessary emphasis on a synchronic line of enquiry and destabilize the argument that retranslation is a mechanistic corollary of ageing; in these cases, the concentration of retranslations in close temporal proximity with each other cannot be explained away in terms of updating.

Susam-Sarajeva instigates another meaningful change in perspective when she considers the absence of retranslation. In opposition to the relatively high frequency of retranslations into Turkish of Barthes, Susam-Sarajeva identifies that the French feminist, Cixous, has rarely been retranslated into English. This prompts her to query whether 'the existing translation achieved the "accomplishment", the completeness and achievement Berman was talking about' (2003: 19), or whether the receiving system was static and therefore no updating was necessary. The conclusion is that neither scenario is very likely; rather, the rarity of retranslation is explained in reference to the prevailing attitude to translation within the Anglo-American feminist context where translations 'were often seen and presented as unproblematic and "transparent"' (2003: 20). In other words, how can translations be deemed deficient, and therefore in need of retranslation, if there are no grounds for deficiency in the first instance? These case studies then lend further weight to the argument that retranslation, or absence thereof, is contingent on the conditions of the receiving system in which it circulates or from which it is excluded. Although the Barthes example shows some concern for improvement as far as terminology is concerned, this improvement is in the service of the target culture discourse, and not the original. Similarly, the history-as-progress model becomes redundant in a context which simply does not identify a need to return to the source.

Retranslation as challenge

A further angle from which to approach retranslation is to consider how existing versions relate to and interact with each other, above and beyond their connection to the source text. Central to this line of enquiry so far has been the issue of challenge, as evinced in Pym's (1998) distinction between 'active' and 'passive' retranslations. These passive retranslations are either separated diachronically by the passage of time, and 'would seem to be responding to long-term processes of linguistic or cultural change in the target community' (1998: 82), or they are separated synchronically by geopolitical or dialectological boundaries. But in both instances, the retranslations are deemed to 'have relatively little disturbing influence on each other' (1998: 82), and are therefore dismissed by Pym as empirically 'redundant' since their study 'can only affirm the general hypothesis that target-culture norms determine translation strategies' (1998: 83). Although Pym's approach to passive retranslations does imply an acceptance of Gambier's (1994) updating argument, it nonetheless criticizes case studies, such as those outlined earlier, which take a rather sweeping view of the influence of norms, thereby 'blindly surrendering causality to target-culture norms' (Pym 1998: 83).

Conversely, Pym stresses the heuristic value of active retranslations; this category appears to be marked and motivated by rivalry, and comparative analyses between these antagonistic versions is more likely 'to locate causes far closer to the translator, especially in the entourage of patrons, publishers, readers and intercultural politics' (Pym 1998: 83). In short, active retranslations are presented as a window on to multiple, extratextual causes of retranslation which extend beyond the limited and limiting consideration of norms. Also of note is Pym's emphasis on re-editions which form part of landscape in which retranslation occurs and can be regarded as 'a good index of public demand' (Pym 1998: 79). Thus, when a (re)translation appears as a re-edition, the validity of that particular version is reinforced; on the other hand, the appearance of a new, active retranslation 'strongly challenges that validity, introducing a marked negativity into the relationship' (Pym 1998: 83) with previous translations. And so, although the challenge stems from external agents, Pym identifies battle lines that are drawn more specifically in the choice of text to retranslate and in the choice of how to retranslate: examples of active retranslations are shown to adapt the source text for a new readership, to correct a previous version (in line with Berman's trajectory of progress), and to counteract limited access to the content of a given work.

Similarly, Venuti frames retranslation as a purposeful act of differentiation which seeks to (re)inscribe particular cultural, religious, economic and so on values into a selected work. Consequently, such retranslations are characterized by a 'crucial awareness [of pre-existing translations] and justify themselves by establishing their differences from one or more previous versions' (Venuti 2004: 25). But, contrary to Pym (1998), Venuti does not problematize the time span which separates the appearance of different versions, since any retranslation appears to have the potential to rival any of its predecessors. Rather, Venuti sees challenge as contingent on a temporal gap insofar as retranslations 'deliberately mark the passage of time by aiming to distinguish themselves from a previous version through differences in discursive strategies and interpretations' (2004: 35). In this context, diachronic movement, whether large or small, activates as opposed to passivates retranslation.

Again, challenge is played out on the level of the text as indicated by the emphasis on linguistic and hermeneutic difference. However, Venuti does delve deeper than Pym into the specific, extratextual causes of translation, situating motivating factors on the levels of canonicity, ideology, economics and the subjectivity of the translator. Of particular note are those retranslations 'designed deliberately to form particular identities and to have particular institutional effects' (2004: 26), such as retranslations within religious or academic institutions that 'define and inculcate' (2004: 26) the desired doctrinal or critical reading of a canonical text. In this instance, the active force of a retranslation is inherent in its ability to 'maintain and strengthen the authority of a social institution by reaffirming the institutionalized interpretation of a canonical text', or to proffer an alternative interpretation in the interests of change and innovation. Similarly, retranslation may come to the aid of a marginal text in its 'bid to achieve canonicity through the inscription of a different interpretation' (2004: 27). This process of recovery is also alluded to by Bollack who notes that 'retranslation can be used to reveal works which have disappeared from the cultural horizon' (2010: 29). A new textual interpretation seems thus to be understood as having a revitalizing and revealing impact on the source text as well within the receiving socio-cultural context.

In addition, Venuti (2004: 29–30) points to the commercial logic behind retranslations, whereby the retranslation of canonical texts becomes more viable given the market demand and the likely expiration of copyrights, while simply producing a revised edition of an existing work will reduce costs further still. When responding to the question of why new retranslations of the classics continue to appear, Abrams, an editor, notes that in this particular scenario 'costs are low – no big author advances are needed – and there is always a chance that a new version will become a hit in colleges, providing an annuity revenue stream' (2013: n.p.). Such are the 'banal editorial reasons' (Ladmiral 2011: 43, my translation) which can and do generate retranslations. In this instance then, emphasis moves away from differentiation and towards ensuring value of the financial kind. But Venuti further recognizes that the decision to retranslate 'may be motivated by no more than the retranslator's personal appreciation and understanding of the foreign text, regardless of transindividual factors' (2004: 30). This focus on the translator's own subjectivity as a catalyst for retranslation has also been placed under the sign of 'idiosyncratic constraints' by Paloposki and Koskinen (2004: 31) and '*the differential work of the translating subject*' by Brisset (2004: 46, original emphasis, my translation). Here, the momentum of a given retranslation can be traced back to a much narrower and individual source, although it is perhaps important to point out that the figure of the lone translator can belie collective efforts, as exemplified by the French team who came together at Université de Lyon II in order to retranslate Joyce (see Samoyault 2010).

It is thus clear from both Pym (1998) and Venuti (2004) that the logic of retranslation as reinterpretation is no longer restricted solely to the service of the source text, as Berman's rationale would imply. But Berman's vaunted return to the original does, however, lend itself nicely to Venuti's foreignizing agenda (see Venuti 1995), and reverberations of this source-oriented move can be heard in the claim that 'To retranslate is to confront anew and more urgently the translator's ethical responsibility to prevent the translating language and culture from effacing the foreignness of the foreign text' (2004: 36).

A dialogue of difference?

Both Pym (1998) and Venuti (2004) stress rivalry and differentiation as central to the production of retranslations, although the empirical evidence on which they base their claims is somewhat limited. In order to arrive at a more detailed picture of how retranslations might stem from and interact with previous versions, it is worth taking a closer look at other case studies which reveal the various forms and degrees of dialogue which can exist between what are essentially multiples of one, that is texts which share a common point of origin.

There are, in fact, a large number of cases which suggest that the argument of retranslation as challenge carries considerable weight. To begin, St André's (2003) examination of retranslation within Sinological circles in the eighteenth and nineteenth centuries proposes argument as the primary stimulus for the phenomenon. Focus on the Chinese novel *Hao qiu zhuan* reveals how Sir John Francis Davis sets his 1829 English retranslation in opposition to the initial English translation in 1761 by Percy (a British merchant) by reinforcing the corrective properties of his own version, and simultaneously arguing against the legitimacy of the first attempt. Two impulses clearly drive this challenge: Davis's 'desire to establish himself as an authority on things Chinese […] and to set standards of fidelity for translation from Chinese' (St André 2003: 64–5). But St André further shows how rivalry may reach across target culture borders. The first English translator of *Fo guo ji*, a fifth-century account of the travels of a Chinese Buddhist monk, works not from the original text, but from a French translation. The tension between the two Sinologist traditions is evident in the replacement of French scholarship (introduction, notes, etc.) with supposedly superior English expertise. There follows four English retranslations, all of which go to great lengths to underscore the errors of their predecessors and thereby lay claim to their own validity. But on an individual level, St André also shows how the versions reveal the different concerns of the retranslators, which range from historiography to philology and accessibility; such individual, subjective readings will inevitably entail a process of differentiation against any readings that have come before.

Yet more preoccupation with the corrective properties of retranslations comes to light in Seth's (2010) study of the French retranslations of Adam Smith: 'In order to legitimize their own work, the [team of] retranslators […] mention the terminological and grammatical choices made by the translator who preceded them' (Seth 2012: 72) – the implication being that the choices encoded in this earlier version are specious, and that the reader should place confidence in the projected authority of this new version. Emphasis is placed elsewhere on retranslation as the realization, or revelation, of the different interpretations offered by the source text. According to Ferry (2010), the two retranslations of Kleist's *Penthesilea* into French 'have brought to light the epic dimension of the play that seems to have somewhat troubled Gracq' (2010: 138, my translation), the initial translator of the piece. Similarly, O'Driscoll shows how Butcher, the English retranslator of Jules Verne's *Le Tour du monde*, 'drew attention to such previously occluded themes as space, time, linearity, circularity, sexuality and Freudian repression' (2011: 253). While these two examples illustrate how retranslation expands the meaning potential of the original, Dutheil de la Rochère's comparative study of selected versions of Perrault's *Cendrillon* into English shows how retranslation can facilitate the ideological aims of the translator within the receiving culture. Here, Angela Carter's retranslation, *Cinderella: or, the Little Glass Slipper*, 'deliberately differentiates itself from Samber [a nineteenth-century predecessor] in order to renew the meaning of Perrault's tale and its moral' (Dutheil de la Rochère 2011: 159, my translation), a renewal which ultimately allows the work to fully covey the feminist retranslator's own emancipatory message.

Hanna's (2006) doctoral thesis also explores the Egyptian drama (re) translations of Shakespeare, from the end of the nineteenth century to the beginning of the twentieth, through the Bourdieusian lens of 'distinction'. In this case, he finds that the retranslators make concerted efforts to differentiate themselves from their predecessors on the linguistic level of the text and in reference to the function of the retranslation. In the first instance, a range of textual strategies such as reinterpretation, the use of footnotes to flag up supposed gaps in other versions, mistranslation and omission, are all pressed into the service of 'pushing the previous translation "into the past" and hence achieving distinction' (Hanna 2006: 223). In the second, the retranslators pursued distinction 'by suggesting that their translations fulfilled functions that were not *purportedly* fulfilled by previous translations' (Hanna 2006: 227, my emphasis), in that their translations brought to light a new literary form or responded to the needs of a new audience. However, the very purportedness of such claims reminds us of Toury's warning that pronouncements from translators can be 'partial and biased, and should therefore be treated with every possible circumspection; all the more so since – emanating as they do from interested parties – they are likely to lean toward propaganda and persuasion' (1995: 65). In this case, as in others, that persuasion aims to discredit the efforts of others, and may or may not be premised on accurate representations of those prior (re)translations.

But whether on a source-oriented lexical, grammatical and thematic level, or on a target-oriented functional or ideological level, all these case studies point clearly towards the way in which retranslation can readily be framed in terms of reinterpretation, differentiation and the inscription of value, as proposed by Venuti (2004). However, this challenge does in fact unfold over several distinct time periods; for example, a century separates the Samber and Carter versions of *Cendrillon* mentioned earlier, and two centuries separate the Adam Smith retranslations. In light of this evidence, Pym's (1998) distinction between active and passive retranslations seems somewhat untenable and restrictive; rivalry can be discerned on a diachronic plane, as much as on a synchronic one.

Furthermore, both Pym and Venuti's oppositional approach can be nuanced by those case studies marked by the absence of challenge or differentiation. Once again, Brownlie's study of the British (re)translations of Zola is illuminating since it uncovers 'instances of past texts "haunting" present ones' (Brownlie 2006: 165, original emphasis), whereby the strategic choices or period flavour of an earlier version are made manifest in a much later one. This phenomenon of haunting is also visible in Proser's 1978 French retranslation of Brecht's *Der Kaukasische Kreidekreis*. According to Mortier, 'It is difficult to say that it is a new translation. In fact, the retranslation by Georges Proser retains some of the wording of Jacob and Pfrimmer's translation' (2010: 145). Although this overlap could be explained by a reticence on the part of the translator to alter previous strategies which work well, Mortier points out that Proser retains some of the earlier mistakes and thus labels it as 'a curious retranslation' (2010: 145). Not only does this particular haunting subvert the Retranslation Hypothesis, it also attests to a coincidence with, rather than a distancing from, its antecedents.

The notion of challenge is also problematized by Ladmiral who claims that 'conversely, the desire to retranslate may stem from a positive identification with those translators who have preceded us' (2011: 36, my translation). Based on his own experience of retranslating part of Kant's *Kritik der Urteilskraft* into French, Ladmiral is at pains to stress that he did not find the previous attempt (by a former teacher) wanting, asserting instead the 'modest ambition of attempting to go beyond it by leaning on it' (2011: 37, my translation). In other words, Ladmiral sets out to use the previous version as an accomplished template that he will further refine, but readily admits that any gains he actually made were negligible. In this instance, the retranslator defers to the extant translated text, strengthening its authority, rather than his own.

Finally, certain lines of enquiry assume, as Chevrel does, that all retranslation 'takes its place straightaway in a continuum and enters into dialogue with at least two earlier components: the original work and the first translation' (2010: 14, my translation). As the already mentioned examples demonstrate, dialogue can be antagonistic, revelatory or reverential. But another potential dynamic is acknowledged by the team of French retranslators working on Cervantes's *Don Quichotte*. They made a conscious decision to consult only the source text, thereby cutting off any communication with their predecessor. According to them, it was simply 'out of the question to go back to Cassou's work: clearly, his edition was an important moment in the history of the French translations of Cervantes's masterpiece and it was appropriate to leave it untouched, out of respect for both its memory and its heirs' (Canavaggio 2010: 159, my translation). A break is thus instigated in the dialogic chain – perhaps out of respect or perhaps out of a certain anxiety of influence, in Bloomian terms. In the latter case, a degree of divergence is implied, but the fact remains that the element of challenge is explicitly downplayed, and that any subsequent differentiation will be incidental as opposed to intentional.

Overview

This book starts from the premise that all literary translation is an act of interpretation which crystallizes a series of (un)conscious (mis)readings of a given source text. It further considers these readings, as Venuti does, to be 'determined not merely by the source text and culture but by values, beliefs, and representations in the receiving culture', at the same time as they are 'provisional, one interpretation among several different possibilities and […] always subject to further interpretation by the range of cultural constituencies in the receiving situation' (2013: 245–6). The present investigation into the behaviour of retranslation will start from the context and move towards the text, with particular focus on whether or not retranslation and challenge are inextricably linked and on whether or not retranslation affects a return to the source text, respectively. Answers will be sought in a case study that is essentially literary in nature. First, the (re)translated works will be scrutinized for signs of how they might have been shaped by their socio-cultural conditions of production, and how, or if, they interact with each other. In broad terms, any restoration of or closeness to the source text will be understood in reference to how the translator has perpetuated the interpretive potential of that work. This is in line with Hatim and Mason's argument that 'since an important feature of poetic discourse is to allow a multiplicity of responses among SL readers, it follows that the translator's task should be to preserve, as far as possible, the range of possible responses' (1990: 11). Berman's teleological paradigm and the Retranslation Hypothesis will thus be used interchangeably in this study, with both schemas mapping out a chronological move from the restricted access to source text potential inscribed in initial translations to the augmented access achieved in later retranslations.

In many respects, this study is anchored in a Descriptive Translation Studies approach, following as it does Toury's methodological procedures: 'translations will […] first be situated within the target system' and then 'mapped on to their assumed sources' (1995: 102) in a series of coupled pairs with a view to identifying translation shifts. However, while the approach adopted here also hopes that 'the findings of [these] individual studies will be intersubjectively testable and comparable, and the studies themselves replicable' (1995: 3), the analysis will stop short of attempting to identify any norms which might underlie the decision-making process. Criticism of the norm-based approach, especially its inattention to issues of power and ideology, have been well documented (see e.g. Gentzler 2001; Hermans 1999b). Of particular note too is the problem that 'it aspires to the status of an empirical or objective or positive science, when norms (unlike, say, rocks) have no positive existence to be empirically described' (Hermans 1999a: 137). In the comparative textual analysis, my focus will be squarely on the rocks, the directly observable and often irregular idiosyncrasies of interpretation which have made their mark on the discursive features of a given (re)translation. However, the subjectivity of the researcher forms an unavoidable part of the analytical horizon here; there is no getting away from or around the fact that the positioning of the (re)translations in their target context and the measurement of the shifts between source and target texts are all a product of my interpretation of those observables. While I have taken steps to ensure that those interpretations are transparent and modelled on clear theoretical and methodological frameworks, I have to add the caveat that there will inevitably be some room for alternative readings.

The corpus itself comprises (re)translations of Flaubert's *Madame Bovary* and George Sand's *La Mare au diable*, the two authors and works having been chosen for the breadth of comparative and especially contrastive perspectives that they offer. Both authors were linked by a devoted friendship one to the other, as evidenced in the extensive correspondence that passed between the two 'troubadours', as they were wont to call themselves, and both works were produced within around ten years of each other in the middle of the nineteenth century – *La Mare au diable* in 1846 and *Madame Bovary* in 1857. However, that is where the similarities end. Flaubert wielded a jaded, caustic pen to write what has been described as 'the first sex-and-shopping novel' (Roberts 2003: vii) in which the moral and financial bankruptcy of the protagonist, Emma, leads to her torrid demise. The backdrop to the story is the petit-bourgeois world of provincial France and the stifling life Emma endures there with her husband Charles, a mediocre, bromidic country doctor. Escapism for Emma comes in the form of daydreams, material goods, adultery and, finally, arsenic. Conversely, Sand's pen was tinged with idealism and hope, painting a virtuous and inspiring portrait of her native Berry region in what is less a work of fiction, than an ethnographic study. Her pastoral tale recounts the physical and emotional journey of the farm-labourer Germain who, recently widowed, finds love with the young shepherdess Marie. The Appendix to the tale, on which this study will centre, uses their marriage as a premise for cataloguing the cultural traditions of the Berry. Information on the source text editions used and the (re)translations studied can be found in the Tables 1.1 and 1.2. Regrettably, this investigation is not exhaustive; in order to keep the data within manageable bounds, only those (re)translations published specifically for a British market will be examined. Effectively, this excludes several US versions, in particular well-known translations of *Madame Bovary* by Francis Steegmuller (1957) and Lydia Davis (2010), to which the British reader may readily have access.

In terms of structure, this book can be divided into two distinct parts, the first of which is dedicated to a contextual exploration of the (re)translations. Chapter 1 will discuss the ways in which paratextual (Genette 1997) and extratextual material can be used as a means of uncovering socio-cultural influences on (re)translation, and Bourdieu's (1996) concept of the literary field will then be presented as a heuristic paradigm on to which these influences can be mapped. Chapters 2 and 3 will scrutinize how the Flaubert and Sand (re)translations, respectively, have been framed by prefaces, notes and so on, advertised and reviewed in Britain. Here, the empirical evidence will be understood in reference to the hierarchical contours of the literary field, especially struggles for economic and symbolic capital, thereby allowing us to discern whether and to what effect the (re)translations were engaged in acts of challenge and differentiation. The second part of the book will turn to comparative issues of a textual nature. Chapter 4 will propose a hybrid methodology which starts with narrative theory (Baker 2006) as a means of highlighting the most salient features of each source text, on the basis of which the benchmarks for comparative analysis can be established. However, the indeterminateness of Flaubert's writing places the expository power of narrative theory under some strain, so, in order to develop a more fine-tuned methodology, the analytical approach will further combine concepts from narratology (voice and focalization) and Halliday's Systemic Functional Grammar (2004). This will be followed by the case study on *Madame Bovary* in Chapter 5 and the case study on *La Mare au diable* in Chapter 6. Both will serve to apprise how the narrative features of the source texts have been interpreted in the successive (re)translations, on the basis of which it then becomes possible to review the supposed progressive trajectory of retranslation. Back translations from the original French will be provided in these chapters, so as to broaden access to the specific examples for all readers. Finally, a synthesis of findings will be provided in the Conclusion, where a new way of thinking about retranslation will also be put forward.

Table 1.1 Source text and (re)translations of *Madame Bovary*

Abbreviations	Source text and (re)translations
MB	Flaubert, G. (1857/1971) *Madame Bovary*, Paris: Éditions Garnier Frères.
TT1 Marx-Aveling	Flaubert, G. (1886) *Madame Bovary*, tr. Eleanor Marx-Aveling, London: Vizetelly & Co.
TT2 Blanchamp	Flaubert, G. (1905) *Madame Bovary*, tr. Henry Blanchamp, London: Greening & Co.
TT3 May	Flaubert, G. (1928) *Madame Bovary*, tr. J. Lewis May, London: J. Lane Bodley Head.
TT4 Hopkins	Flaubert, G. (1948) *Madame Bovary*, tr. Gerard Hopkins, London: Hamish Hamilton
TT5 Russell	Flaubert, G. (1950) *Madame Bovary*, tr. Alan Russell, Harmondsworth: Penguin.
TT6 Wall	Flaubert, G. (1992) *Madame Bovary*, tr. Geoffrey Wall, Harmondsworth: Penguin.
TT7 Mauldon	Flaubert, G. (2004) *Madame Bovary*, tr. Margaret Mauldon, Oxford: Oxford University Press.
TT8 Thorpe	Flaubert, G. (2011) *Madame Bovary*, tr. Adam Thorpe, London: Vintage.

Table 1.2 Source text and (re)translations of *La Mare au diable*

Abbreviations	Source text and (re)translations
MD	Sand, G. (1846/1999) *La Mare au diable*, Paris: Gallimard.
TT1 Anon	Sand, G. (1847) *Marie*, tr. Anon., London: Chapman & Hall.
TT2 Anon	Sand, G. (1847) *The Haunted Marsh*, tr. Anon., London & Belfast: Simms & McIntyre.
TT3 Shaw	Sand, G. (1848) *The Devil's Pool*, tr. Francis G. Shaw, London: H.G. Clarke.
TT4 Sedgwick	Sand, G. (1895) *The Devil's Pool*, tr. Jane M. & Ellery Sedgwick, London: J.M. Dent.
TT5 Miles	Sand, G. (1929) *The Devil's Pool*, tr. Hamish Miles, London: Scholartis Press.
TT6 Cowan	Sand, G. (1966) *The Devil's Pool*, tr. Antonia Cowan, Glasgow: Blackie & Co.
TT7 Brown	Sand, G. (2005) *The Devil's Pool*, tr. Andrew Brown, London: Hesperus Press.

1

Multiples of One: A Socio-cultural Approach

Introduction

The influential role of context in the production and reception of translations has long been at the forefront of thinking in Translation Studies. Ever since the 'cultural turn', much emphasis has been accorded to questions such as the position of translated literature in the polysystem of a given target culture (Even-Zohar 1990), the interrelated mechanisms of patronage, ideology, economics and poetics which constrain translation as rewriting (Lefevere 1998) and the sociological factors which shape the processes, products and agents of translation (e.g. Gouanvic 1999; Helibron and Sapiro 2002; Wolf and Fukari 2007). A socio-cultural approach will also be implemented here, and this chapter will outline the methodology used to reveal and interpret the specific contextual dynamics that have acted on the decisions to (re)translate, the physical appearances of the (re)translations, the relative values accorded to those (re)translations and the nature and extent of any interactions between these multiples of one. Although Chesterman views the use of the 'the compound concept of the "sociocultural" ' as 'a bit lazy' (2006: 10), in that the conflation of the two levels disallows a distinct mapping of each, the fact that translation itself emerges from a synthesis of both cultural and sociological structures suggests that a combined approach is nevertheless feasible. As Wolf puts it, 'cultural and social practices – and consequently their theoretical and methodological conceptualization – cannot be regarded as detached from one another' (2007: 6). The analytical purview of this contextual study will, accordingly, stretch over both strata, understanding (re)translation as a complex socio-cultural object, the stuff of ideas and people and subject to the realities of contextual circumstance.

In broad terms, this socio-cultural investigation will draw on the work of French sociologist, Pierre Bourdieu, who, as Inghilleri notes, has been informing translation research for more than a decade, 'offering a more powerful set of concepts than norms or conventions to describe socio-cultural constraints on acts of translation and their resulting products' (2005: 126). In point of fact, one of the first attempts to use Bourdieu as a means of moving beyond norms is to be found in the work of Simeoni (1998). There, attention is shifted away from the notion of translation as an exclusively norm-governed activity and towards the agency of the translator, viewed through the lens of *habitus*: 'It seems to me that Toury places the focus of the relevance on the preeminence of what controls the agents' behavior – "translational norms".' A habitus-governed account, by contrast, emphasizes the extent to which translators themselves play a role in the maintenance and perhaps the creation of norms (Simeoni 1998: 26). In other words, the habitus of the translator – the set of dispositions, habits, skills, tastes and so on acquired through everyday experiences since childhood – will predispose that translator to behave in a particular way, with or against the grain of norms, which in turn will shape the translation. However, in much the same way as Brownlie criticizes a broad-based norms approach for its tendency 'to neglect complexities' (2006: 155) in the socio-cultural environment, so too has the universalism of habitus been taken to task by Lahire who argues that it 'is impossible to predict the occurrence of a particular social behavior like the fall of bodies can be predicted from the universal law of gravitation' (2003: 353).

Consequently, this study will not engage with the notions of norms and habitus, and aims instead to draw out those very intricacies of context which have brought about (re)translation at a particular moment, in a particular manner and for a particular purpose. In addition, the absence of sufficient background information on the social status, education, professional history and so on of each and every (re)translator frustrates any attempt to bring habitus to the fore in any sustained or meaningful way. Concrete data on the socio-cultural lines of influence are, however, recoverable from the paratextual and extratextual material that is related to the (re)translations. By exploring how the (re)translations have been packaged, marketed and received, insights can be gained into the individuals and institutions involved in the circulation of the target texts, their attendant motivations and constraints.

Furthermore, the paratextual and extratextual clues to (re)translation behaviour will be explored in reference to another of Bourdieu's key concepts: the literary field. Bourdieu defines the literary field as: 'a force-field acting on all those who enter it, and acting in a differential manner according to the position they occupy there [...] and at the same time it is a field of competitive struggles which tend to conserve or transform this force-field' (1996: 232). On the basis of this definition, it is possible to glimpse certain parallels between the structures of the literary field and those of Even-Zohar's polysystem, namely the differentiation of positions, the emphasis on dynamism and struggle as a modus operandi and the dialectic of conservation or innovation. But Bourdieu is anxious to distance himself from the formalist model of systems, arguing that it is not possible to conceive of culture as an autonomous system with 'an immanent propensity to transform itself by a mysterious form of *Selbstbewegung* which finds its principle only in its internal contradictions' (1996: 198). This rejection clearly applies to the abstract relations of polysystem theory, and certainly ties in with Hermans' criticism of Even-Zohar's model that 'the stakes remain invisible [...] as if the whole thing were on automatic pilot' (Hermans 1999b: 118). Rather, Bourdieu proposes a space where the 'principle of change in works resides in the field of cultural production and, more precisely, in the struggles among agents and institutions' (1996: 234), and it is the identification of these struggles, the agents and the institutions that will allow us to build up a more detailed picture of (re)translation behaviour in context.

The parameters of Bourdieu's literary field have already set the scene for a number of investigations in Translation Studies. For example, Gouanvic (1997, 1999) retraces the establishment of a French science fiction field that relied on translation imports from the United States and was the site of struggles between the various translators, editors and publishing houses and critics involved. Casanova (2002, 2004) explores the dynamics of global literary exchanges between national fields, understanding translation as an '"unequal exchange" occurring in an extremely hierarchical universe' (2002: 7, my translation); for dominant languages, translation serves as a means of appropriating symbolic capital, and for the dominated, translation offers a path towards recognition. And Hanna (2005) also charts the emergence of an Egyptian field of drama translation, the dynamics of which are delineated in reference to the agents involved in translating Shakespeare, their agendas and power relations. Specifically, Hanna draws on Bourdieu's heuristic notion of 'trajectories', the '*series of positions* successively occupied by the same agent or the same group of agents in successive spaces' (Bourdieu 1996: 258, original emphasis), to bring to light the relative and shifting positions of the translators within the field. This notion is particularly pertinent when it comes to the study of retranslations as it allows for a diachronic mapping of, not simply how one translator or one publishing house has fared in the struggles of the field, but also how one source text moves through those hierarchies in its multiple, successive target language instantiations.

Sociological approaches to translation are often classified according to three main lines of enquiry: product, agents and processes (e.g. Chesterman 2006: 12; Wolf 2007: 13). This study will situate itself within the parameters of the first two categories as this is what the available empirical data dictate; the paratextual and extratextual material allows us to look in more detail at who was involved in the production of the (re)translations, what the finished products look like and how they were marketed and received, but they regrettably reveal little, if any, information from behind the scenes in terms of how the translation was commissioned, whether the publisher provided the translator with a specific brief and other such editorial, economic, political and so on negotiations. The following sections will discuss in greater depth the concepts used to probe the creation of the (re)translations, providing more precise definitions of the paratext and the extratext, as well as elaborating on the structures, stakes and agents of the literary field on to which the empirical evidence about the (re)translations will be mapped.

An overview of paratext

The starting point of this socio-cultural analysis of (re)translation will be the identification and scrutiny of what Genette has labelled paratextual material, namely all the verbal or non-verbal material which frames and extends a given text. More precisely, the paratext 'constitutes a zone between text and off-text, a zone not only of transition but also of *transaction*: a privileged place of a pragmatics and a strategy, of an influence on the public, an influence that […] is at the service of a better reception for the text and a more pertinent reading of it' (Genette 1997: 2). Hence, paratext becomes a fundamental object of enquiry for the study of (re)translations as it will reveal the strategic (ideological, cultural, economic, etc.) manoeuvrings via which a given work presents itself to a given readership, while also offering insights into the dynamics of how (re)translations might interact with one another and how they are positioned in relation to constantly evolving socio-cultural contexts.

Genette draws a distinction between the two component parts of paratext: peritext and epitext. This differentiation is primarily spatial in nature: the former relates to material which physically surrounds a given text, and the latter to material which finds itself external, but nevertheless linked, to the text. A more detailed typology of the two components will be outlined next in order to clarify where such material can be found and to delineate its boundaries.

Peritext

Essentially, peritext is everything that is situated 'within the same volume' and includes 'such elements as the title or the preface and sometimes elements inserted into the interstices of the text, such as chapter titles or certain notes' (Genette 1997: 4–5). This description can be further refined to take into account more specific categories. The first of these is the publisher's peritext, which comprises any material tied to editorial strategy, for example the material format, the book cover, the information on the title page (name of author, publisher, translator; edition; date; etc.), dedications and biographical or critical information on the author. Likewise, titles, dedications, inserts and epigraphs also serve to mediate the relationship between the text and the readers. Finally, prefacing material includes a whole gamut of elements such as introductions, prologues, notes, notices and postfaces. Here, a further distinction can be drawn between the 'authorial preface' and the 'allographic preface' (Genette 1997: 12), where the former relates to material produced by the author and the latter to material produced by an authorized third party.

Epitext

The epitext is 'any paratextual element not materially appended to the text within the same volume, but circulating […] in a virtually limitless physical and social space' (Genette 1997: 344). Again, further distinctions can be made with regard to its boundaries: '*publisher's, semiofficial allographic, public authorial,* and *private authorial*' (Genette 1997: 345, original emphasis) epitexts all come into view in Genette's typology. The remaining categories converge on the figure of the author: a semiofficial allographic epitext is any piece of writing carried out by a third party which has been passably authorized by the author; the public authorial epitext includes those occasions on which the author addresses an audience through self-commentary, interviews, conferences and so on, while the private authorial epitext covers material such as correspondence, diary entries and pre-texts (outlines, drafts, etc.).

Towards a translatorial paratext[1]

Translation Studies has had frequent recourse to paratextual analyses as a means of situating translated works in their wider socio-cultural context. But all too often, the expediency of this strategy has allowed the relationship between translation and paratext to evade critical evaluation. First and foremost, we should ask the question: what room is there for translation in Genette's paradigm? For the above typology focuses on the author, the publisher and the (semi) authorized third party, and none of these categories make explicit room for the translator. In his conclusion to *Paratexts*, Genette merely acknowledges that translation is a practice 'whose paratextual relevance seems to [him] undeniable' (Genette 1997: 405), and regrets not having had the opportunity to elaborate further on this connection. Approaching this limitation from a Translation Studies perspective, Tahir-Gürçağlar criticizes Genette on a number of counts, beginning with his apparent 'reluctance to tackle the problematic aspects of elaborating translation as paratext' (2002: 45–6). In so doing, she interprets the relationship between translation and paratext as a wholly analogic one, in the sense that translation functions as an accompaniment to or a commentary on the source text. Hence her second criticism; given that all paratext is subordinate to its text in Genette's model, accordingly all translation 'will serve only its original' (2002: 46) – a servitude which has long been rejected in translation scholarship.

However, Tahir-Gürçağlar does not fully consider the conditions which Genette places on the relationship; the paratextual relevance of translation comes to the fore 'particularly when it is more or less revised or checked by the author […]; and all the more so when the entire task is undertaken by the author alone' (1997: 405). In other words, the relationship is predicated specifically on a correspondence between authorized or self-translation and paratext. Given that the principal stake of the paratext is to 'ensure for the text a destiny consistent with the author's purpose' (1997: 407), the commentary on the original that is inherent in the translation must also be aligned with authorial design. Once any process of rewriting occurs beyond authorized or self-translation, the parallels between paratext and translation necessarily collapse. It follows that Tahir-Gürçağlar's criticism must be refined. It is not the case that Genette posits a widespread and subservient analogy of translation as paratext; rather, it is the translator as commentator who is subordinate to the author-translator as commentator.

As already outlined, Genette accepts that not all paratextual material stems directly from the author, identifying contributions in the shape of the publisher's paratext and third party prefaces. It is in respect of this latter category that Genette alludes to translation as a common site for allographs that appear later than the original text (1997: 264). But he briefly problematizes this phenomenon in a footnote: 'The translator-preface-writer may possibly comment on, among other things, his own translation; on this point and in this sense, his preface then ceases to be allographic' (1997: 264). On the one hand, the translator is affirmed as a valid commentator on his or her translation work and sees his or her position elevated above that of third party. On the other hand, however, this elevation is tempered; Genette does not go so far as to endorse the translator as (authorial) commentator on the original, with the result that the translator is bereft of any clear-cut position within the paratextual model. In response to this indeterminateness, I would like to supplement Genette's paradigm with a 'translatorial paratext', thereby placing stronger emphasis on the tangible and mediative paratextual presence of the translator. Both the analogic and concrete interpretations of the translator in Genette's concept of paratext serve to confirm Venuti's conceptualization of the 'translator's invisibility', occasioned in part by 'the individualistic conception of authorship [which] devalues translation' (1995: 7), and which is very much in evidence in Genette's work.

In essence then, the additional category of the translatorial paratext will help to discern the extent to which the translator plays an active role in the cultural mediation of their (re)translation and to identify whether or not they have engaged, positively or negatively, with versions of the text which have gone before. When aligned with an exploration of the publisher's peritextual and epitextual material, a clearer picture can be drawn of the material, social, cultural and economic conditions under which a given (re)translation was initiated and produced. Furthermore, the absence of any translatorial paratext is also telling, and the significance of, for example, prefaces by other writers will be explored in reference to questions of agency and consecration below.

Extratext

In addition to paratextual material, this empirical study will also take certain categories of extratextual material into consideration, namely those articles and reviews that are related to the translations, the translators, the publishers and/or the source text authors. Genette warns that 'Inasmuch as the paratext is a transitional zone between text and beyond-text, one must resist the temptation to enlarge this zone by whittling away in both directions' (1997: 407). In other words, paratext occupies a particular interim position and its boundaries should be explicitly demarcated. Therefore, a clear line must be drawn between paratextual material, which is closely linked to the text having stemmed from the translator, author, publisher and/or authorized third party, and extratextual sources of information on (re)translation such as reviews which are often, and erroneously, discussed in Translation Studies under the heading of the former.

As sites of information on how a given translation has been received, reviews may offer insights into whether or not that version has been judged deficient or admirable, into the reputation of the author, work or translator, and into the relationship between the retranslation and its precedents. On the one hand, the opinions expressed by the critics will shed more light on textual approaches to retranslation by exposing which versions might have been deemed in need of betterment. On the other hand, the reviews will bear witness to factors in the wider socio-cultural context which have left their imprint on the phenomenon of retranslation, thereby underscoring the restrictions of textual lines of enquiry in the first instance. All of these, the available paratextual and extratextual material, will be scrutinized in the following two chapters and the struggles, stakes and hierarchies that they reveal will be represented in relation to Bourdieu's literary field, the specific structures of which are set forth next.

Mapping the literary field

Retranslation and the struggle for symbolic and economic capital

The structure of the literary field can superficially be represented as 'synchronic oppositions between antagonistic positions (dominant/dominated, consecrated/novice, orthodox/heretic, old/young, etc.)' (Bourdieu 1996: 239). However, below the surface, this oppositional structure comprises two intersecting axes: external and internal hierarchization. Firstly, the 'principle of external hierarchization' (Bourdieu 1996: 217) is a consequence of the forces exerted by the field of power, that is by the agents and institutions who have an interest (economic, political etc.) in the struggles of the literary field. This particular structure responds to 'the criterion of *temporal success* measured by indices of commercial success' (Bourdieu 1996: 217, original emphasis), with that success subsequently being converted into economic capital for those authors or works which find the greatest recognition amongst the public at large. Conversely, the 'principle of internal hierarchization' (Bourdieu 1996: 217) responds to a more restricted logic; prestige, or symbolic capital, is to be gained from exclusivity, that is from the recognition which stems from other artists alone, and not from the masses. Furthermore, these two hierarchical principles are inversely proportional to one another: 'economic profits increase as one goes from the "autonomous" pole to the "heteronomous" pole, or, if you will, from "pure" art to "bourgeois" or "commercial" art, whereas specific [symbolic] profits vary inversely' (Bourdieu 1996: 250). In other words, art which is commercially successful is high in economic capital, but low in symbolic capital, while the reverse is true of more esoteric artistic endeavours. Nevertheless, this general rule does not preclude instances where symbolic capital can be converted into economic capital in the long term, and vice versa.

It is precisely this interplay between the two principles of hierarchization which generates struggles in the literary system, where the accumulation of economic or symbolic capital is at stake. Or, as McDonald succinctly puts it, it is the battle between the 'purists and the profiteers' (1997: 15). Thus, at the two extreme ends of the autonomous and heteronomous poles we find 'the defenders of the most "pure", the most rigorous and the narrowest definition of belonging' and those who wish to 'to reduce the business of art to the business of money' (Bourdieu 1996: 223). It follows that any act of (re)translation will be subjected to the external and/or the internal forces at play in the literary field, becoming collateral in the respective attempts of the translator or the publisher to secure economic or symbolic capital.

Gouanvic argues that 'Symbolic capital is not acquired – in the case of the writer – essentially by heritage but by recognition, which must be constantly regained through new works published in the literary field' (2005: 161). In turn, the translator 'benefits from the symbolic capital invested in the original work', and also 'intervenes as an agent who confers on the author and on the work a quantity of capital by submitting it to the logic of the target field' (2005: 161–2). In this sense, the transfer of a source text into a target culture can be considered mutually beneficial (or disadvantageous, depending on the position secured), but it is also necessary to bring the agendas of other interested parties into focus in order to identify their own particular capacities for the generation of symbolic capital. Also of pertinence is Gouanvic's observation about the impermanence of recognition and its recapturing through the production of new works. If retranslation is viewed in light of this rationale, then the continued generation of new versions of a given ST can be understood as part of the apparatus whereby translators, editors, publishers and others work towards the attainment of symbolic capital.

At the other end of the scale, retranslation too can be implicated in the accrual of economic capital. Heilbron and Sapiro (2002: 3) warn against the dangers of failing to distinguish between a general economic market for goods and the specific market for symbolic goods since 'a substantial proportion of the process for importing foreign literary works is based on the logic of restricted production' which values literary merit above best-seller status. That said, it is also important to bear in mind that those works which come with the label 'classic' are generally consumed in large numbers, and that there may be other constellations of factors in a literary field which do create a clear supply and demand situation. Therefore, general market conditions cannot be wholly disregarded, and the study of the paratextual and extratextual material in Chapters 2 and 3 will seek to determine the extent to which the (re)translations have been driven and determined by economic forces, in terms of both restricted and wholesale production.

Retranslation, legitimization and agents

The ongoing struggles for economic and symbolic capital mean that the literary field is in a perpetual state of change, as agents vie to occupy new positions, or maintain or improve the ones in which they already find themselves. One of the fundamental sites of competition is 'the monopoly of literary legitimacy' (Bourdieu 1996: 224). By acquiring legitimacy, the right to belong, agents also acquire the right to 'define boundaries, defend them and control entries' (Bourdieu 1996: 225); in short, the securance of legitimacy equates to the securance of the very boundaries of the field itself, and the power to determine who can enter the field and who gets pushed out. This particular struggle is played out between those who occupy an established and dominant position within the field and the newcomers, and it is this latter category of agents who need to make their mark on the field in order to ensure their survival. As Wolf observes, 'the agents dominating the field of production and the market through the various forms of capital they have been able to accumulate in earlier struggles, are at odds with the newcomers, who, on their turn, stand for discontinuity, rupture and subversion' (2011: 10). Whereas the dominant agents will do what they can to preserve the configuration of the literary field as it stands, the newcomers will attempt to redraw the field, to bring about its reconfiguration, by clearly differentiating themselves. Each newcomer in the corpus of the Flaubert and Sand retranslations will consequently be explored for any indication of challenge through differentiation, and for any sign as to how successful or otherwise that challenge was. But, while acknowledging, as Chesterman does, that the literary field is 'more characterized by competition than by cooperation' (2006: 19), and bearing in mind that retranslation has also been placed under the sign of challenge and differentiation, we should remain alert to any instances where the struggles of the field might be realized and reinforced by virtue of cooperation.

In other words, we should not be blind to scenarios in which (re)translations function as a collective in terms of their positioning and relative accumulation of economic or symbolic capital within the field.

Up to this point, the agents circulating in the literary field and their powers of legitimization have been discussed using rather general terms. A more nuanced approach can be gleaned from the work of Casanova (2002) who positions the agents of the literary field along a continuum of legitimization, or what she terms 'consecration'. At the lowest, least powerful end of the spectrum are the 'ordinary mediators' who inform the field about literary innovations from abroad, and the claim that they are 'almost "invisible" ' (2002: 17, my translation) is certainly substantiated by the present study since, as mentioned before, the specific processes which underlie each (re)translation are irrecoverable. At the other end we find the 'consecrated consecrators' (2002: 18, my translation) who already enjoy individual legitimization through their charisma or institutional legitimization through, for example, their academic affiliations. In those cases where a (re)translator is himself or herself already consecrated in the target literary field, the (re)translation, by a process of osmosis, can also lay claim to a high degree of legitimization. Similarly, Casanova notes that if both translator and source text author have accrued symbolic capital, then 'we can talk about a sort of inter-consecration or exchange of capital' (2002: 18, my translation). Conversely, if the translator is somewhat lacking in terms of consecration, then this exchange of capital 'is transferred to other, better equipped mediators' (2002: 19, my translation) such as prestigious preface writers or critics. And so the analyses of the paratextual and extratextual material will further take into account the positioning along this continuum of legitimization of the agents who emerge as visible in the production of the Flaubert and Sand (re)translations.

Finally, the potential highlighted here for source author and target agents to exchange capital also reminds us of Casanova's international perspective on translation and the need to consider not only the trajectories that shape national literary fields, but also the relative positions of power that shape transfer between those fields. In Casanova's terms, the transfers which concern us occur across two dominant, as opposed to dominated, languages; both French and English can be defined as having, 'by dint of their specific prestige, their maturity [...] a high volume of literary capital' (2002: 9, my translation). But although the repeated transfers of this case study may take place amongst equals, there are still external economic and political forces which may fashion the timing and the form of the (re)translations, while the source authors may or may not find a positioning inside the target literary field that equates to their positioning at home. Again, the empirical evidence will be scrutinized for any indications as to how the interrelationship between the two literary fields might have exerted and influence on the production and the circulation of the (re)translations.

Summary of the methodological approach

Bourdieu claims that each new work that enters the literary field will 'occupy a distinct and recognizable position in the historically constituted space of coexisting (and therefore competing) works' (2002: 240). By charting the positions occupied by the (re)translations, individually and in relation to extant target language versions of the same source text, the trajectories which emerge will provide a more detailed map of the behaviour of retranslation which surpasses any linear or text-bound consideration of the phenomenon. The hierarchies of the British literary field and its interaction with the source literary field should bring to light struggles over economic and symbolic capital and legitimization which might impact the hows and whens of (re)translation.

The bedrock of this analytical approach is the paratextual and extratextual material that frames or is linked to the (re)translations. The paratext can first be used as a means of locating evidence for the type and extent of interactions between the (re)translations, so as to better assess the assumption that (re) translations are motivated according to a logic of challenge and rivalry. It may simultaneously provide indications about the (economic or symbolic) impetuses for retranslation, the mechanisms through which the agents strived to maintain or improve their positions, as well as the relative legitimization, or consecration, of the agents involved. Likewise, the examination of extratextual reviews and articles will illuminate how a particular work (ST or TT), translation or author has been received within the British literary system, thereby allowing conclusions to be drawn about the relationship between the source and target fields, as well as the success (or otherwise) of the agents' struggles in the latter.

In short, it is the overarching logic and structures of Bourdieu's literary field that guide the scrutiny of the paratextual and extratextual material in the first instance. The findings can then be mapped back on to the hierarchies of the field as a means of isolating the specific trajectories of each (re)translation and then seeing how they interact with each other. The contextual factors which have an impact on the phenomenon of retranslation can thus be untangled and viewed with more clarity.

2

Re-encounters with *Madame Bovary*[1]

Introduction

The history of the British translations of *Madame Bovary* begins in very close proximity to Flaubert himself, with the author proclaiming the very first version, carried out under his own gaze by Juliet Herbert, English governess to his niece, to be no less than a 'chef d'œuvre' (1929a: 26). However, Flaubert's attempts to secure a publishing deal in London for the translation were thwarted, leading him to turn his back on the endeavour of translation with the declaration that he was 'ready to abandon it all' (1929a: 26). He thereby seals the fate of Herbert's work, which never makes an appearance in print; and the manuscript has now long since been lost in the annals of obscurity. And yet this faltering start does not set the tone for the subsequent fate of *Madame Bovary* translations in the British literary system. Rather, from amongst Flaubert's entire body of work, it is indeed *Madame Bovary* which has undergone the highest volume of retranslation. The novel has been translated in the British literary system, in full, eight times, over a period which spans from the end of the nineteenth century to present day, while a plethora of reprints and re-editions has further served to ensure its consistent presence throughout this time, as highlighted in Table 2.1. Every attempt has been made to ensure that this survey is as comprehensive as possible, although, as Paloposki and Koskinen point out, 'An all-inclusive list for any one target language is nearly impossible' (2010: 36).

In light of the multiplicity of TL versions, this chapter will investigate the behaviour of the (re)translations of *Madame Bovary* in terms of the impact exerted by their socio-cultural conditions of production, while remaining alert to any relational dynamics that might hold between existing versions. To this end, a paratextual analysis will be undertaken which draws on Genette's (1987) notions of peritext and epitext, that is the supporting material, such as prefaces, introductions and advertisements, found within and around the various editions of the work, and will further include the supplementary notion of 'translatorial paratext', as discussed in Chapter 1. Extratextual material, namely newspaper reviews, will also be examined in order to determine how the (re) translations have been received. The opinions expressed in both the paratext and extratext will be framed in reference to Bourdieu's model of the literary field, where both external (economic, political, etc.) pressures and internal struggles over symbolic capital in particular will determine the status and position of a given (re)translation within the hierarchical construct. The extent and nature of any visible synergies between different versions can further be used as a means of nuancing the assumptions held by Pym (1998) and Venuti (2004) that retranslation is tantamount to challenge. Largely, this approach is intended to paint a more complete portrait of the way in which *Madame Bovary* has been diffused and received over time in Britain, and to unravel the behaviour of retranslation further still by considering the phenomenon from a range of perspectives.

Table 2.1 (Re)translations and re-editions of *Madame Bovary*

Year	TT	Publisher
1878	Partial Saintsbury	Fortnightly Review
1886	TT1 Marx-Aveling	Vizetelly & Co.
1892	TT1 Marx-Aveling	Gibbings & Co.
1905	TT2 Blanchamp	Greening & Co.
1906	TT1 Marx-Aveling	Maclaren & Co.
1910	TT2 Blanchamp	Collin's Cleartype Press
1913	TT1 Marx-Aveling	A.M. Gardner & Co.
1922	TT1 Marx-Aveling	J. Cape
1928	TT3 May	J. Lane Bodley Head
1928	TT1 Marx-Aveling	J.M. Dent
1929	TT2 Blanchamp	London Book Co.
1930	TT1 Marx-Aveling	J. Cape
1931	TT3 May	J. Lane Bodley Head
1932	TT1 Marx-Aveling	J. Cape
1934	TT1 Marx-Aveling	J.M. Dent
1936	TT1 Marx-Aveling	J. Cape
1941	TT1 Marx-Aveling	J.M. Dent

(*Continued*)

Table 2.1 (Re)translations and re-editions of *Madame Bovary* (*Continued*)

Year	TT	Publisher
1946	TT1 Marx-Aveling	Camden Publishing Co.
1948	TT4 Hopkins	Hamish Hamilton
1949	TT1 Marx-Aveling	Camden Publishing Co.
1950	TT3 May	Nonesuch Press
1950	TT5 Russell	Penguin
1952	TT1 Marx-Aveling	Folio Society
1953	TT3 May	Collins
c.1959	TT3 May	Murray's Book Sales
1959	TT4 Hopkins	OUP
1961	TT5 Russell	Penguin
1975	TT5 Russell	Penguin
1978	TT5 Russell	Penguin
1981	TT4 Hopkins	OUP
1984	TT5 Russell	Penguin
1987	TT4 Hopkins	OUP
1992	TT6 Wall	Penguin
1995	TT6 Wall	Penguin
1998	TT4 Hopkins	OUP
1999	TT4 Hopkins	OUP
2000	TT6 Wall	Penguin
2001	TT6 Wall	Penguin
2003	TT1 Marx-Aveling	Collector's Library
2003	TT6 Wall	Penguin
2004	TT7 Mauldon	OUP
2006	TT6 Wall	Penguin
2007	TT1 Marx-Aveling	The Independent
2007	TT6 Wall	Penguin
2008	TT7 Mauldon	OUP
2009	TT1 Marx-Aveling	Arcturus Publishing
2011	TT3 May	Harper Collins
2011	TT8 Thorpe	Vintage
2012	TT1 Marx-Aveling	Egoist Press

Entry conditions

That the two literary systems of France and Britain were closely interlinked during the nineteenth century is beyond doubt; writers, ideas, styles and genres circulated relatively freely between the two poles. But to begin with, this mutual influence owed very little to translation. As Bourdieu notes, the literary field is based on a 'principle of internal hierarchization' (1996: 217) whereby each entrant occupies a position relative to its perceived degree of symbolic capital; given that 'the wealthiest and most literate segment of society could read much foreign literature without the help of translation' (Hale 2006: 36), as was most certainly the case as far as French was concerned, it follows that the educated elite, who occupied a dominant position in the internal hierarchy, granted prestige to the French STs themselves, marginalizing translation to a peripheral position. However, in order to fully set the scene for the first published translation of *Madame Bovary* into English, it must be said that such incorporation of French literature in its original form was tempered by a latent distrust of foreign morality. Such suspicion is nowhere more evident than in the ultra-conservative *Quarterly Review* which in 1862 denounces *Madame Bovary*, side by side with Napoleon III, purporting that:

> his era enervated the minds of its inhabitants with a literature as filthy, as frivolous, and as false as ever sapped the morals of a nation, or made the fortune of a publisher. Such works as 'Madame Bovary', […] poisoned by the nastiness of a prurient mind and set out with all the artifice of a showy pen, are not so much outrages on decency as signs of the times amid which they crawled out of the dunghill – their author's brains. (272–3)

Thus, while the symbolic capital of French STs may have been considerable in the higher echelons of society, the internal logic of the literary field is at the same time susceptible to pressure from the external field of power, which in this instance equates to the moral authorities of Britain who have a stake in preventing the spread of this alleged pernicious threat from abroad amongst all levels of society.

TT1 Marx-Aveling: Initial negotiations

A gap of almost thirty years separates the publication of the ST and the appearance of the initial British version in 1886, translated by Eleanor Marx-Aveling, daughter of Karl Marx, and published in London by Vizetelly & Co.

Undoubtedly, the prevalence of the already mentioned conditions held the translation at bay, and may perhaps go some way to explaining why Flaubert himself was unable to fix a publisher: any interested parties would already have had access to his work in the original, whilst an act of translation may have attracted the unwanted attention of the censors. But, a literary system is in a constant change of flux, and one of the major driving forces is 'the appearance of new categories of consumers who, having an affinity with the new producers, guarantee the success of their products' (Bourdieu 1996: 253). Thus, as a new mass reading public emerges in Britain in the wake of educational reforms, publishers begin to produce cheaper works of fiction: one way in which to meet this growing new demand for affordable and popular literature is to supplement one's catalogue with translation, not least since uncertain and unenforced copyright laws and the low rate of pay for translators meant that this option was a cost-effective one. In this respect, the initial translation is destined for the mass market, as opposed to the restricted, purist one. Likewise, the putative moral threat posed by Flaubert appears to have lessened with time; already by 1878, the shockwaves created by the author's trial in Paris have subsided as critic and academic George Saintsbury claims that 'the prosecution is now defended by nobody' (1878: 577), while in the year of Marx-Aveling's translation, Flaubert is being classified as 'one of the high priests' (Kennard 1886: 693) of fiction.

However, despite the field appearing ripe for *Madame Bovary* towards the end of the century, the history of the Marx-Aveling translation is a turbulent one. To begin, Vizetelly & Co., established in 1880 and therefore a relatively new entrant into the publishing world of London, came under attack by the National Vigilance Society, formed 'ostensibly for the purpose of protecting boys and girls against what was called "pernicious literature"' (Vizetelly 1904: 257). Their primary grievance was the company's translations of Zola, notably versions of *L'Assomoir*, *Germinal* and *Le Ventre de Paris*, and Henry Vizetelly found himself twice convicted on charges of obscenity. Indeed, *Madame Bovary* was itself implicated in the charges, but given the apparent turn in critical opinion, 'the summons respecting that work was eventually adjourned sine die' (Vizetelly 1904: 257). Ultimately though, the publisher who had first introduced *Madame Bovary* to the masses was unable to recover financially from the prosecutions, and the company was ruined.

Furthermore, Marx-Aveling's translatorial peritext would seem to suggest a lingering wariness among the public at large. Hence her assertion that 'Flaubert is still so little known in England, his work so completely misunderstood, that some words of introduction to this translation – the first English one of "Madame Bovary" – are a necessity' (1886: vii). The translator's introduction can be read as an attempt to counteract the author's muddied reputation, not least by underscoring that 'in Flaubert we have the direct antithesis of Zola' (1886: xvi). By distancing the work of Flaubert from that of Zola, Marx-Aveling is essentially distancing her publishers from their own scandal; this work of innocence by dissociation thus demonstrates how the translatorial peritext can simultaneously serve the needs of an editorial one.

Marx-Aveling's introduction also addresses the text itself in its allusion to translation strategies. Here, the translator adopts a position that might be taken for self-effacement:

> no critic can be more painfully aware than I am of the weaknesses, the shortcomings, the failures of my work; but at least the translation is faithful. [...] It is pale and feeble by the side of its original. Yet, if it induces some readers to go to that original, if it helps to make known to those who cannot thus study this work of the greatest of French novelists after Balzac, I am content. (1886: xxii)

It is important to note that the negative attributes are accompanied by two very persuasive concessions: the watchword 'faithful' is a powerful counterbalance to the previous caveats, while the translation is further validated by the emphasis on accessibility above and beyond style. The paratextual posturing of Marx-Aveling in relation to the extratext and the text therefore reminds us that we are dealing not only with 'a space of *authorial* ruses, side-steppings and evasions' (del Lungo 2009: 105, my emphasis and translation), but of translatorial ones as well. Indeed, the very visibility of Marx-Aveling, realized through this translatorial peritext, may also be considered an attempt to exploit the symbolic capital of her father, Karl Marx; even a partial transfer of this capital may have been deemed sufficient to hasten the process whereby Eleanor could make a name for herself.

Admittedly, Marx-Aveling's manoeuvrings did not lead to positive reviews; for example, *The Athenaeum* greets her efforts at the time as having been carried out:

> with more zeal than discretion. [...] The translation is laborious, but unequally effective. Mrs. Aveling seems to have thought it incumbent on her to translate as far as possible word for word, and this can never result in anything but an unsatisfactory version when two languages so different in genius as French and English are concerned. Besides, even her word-for-word system has not been

> successfully carried out. […] [W]hen a writer takes such superhuman trouble as Flaubert did to choose exactly the words and phrases that suited his meaning, and no others, it is incumbent on his translator not to be content with a mere approximation. (Anon 1886: 429–30)

In other words, the translatorial peritext does nothing to dispel outside criticism, and by extension, to refute Berman's claim that initial translations are in some way deficient. Nevertheless, it would appear that the text has prevailed despite this dubious reception: Marx-Aveling's version has been reissued at least twenty-one times, by fifteen different publishers, with the most recent reprints appearing in 2012.

Besides the evident economic incentive of an expired copyright, the frequency with which this version has been reprised by publishers would suggest that the translation has an appeal that extends beyond its reputation of 'mak[ing] little attempt to match Flaubert's highly worked style' (France 2006: 241). However, the vast majority of these reprints omit the translator's original introduction. As Genette notes, the 'duration of the paratext is often intermittent' (1997: 6) as a consequence of its functional character; in this instance, the perpetuation of Marx-Aveling's work well beyond its immediate temporal point of entry, that is beyond the reach of the Victorian censors, is offset by the discontinuation of her introductory stratagems. But on another level, the very presence of Marx-Aveling's translation suggests that the teleology of retranslation may be somewhat more confused than previously allowed for. We now have a situation where the initial translation reappears after the most recent retranslation; not only does this perplex the history-as-progress logic of the Retranslation Hypothesis, but it also frustrates Pym's seemingly clear-cut differentiation between passive and active retranslations. For, while Pym regards passivity as being determined by the passage of time, which supposedly ensures that 'knowledge of one version does not conflict with knowledge of another' (1998: 82), Bourdieu views the temporality of the literary field in less linear terms. Instead, he asserts that:

> agents and institutions engaged in the game are simultaneously contemporaries and temporally discordant. The field of the present is merely another name for the field of struggle (as shown by the fact that an author of the past is present to the exact extent that he is still at stake). Contemporaneity as presence in the same present only exists in practice in the struggle that synchronizes discordant times or, rather, agents and institutions separated by time and in relation to time. (Bourdieu 1996: 158)

In other words, the fundamental dynamic of struggle that structures the field bends time in on itself, allowing products and producers who entered the field at a comparatively remoter point to remain in the game at a later stage. The synchronizing properties of the field cannot then be abstracted into a schema which has been based on a chronological opposition between now and then, and the explanatory power of 'passive' retranslations is subsequently limited.

But how do we account for the endurance of versions such as this initial translation whose reproduction integrates them firmly within the fray of the literary field? One answer may be traced back to the close temporal proximity of Marx-Aveling's work to the original, which marks it with a certain authenticity. As Steiner comments, 'Read now, what is frequently an imperceptive version is steadied by its period flavour' (1998: 396); despite its perceived shortcomings, it is an antiquated feel which may have contributed to the continuation of this initial translation. Similarly, Barnes notes that 'some of us continue to read the Garnett translations [of Chekhov]. Mainly because they do the time-travelling work instantly, and give a better illusion of being a reader back then' (2010). Viewed in this light, the fate of the textually aged translation is reframed; instead of being condemned to obsolescence, it is precisely the caducity of the linguistic and cultural norms which endow the initial translation with its 'time-travelling' capabilities, allowing the reader to be projected backwards and thereby increasing the work's legitimacy as a vestige of the original setting.

Splicings

Yet more confounding variables come to light in respect of the status which the Marx-Aveling translation attributes to itself as 'the first English one of "Madame Bovary"' (1886: vii). It is significant that the British public had, in actual fact, access to a partial translation of some key passages of the work as early as 1878 when George Saintsbury published an essay on Flaubert in the *Fortnightly Review*. Here, Saintsbury incorporates the translation of three lengthy passages from the work; an extract from I.7 (in which Emma questions her decision to marry Charles) is employed as a means of illustrating Flaubert's style, while two passages are taken from II.12 (where Charles' dreams for the future are juxtaposed against those of Emma) in support of what Saintsbury holds to be a 'masterpiece of ironical contrast' (1878: 580–1). This practice was not uncommon in such British periodicals where 'reviews covered both foreign literature, sometimes offering extracts newly translated by the reviewer, and

English translations' (France 2006: 143); the Saintsbury translation can thus be accredited as the first real point of entry granted to the ST.

Unquestionably, Marx-Aveling's version can still lay claim to the status of the first definitive translated version; but, the boundaries of retranslation become blurred since her work now incorporates a retranslation of the earlier passages. This typology becomes even more disordered when we uncover the paratextual and textual manipulations ensconced in the J.M. Dent reprint of Marx-Aveling's translation, first issued in 1928. In her biography of Marx-Aveling, Kapp remarks in passing that Dent drops the original introduction to the work (1976: 99); however, this exclusion merits a closer investigation. In fact, not only is the introduction removed, but it is also replaced by Saintsbury's aforementioned article, retaining his translation of the three passages. Nor does the substitution end there; rather, an exploration of the text itself reveals that the Marx-Aveling passages have also been removed and replaced by those which Saintsbury has translated and which now appear in the new introduction. This stealthy act of grafting one version onto another means that Dent has issued a hybrid translation framed by a hybrid peritext. In the first instance, Berman's straightforward move from defective initial version to retranslation is once again distorted by the composite nature of the target text. In the second, an article that was at once extratext (review) and text (translation) has now become peritext – part allographic, part translatorial.

TT2 Blanchamp

And so, what of the more clearly defined retranslations? Implicit in Berman's conception of retranslation is the idea that each new version will surpass and displace that which has gone before; this evolution further resonates with the Bourdieusian phenomenon of definitional conflicts, wherein 'One of the central stakes in literary (etc.) rivalries is the monopoly of literary legitimacy' (1996: 224). In other words, each new retranslation will challenge extant versions for the right to become the definitive, legitimate translation, eclipsing all others, and if we follow Berman's history-as-progress model, the newer the retranslation, the better equipped it will be to make its challenge.

But the rush to take up this gauntlet of retranslation is not in evidence at the turn of the century: as Newman writes in *the Fortnightly Review* in 1895, 'if translation be any index to the English appreciation of a foreign author, it cannot be said that Flaubert's following in this country is very large' (813). It may well be that the fate of Vizetelly & Co. has left a lingering taste in the mouths of other publishers, and as a consequence neither *Madame Bovary* nor other works by Flaubert are destined as yet for mass, popular consumption.

Such reticence may indeed explain both the delay in the appearance of the first retranslation and its form: published in the Lotus Library series of Greening & Co. in 1905 and 'done into English' by Henry Blanchamp (almost two decades after the Marx-Aveling translation), this version is, like that of Saintsbury, partial. However, on this occasion, the guiding principle may have been one of brevity, if not of expurgation, particularly towards the end of the novel: gone is the obsequious portrayal of Homais in the company of M. Larrivière, gone is the vigil held by Homais and M. Bournisien at Emma's deathbed, and gone is the blind beggar. Similarly, the novel is brought to an abrupt end with the words Charles 'fell to the ground; he was dead' (TT2 Blanchamp 263), hence no post-mortem for Charles, no banishment of Berthe to the cotton mill and no *croix d'honneur* for Homais.

The textual absences are mirrored on a peritextual level as there is no translatorial introduction, while the publisher's advertisements tell us only that the work was sold for the modest price tag of 1s. 6d. However, this relative lack of framing in itself speaks volumes. The price allows us to surmise that the Lotus Library, which also issued translations of Maupassant, Musset and Zola, had a more popular audience in its sights. Whether the cuts made to the ST were done so out of a sense of catering for this new readership – whose attention spans were perhaps not so developed as those of the literary elite – or out of a sense of cautious propriety is unclear. Nonetheless, in respect of this latter point, it is evident that while religiously sensitive material may have been deliberately removed, all seduction scenes and a good part of the death scene remain intact. Writing in 1904 on his father's publishing endeavours, Ernest Vizetelly alludes to the lack of demand for 'works of high repute in France', rather 'it soon appeared that if French fiction was to be offered to English readers at all it must at least be sensational' (1904: 249). Lack of paratextual evidence means that the particular strategies of Greening & Co. can only be surmised, but this edition may wish to strike a balance between readability, titillation and decorum; by curtailing the length of the novel, retaining some of the more spirited scenes whilst removing the most injurious, the popular reader will be presented with a Flaubert that is at once accessible and entertaining – a far cry from the uncertainty of the ST. Peritextual commentary on the work would thus be an unnecessary distraction. It is not Flaubert's literary merit which is at stake here, rather uncomplicated access to Emma's infamous story in its abridged form.

According to the Retranslation Hypothesis, this version should have permitted closer access to the source text; evidently, market conditions mean that the reverse is true. As to its persistence, the Blanchamp translation is only reissued twice (1910; 1929) and hereafter falls into obscurity. Conversely, it is framed chronologically on both sides by re-editions of the Marx-Aveling translation; thus, this initial translation appears to have staved off any challenge presented by the newcomer and resists being superseded.

TT3 May

With the subsequent new retranslation comes a new approach, not to mention a conspicuous attempt to break with the previous versions, or in the words of Bourdieu, 'make a name for oneself' (1996: 239). In 1928, J. Lane (The Bodley Head) issued a translation of *Madame Bovary*, carried out by J. Lewis May and presented in a luxurious, illustrated edition. Although ungenerously described by one reviewer as 'one of those unfriendly monumental tomes which make a meretricious bid for popularity at Christmas time' (Holbrook 1928: 202), the same nevertheless welcomes the translator's efforts, claiming that 'Mr. May has given us "Madame Bovary" in a more becoming English dress than any of those who have hitherto attempted the "insurmountable" task' (Holbrook 1928: 202). Furthermore, the article proffers an interesting reflection on the state of Flaubert translations at that time:

> If we had treated France as badly as we have treated Flaubert, diplomatic relations might have been cut off. […] Although we have in English a complete Anatole France, a nearly complete Proust and the beginning of a complete Stendhal, we have no complete Flaubert. It is in fact far worse than that; we have scarcely any translations of any of his works which begin to give him adequate representation in our language; some of the attempts to translate him are beneath contempt, the remainder survive by lack of competent opposition. (Holbrook 1928: 202)

Notably, it is within this category of 'competent opposition' that the May version actively seeks to inscribe itself, and nowhere is this tactic more evident than in the translator's introduction to his work. Here, it is stated in no uncertain terms that 'Flaubert, at least so far as Madame Bovary is concerned, has not been particularly well served by his translators', who 'have failed to recognise the nature and importance of the task before them' and despite May's normative protestation that he 'alas! could only dimly and imperfectly express'

(1928: xvii–xix), Flaubert's style, the prevailing implication is that this version rises to the occasion, serves Flaubert well and, in so doing, ought to dispense with those flawed attempts that have come before. What then comes to light in this retranslation is the very earliest evidence of rivalry in retranslation given its overt antagonism towards other extant versions within the literary field in order to challenge their legitimacy.

In spite of such lofty ambitions, the appearance of the May retranslation does not succeed in securing a dominant position for itself, nor does it mark a rupture in the established order of things: reprinted once in 1931 by J. Lane Bodley Head, and then reissued four times (1950; 1953; c.1959; 2011), this particular translation still pales in quantitative comparison against the deluge of reprints of the Marx-Aveling version. Indeed, over the period of the next two decades alone, the initial translation will appear at a rate of almost once every two years (1928; 1930; 1932; 1934; 1936; 1941; 1946; 1949; 1952), alternating between the two main publishing companies of J. M. Dent and J. Cape until 1941, then adopted by the Camden Publishing Co. and Nonesuch Press for the remaining years. Of course, this prevalence is in large part circumstantial: spanning the dark decade of the thirties, World War II and its aftermath, this concentration of reprints certainly responded to the gloomy financial climate, as well as to the shortages, economic or otherwise, as imposed by the war: no copyright restrictions on the Marx-Aveling version means no need to commission a costly and a time-consuming new translation.

In addition, both the Dent and Cape imprints catered for a well-defined market. As far as the former was concerned, the Everyman's Library was targeted precisely at everyone so that 'The knowledge to be derived from the series would benefit not only men like J.M. Dent himself, who had little formal education, but anyone, of whatever standard of education, who was willing to continue learning' (Mumby 1974: 323). Jonathan Cape, in turn, 'wanted the reader to have the benefit of the cheapest possible prices' (Mumby 1974: 357), issuing pocket-sized editions in the Traveller's Library series. Thus, the guiding principles were those of accessibility and price, and the readership of the two houses undoubtedly overlapped. Furthermore, Marx-Aveling's peritextual claims of faithfulness tempered by stylistic inadequacy may also have helped to flag up its potential to Dent and Cape as a good match for its readership: more instructive in terms of its completeness than the Blanchamp version, and less daunting in terms of its language than May's contribution. In many regards, the initial translation becomes the only viable option, with its fate inextricably caught up in the cultural conditions of the literary field.

TT4 Hopkins and TT5 Russell

The following two new retranslations appear in quick succession: Hamish Hamilton issues a version by Gerard Hopkins in 1948, while Penguin launches its Alan Russell translation in 1950. Hopkins's *Madame Bovary* is integrated into the Novel Library series which, according to the work's dust jacket, boasts a policy of presenting, 'at a price within the bounds of every reader's purse, novels of excellence'. The appearance of the Hopkins's version under this particular imprint is fleeting, but it is taken up by Oxford University Press (OUP) in 1959. It is at this point that we can note the very beginnings of an evident competition between the houses of Penguin and OUP as far as the publication of *Madame Bovary* is concerned.

There are certainly no obvious paratextual signs of altercations between the Russell and Hopkins translations; the former takes the opportunity in his introduction to the context in which *Madame Bovary* was written, including an overview of the life, concerns, troubles and works of Flaubert. Contrary to the Hamish Hamilton edition, Hopkins is given a voice in the OUP text; in his foreword, the tactic is somewhat different, and although he briefly outlines a history of the ST, the bulk of his thoughts are centred on the translation problems specific to Flaubert (the 'mot juste'; syntax; the use of the imperfect tense; sociolect). Neither Russell nor Hopkins makes reference, positive or depreciative, to any previous translation attempts. On face value, this lack of posturing might be viewed as symptomatic of the differing agendas of the two publishing houses. Little needs to be said about the paperback revolution set in motion by Penguin which furnished the masses with affordable and well-designed books, while OUP set their sights on a more academic market. In sum, different readerships, different (non-conflictual) strategies.

But it is significant that by now *Madame Bovary* has found its place in the literary canon, with the two publishers issuing the work in series dedicated to the classics; therefore, some overlap in readership is to be expected. An OUP advertisement for *Madame Bovary* in *The Guardian* takes this encroachment further still, stating that 'these good looking volumes are so cheap, yet they last a lifetime' (Anon 1959: 14). By staking a claim for design and affordability they clearly move into Penguin territory, and by emphasizing durability they launch a very thinly veiled attack on the paperback format. It follows that rivalry is observable on the epitextual level, while the peritexts appear to disengage from blatant acts of competition. Nevertheless, the absence of challenge in the peritexts can equally attest to the presence of a particular strategy: rather than draw attention to potential translation alternatives, a tacit rejection of their very existence may go some way to securing one's own survival. This subtle dissimulation points once more to the problematic nature of active retranslations as understood by Pym, since it is the apparently passive peritextual stance which propels the challenge forward.

As the economic struggle for survival in the publishing world becomes fiercer, the vying for dominance becomes more overt. In 1981, OUP takes the decision to issue a revised version of Hopkins's translation, replacing his translatorial peritext with an allographic one, namely an introduction by Oxford academic Terence Cave and a wealth of explanatory notes. Inherent in this move is a conscious attempt to appeal to a specifically academic market, along with evidence that the publishers hold with a 'new equals improved' ethos. In the first case, the new paratextual material can be regarded as an act of symbolic violence, that is a deliberate attempt at domination through accumulated prestige, where the aim is to create a 'monopoly of the power to say with authority who is authorized to call himself writer (etc.)', in this case, the allographic commentator. In opposition to the Hopkins foreword, in which he claimed that the difficulties of translation 'assume enormous and insurmountable proportions' (1959: viii), no aspersions are cast as to the quality of the translation in the revised version. Rather, the intellectual weight of the introduction bolsters its claim to legitimacy; as Casanova has pointed out, if the consecrating potential of the translator is not sufficient, then a process of 'inter-consecration' (2002: 19) can take place, bolstering the symbolic (or literary) capital of the work through the presence of a more prestigious, and in this case academically legitimized, agent. Secondly, the publishers initiate a tactic of renewal which will be perpetuated in the years to follow, and which appears to be intuitively attuned to Berman's progressive model of retranslation.

TT6 Wall

Penguin responds to the OUP revision by upping the ante, and in 1992 they replace their oft reprinted Russell version with an entirely new translation by Geoffrey Wall. This too is framed by a comprehensive introduction (albeit pitched at a more general level), and by a considerable number of notes. However, where it distinguishes itself from the OUP edition is in its engagement with and acknowledgement of earlier translations in the translatorial peritext:

> Translating afresh the already translated classic, the translator is drawn into dialogue with his or her precursors. Though I was working on different principles, and though I have found that I eventually disagreed with some of their most cherished efforts, I have profited from the posthumous conversation of three previous translators of *Madame Bovary*: Eleanor Marx, Alan Russell and Gerard Hopkins. (Wall 1992: xx)

This reflection on the act of retranslation is telling in many ways: firstly 'afresh' has connotations of progress, of betterment, and inscribes the version into Berman's specific vision of retranslation. Secondly, in this literary field where existence and difference go hand in hand (Bourdieu 1996: 239), the self-positioning, based on differentiation and disagreement, in relation to his precursors is pertinent. Thirdly, this is the only occasion when there is explicit recognition of the fact that the translator has in fact drawn on the work of others, thereby emphasizing the arteries of influence which may be posited between extant versions. In his article, 'Retranslating Madame Bovary', Wall elaborates further on this conversation, explaining that 'Whenever I got stuck I would turn to them […] I discovered a happy plurality of voices available to me' (2004: 95). However, such influence is only given limited reign, and as with the above note, a chord of dissention is struck: 'for all their virtues, neither Hopkins nor Russell were to be trusted', while Marx-Aveling's translation 'falls down at those moments where Flaubert has invested, imaginatively, in his subject-matter' (2004: 96). Thus, it is ultimately in the spirit of contradistinction and improvement that the Wall translation presents itself, thereby supporting the assumption that challenge and differentiation go hand in hand, and that time begets progress – on the outward level of posturing at least.

TT7 Mauldon

Mirroring Penguin's move, OUP issue a brand new translation by Margaret Mauldon in 2004. According to the publisher's online catalogue, this 'new translation by award-winning translator Margaret Mauldon replaces the slightly old-fashioned one by Gerard Hopkins', while 'Respected critic and writer Malcolm Bowie has written a wide-ranging and original new introduction to the novel' (OUP). Once more, the currency of the paratext is one of symbolic capital, gleaned from the prestige of the translator and from that of the allographic author in a further example of inter-consecration. However, the allusion to the 'old-fashioned' Hopkins version also points to another key consideration in the study of retranslations: the ageing of the TT. In this instance, OUP are acting on the presumption that the outdated language of the work which first appeared in 1950 necessitates a new version for modern times. Their behaviour apparently confirms the universal feature put forward by Berman that translations age (1990: 4), and emphasis is even placed on the necessary rejuvenation of peritextual material too, since the introduction is lauded as both 'original' and 'new'.

But, as Genette warns: '*attention au paratexte*!' (1987: 413, original emphasis). For the paratext is a construct, an artifice potentially underpinned by (im) posturing. As such, the reader should be wary of any claims made there; it is an easy task to assert in the blurb that 'Margaret Mauldon perfectly captures the tone that makes Flaubert's style so distinct and admired' (TT7 Mauldon outside back cover), but it is a less easy task for the translator to fulfil those professions of perfection in the text itself. By way of brief illustration, I refer to the review of Mauldon's translation by Clive James who shrewdly observes that 'Despite the heavy endorsement from Professor Bowie, her accuracy is not always beyond cavil' (2004: 179), especially given her anachronistic use of the twentieth century idiom, 'No way!'. Indeed, James signals the fallacy of the paratext when he questions Mauldon's decisions to retranslate, and echoes the benefits which we have seen earlier of closer temporal proximity to the original: 'Why try to improve on it [Russell's translation] if all she can offer is prose that sounds – *purportedly* sounds – less dated? Isn't a dated style what we want?' (2004: 178–9, my emphasis). Rather than accept the offering on face value, James shatters the illusion developed in the paratext that an ageing (re)translation is an unwelcome one, lauding the capacity of earlier texts to reposition the reader closer to the original on the space-time continuum, as both Steiner (1998) and Barnes (2010) do earlier.

A certain degree of collusion can be surmised in the stances adopted by both Penguin and OUP, that is in their apparent affinity with and the perpetuation of the idea that translations need to be updated or renewed. By codifying retranslation as renewal and improvement, the publishers are simultaneously defining the terms of the game within the literary field and ensuring future opportunities for challenge and domination. The broader the circulation (or exploitation) of the idea that translations age, the more effective the marketing strategy that 'new equals improved', resulting in higher economic yields and ensuring further demand for updated versions along the way.

In addition, the prevalence of OUP and Penguin from the 1960s onwards seems to have more or less arrested the appearance of retranslations in other imprints for some fifty years. One explanation for their prevalence is the grandeur accorded to these particular retranslations, not as a result of any inherent linguistic excellence, but as a consequence of the symbolic capital which the publishers have in abundance. It is worth remarking that, around the same time as OUP and Penguin come to saturate the market, there is also a significant decline – if not an outright halt – in translation reviews. This phenomenon undoubtedly ties in with Venuti's (1995) assertion of the 'invisibility of the translator', but it also points to the tendency to willingly confer authority onto these publishing institutions, issuers and guardians of the literary canon; their legitimacy is such, there is no perceived need to question their retranslations (or as Venuti might see it, no interest in posing the question). In turn, this leaves the way open for these leading publishers to specify themselves when the time is right to retranslate; viewed in this light, retranslation is far removed from concerns over textual deficiency, instead it plays a fundamental role in the power struggles within the literary system.

TT8 Thorpe

The stemming of retranslation does not hold indefinitely though, and the latest translation, published in 2011 by Vintage under their Classics imprint, makes its entry into the landscape and hierarchies of the British literary field. Emblazoned on the front cover in capital letters is the text's unique selling point: '*NEW TRANSLATION BY ADAM THORPE*'. Or rather, its not so unique selling point as the same formulation also appears on the Mauldon version, with the same positive, symbolic emphasis on novelty and the same positive, symbolic naming of the translator – for whether or not the book buyer or peruser is familiar with the translator, it is this very act of naming which is intended to send out a message of authority and ultimately trustworthiness, which in turn is expected to translate into economic capital. A shift in marketing trends is perhaps now bringing Venuti's invisible translator out of the shadows, not in the name of unmasking the foreign, but of showcasing the legitimacy (real or purported) that the presence of their name infers.

The editorial peritext on the inside of the translation continues in the same vein, affirming that:

> This stunning new translation, by the celebrated novelist Adam Thorpe, delicately and meticulously transposes the rhythms, tones and poetry of *Madame Bovary* and brings us closer to its shifting depths. It is destined to become the definitive translation of our time. (TT8 Thorpe inside dust cover)

The resonance with Berman's (1990) notion of the *grande traduction* is striking: according to the publishers, not only will this version serve to better illuminate the hitherto obscured nuances of the original, but it will also have a demonstrable impact within the receiving culture, suppressing the need for future retranslations. Again, there is something of a happy complicity between the meme of retranslation as rejuvenation and the marketing manoeuvres of the publishing company.

Of course, implicit in the proclamation of definitiveness is that of differentiation. The challenge launched against the merit of previous (re) translations may be subtle (naming no names, as was the case in the TT4 Hopkins and TT5 Russell), but its supposed authority nevertheless extends both backwards and forwards. The differentiating stratagem is also discernible in the translator's notes where Thorpe underscores his choice to 'only use pre-1857 vocabulary and expressions' to ensure that the novel be 'placed back in its own context' (2011a: n.p.). In opposition to its immediate predecessor, the translator rejects any attempt to update the language of the work – maybe having paid heed to the reprimands of James (2004) above – and affirms that he has modelled his style on the work of Henry James and James Joyce. This allusion cannot be viewed as entirely innocent either; by aligning his work with that of two great modernists, the translator surely hopes to generate yet more legitimacy through the assimilation of residual symbolic capital. Indeed, this overt posturing also attests to how the dynamics of the field have changed since Marx-Aveling's time and her comparatively more humble stance.

More so than any other previous translator, Thorpe is also very visible on the level of the translatorial epitext. While Wall (2004) produced an article on his retranslating experience in a French academic journal, some twelve years after the publication of his version, Thorpe has been able to reach a wider and more contemporary audience in his piece for *The Guardian* which carries the title 'Madame Bovary: the Everest of translation' and which coincided with the release of his retranslation in October 2011. In this respect, the translatorial epitext cannot be disassociated from strategies of self-promotion and book promotion. If *Madame Bovary* was indeed Thorpe's Everest, then the translator accordingly becomes the intrepid and conquering adventurer, staking a claim for his 'great translation' at the summit. In contrast to Wall, the ascent was achieved without the assistance of previous translators, for in an act of differentiation and symbolic violence, these are stealthily brought into the analogy not as helpful Sherpas, but as 'foolhardy expeditions' which crowd the slopes (Thorpe 2011b). A more overt challenge is then made to his predecessors with reference to the Flaubertian fixation on the indivisibility of idea and form: 'This was crucial to get right, not only because it was what previous translators had largely omitted, but because I'm obsessed by the same equation in my own work' (Thorpe 2011b). There are two corollaries to this particular vying for position: firstly, we hear yet another echo of Berman's reasoning – in this instance that retranslation, especially the great ones, will restore the essence of the original – which lends itself well to manoeuvres of legitimization. Secondly, the emphasis on the mutual obsession of Flaubert the writer and Thorpe the writer is a further means of reinforcing the symbolic capital of the translation, in much the same way as the allusions to Joyce and James were.

Further sites of epitexual visibility for Thorpe are his public lecture delivered at Cardiff University in January 2013 with its suitably alluring title 'My Nights with Emma B', which is now available online (2013), as well as the author's website (2014a) and Facebook page (2014b). It may indeed be possible to identify a correlation between the enhanced online presence of the translator and the return of translation reviews which, as mentioned earlier, had previously reached something of an impasse. These reviews are also resoundingly positive: for example, novelist Philip Kerr (2011) selects the 'stunning and heartily recommended' translation as one of his 'Books of the Year' in *The Scotsman*, while another novelist Russell Kane (2012) professes in *The Independent* that Thorpe's translation is 'to die for'. Praise indeed, and praise which will surely generate economic revenue. But the question remains as to whether the creation of symbolic value can be tied solely to the merits of the translation itself, or whether it can also be tied to a certain degree of self-fulfilling prophesying by Thorpe, who had the opportunity to clearly articulate the fruits of his labour.

Interestingly, this is the first retranslation in the corpus where the translator and publisher have been in a position to fully harness the marketing potential of online media. I would argue that in light of this broad, symbolic and economic capital-generating platform, the supposed invisibility of the translator must be rethought. For as Bourdieu points out, 'great upheavals arise from the eruption of newcomers who […] import innovation regarding products or techniques of production, and try or claim to impose on the field of production, which is itself its own market, a new mode of evaluation of products' (1996: 225). The arrival and consolidation of the Internet has undoubtedly created one such upheaval in the literary field, redrawing virtual lines in the sand and facilitating the increased presence of the translator; the evaluative currency of invisibility may find itself devalued in this new configuration.

Multiples of one

Thorpe emphasizes the positive, as opposed to the antagonistic, aspects of retranslation in his observation that 'Having several good translations is no bad thing – they are autonomous creations, yielding different aspects of the original text' (2011b). Evidently, he is including his own version under the banner of good, but the categorization of retranslations as 'autonomous' nevertheless raises an interesting question: to what extent can we assume that retranslations are purely independent entities? For retranslations are necessarily multiples of one; far from effacing each another, the texts form a certain collective, presided over by the immutable title of *Madame Bovary* and inescapably bound together by their common heritage. Indeed, there is a place for this aggregate within the dynamics of the literary field since Bourdieu recognizes that 'The history of the field is truly irreversible; and the products of this relatively autonomous history present a kind of *cumulativity*' (1996: 242, original emphasis). Each successive (re)translation thus enters into the struggles of the field to adopt a position which can be framed not only in individual terms, but also in relational terms, that is against the accumulated history of the field in general, and of the corpus of *Madame Bovary* (re)translations in particular.

If we shift our focus towards how the corpus functions cumulatively, then we also have to take into consideration the dynamics of the literary field which might lead to 'the *wearing out of the effect* of consecrated works' (Bourdieu 1996: 253), not least because this loss of impact is intrinsically linked to reiteration: 'It is primarily the result of the routinization of production [...] and arises from the repeated and repetitive application of proved procedures and the uninventive use of an art of inventing [the] already invented' (Bourdieu 1996: 253). And so, even if a given work reaches a canonical status, there may be a rupture in the configuration of the field at any point which challenges the enduring, routine position of the work and relegates it to an outdated one. However, if retranslation is understood as an inventive, innovative procedure, one which reinvents the already invented by revealing more and more of its facets, then retranslation simultaneously becomes a procedure of defamiliarization and a ballast against banalization. The paratextual insistence on newness in the retranslations discussed above thus adopts an additional layer of significance. The device is not merely one of differentiation from previous (re)translations, but of differentiation per se, signalling that a new image has been overlaid on to the composite face of *Madame Bovary*. As the layers build up, the threat of wearing out diminishes, ensuring the survival of this 'belle infidèle' within the boundaries of the British literary system.

Conclusion

This digest of the paratextual and extratextual material related to the British *Madame Bovarys* has gone some way to disclosing the dynamics of the British literary field – the stakes of the game, the players, the strategies and how they have changed over time – as well as identifying the impact of those dynamics on the (re)translations on an individual, interactive and collective level. In so doing, it has also brought to light several significant examples of (re)translation behaviour which suggest that our critical approach to the phenomenon should be broadened.

Hybrid textual properties are evidenced in the (re)translations of *Madame Bovary*; the paratextual and textual splicing of the partial Saintsbury version with the Marx-Aveling version unsettles one of the cornerstones of previous thinking on retranslation, namely the fallibility of *the* initial translation. The conceptualization of any (re)translation as an indivisible entity may thus blind the researcher to the knottier, more muddled intricacies which arise from these texts which reiterate both the source text and, potentially, fragments of each other.

In light of the fact that the internal logic of Bourdieu's literary field is one of differentiation and struggle, it is scarcely surprising that we should find practices in support of Venuti's claim that 'retranslations are designed to challenge a previous version of the foreign text' (2004: 32). From TT3 onwards, the retranslations become embroiled in the pursuit of symbolic and economic capital; some are more overt in their legitimizing machinations than others, and some are more successful in securing the desired capital than others. This study has also emphasized the extent to which rivalry is played out on a distinctly paratextual level, where the eagerness on the part of publishers to showcase their retranslation as a 'new translation' can be read as a differentiating strategy which effectively exploits the idea that new equals improved. This improvement may not be visible within the text itself, but its very implication serves to enhance the authority and the position of the retranslation within the field, while also projecting forward to stimulate future retranslation possibilities.

In addition, the notion that retranslations will rival *anterior* versions is confounded by the persistent presence of TT1 Marx-Aveling over the decades. Not only does this presence signal the economic and symbolic capital to be gleaned from an expired copyright and period flavour respectively, but it also further attests to the ineffectiveness of Pym's (1998) dialectic of passive and active retranslations. Bourdieu's model of the literary field does not allow for a distant, inert past; the present configuration of its boundaries is borne both of contemporary and historical struggles, and as long as a particular work or agent has the capacity to influence the shape of those boundaries, as the Marx-Aveling translation does, there can be no dismissive charges of inactivity.

Finally, the anatomy of Bourdieu's literary field has also invited a consideration of how the English versions of *Madame Bovary* function as a collective, with this cumulative approach adding a new dimension to the conceptualization of retranslation. In this case, the multiplicity of (re)translations ensures strength in numbers, or rather, strength in interpretations; each successive version rejuvenates the canonical work by injecting it with alternative readings, and these new slants together safeguard against a potentially deconsecrating process of over-familiarization.

3

On Shifting Sand: Relocating *La Mare au diable*

Introduction

As was the case in the preceding chapter, the lines of enquiry will extend beyond the text to consider the various positions which the (re)translations of *La Mare au diable* take up within the British literary system, as indicated by a close scrutiny of paratextual and extratextual material. It will consequently be possible to examine how socio-cultural factors, not least the search for economic and symbolic capital, have shaped the appearance of and interaction between these (re)translations. It is of note that the pastoral tale can lay claim to the accolade of being the most retranslated work from Sand's extensive œuvre in Britain: the greatest concentration of translation comes in the mid- to late nineteenth century when four different versions are in circulation, but the rate decreases with time as only two new retranslations of the work appear in the twentieth century, falling to one in more recent times (see Table 3.1 below). But despite the comparative frequency with which the work was imported into the literary system, Massardier-Kenney observes that 'English translations are absent from studies on the reception of Sand's works abroad' (2004: 71, my translation). This study will subsequently seek to redress this oversight by better clarifying the shifting fortunes of *La Mare au diable* and its author within the context of the British literary system.

Table 3.1 (Re)translations and re-editions of *La Mare au diable*

Year	TT	Title	Publisher
1847	TT1 Anon	*Marie*	Chapman & Hall
1847	TT2 Anon	*The Haunted Marsh*	Simms & M'Intyre
1848	TT3 Shaw	*The Devil's Pool*	H.G. Clarke
1850	TT3 Shaw	*The Enchanted Lake: a tale*	George Slater
1855	TT3 Shaw	*The Enchanted Lake, a tale*	W. Tweedie

(*Continued*)

Table 3.1 (Re)translations and re-editions of *La Mare au diable* (*Continued*)

Year	TT	Title	Publisher
1861	TT3 Shaw	*The Devil's Pool*	Lea's Sixpenny Library
1884	TT2 Anon	*The Haunted Marsh*	Weldon & Co.
1895	TT4 Sedgwick	*The Devil's Pool*	J.M. Dent
1911	TT4 Sedgwick	*The Devil's Pool*	J.M. Dent (Everyman's Library)
1923	TT4 Sedgwick	*The Devil's Pool*	J.M. Dent (Everyman's Library)
1929	TT5 Miles	*The Devil's Pool*	Scholartis Press
1930	TT4 Sedgwick	*The Devil's Pool*	J.M. Dent (Everyman's Library)
1933	TT4 Sedgwick	*The Devil's Pool*	J.M. Dent (Everyman's Library)
1966	TT6 Cowan	*The Devil's Pool*	Blackie & Co.
2005	TT7 Brown	*The Devil's Pool*	Hesperus Press

Uncertain beginnings: 1847–1884

Prior to the appearance of the initial translation of *La Mare au diable* in 1847, the critical attitude towards Sand in Britain was somewhat ambivalent, not least as a consequence of the now infamous invective against French novels by Croker in *The Quarterly Review*, in which Sand figured prominently alongside Hugo and Balzac as 'conductors of contagion' (1836: 66). Even as early as 1847, *Howitt's Journal* recognizes that 'the Quarterly succeeded for a time in tabooing her works, and closing the eyes, ears, and hearts of the British reading public against her' (Anon 1847c: 128), but for a good many years, reviews of the author and her works are characterized by a tempered estimation in which praise and moral caveats meet. Take for example an article which appeared in *The Mirror of Literature, Amusement and Instruction* of June 1842: here, Sand is lauded as 'not only the most remarkable woman, but the most remarkable writer of the present century' (Anon 1842: 395), and despite claiming that they will 'attempt a just and impartial consideration of one whose name is in some quarters synonymous with vice', they nevertheless 'confess the truth of many of the charges brought against her' (Anon 1842: 395). Likewise, *The Foreign and Colonial Quarterly Review* speaks the following year of 'the perpetual encounter at every page of principles the most inconsistent with our own ideas of right and wrong, and sentiments revolting to our feelings' (Anon 1843: 486), which is then accompanied by the concession that 'it is impossible to read her volumes [...] without being aware that they possess some merit' (1843: 486).

TT1 Anon

The first translation of *La Mare au diable* appears amidst what Bourdieu terms 'conflicts over *definition*' (1996: 223, original emphasis); no one clear-cut attitude towards Sand prevails in the system at the time of its entry in 1847, with each interested party vying for the legitimatization of their own conception of the author and for the corresponding opening or closing of the field boundaries to her works. However, there is evidence to suggest that the initial translation takes deliberate measures to remove itself from this definitional struggle over Sand. One obvious distancing device is the choice of title, *Marie*; even more telling is the fact that Sand's name is nowhere to be found in the edition. Thus, TT1 Anon does not immediately flag itself up as belonging to Sand's oeuvre and as such may fly under the radar of the debate. Similarly, an advertisement (editorial epitext) in *The Examiner* simply alludes to the work as 'A tale from the French with four illustrations' (Anon 1847e: 432), thereby sidestepping any direct connection with the author, while the accompanying excerpt from a review in the *Literary Gazette* merely states:

> There is a sweetness of sentiment that runs through the whole, and a simplicity touching with admirable truth upon human motives, and feelings, and sources of action, which must render 'Marie' very popular. It is at once playful and pretty, yet acute and profound. (Anon 1847e: 432)

Again, there is nothing in this vague description that would allow the work to be traced back to Sand. It is of note that the *Literary Gazette* review also includes a somewhat cryptic allusion to the origins of the work which is left out of the advertisement:

> We have a dreaminess about the birth and parentage of this charming story; but as its education (i.e. translation and editing) as well as its innate nature, make it quite different from many of its family, brothers and sisters, we will say nothing about it. (Anon 1847a: 468)

In effect, any direct reference to the source is avoided, and although Thomson argues that the 'Berry novels, written at the end of the 1840s, completed the acceptance of George Sand by reviewers' (1977: 27), such oblique recognition of her pastoral tale implies that the controversy surrounding the name of the author is still so tangible as to warrant the silence of the reviewer, but not so great as to prevent him providing a clue for the more enlightened reader as regards the heritage of the work. No such hints are to be found in *The Critic*, however, where the reviewer identifies *Marie* as a 'little tale descriptive of the simple life and manners of the French peasantry […]. The author prefaces *his* little volume with a sort of discourse on the happiness or misery of a cultivator of the soil' (Anon 1847b: 197, my emphasis). Thus, the concealment of the Berry region and the gender of the author both serve as a means of severing ties to Sand. The very fact that this initial version does not appear in any surveys of or discussions on the translations of Sand today appears to confirm the success of its dissimulation.

Nevertheless, TT1 Anon does have its cover blown at the very moment of its publication, firstly by the reviewers of *The Athenaeum* who state that 'we should be false […] to every true principle of taste were we not to authenticate – so far as we can do it – this "Marie" – a simple and graceful translation of "*La Mare au Diable*"' (Anon 1847f: 762). The second exposure comes at the hands of one incensed Matilda M. Hays, who was at the time involved, as editor and translator, in an ambitious project to translate all the works of Sand into English. In a review of TT1 Anon for *Howitt's Journal* she writes:

> The mode of publication adopted with this beautiful little work, strongly reminds one of the fox in the fable, who, concealing his head, fancied that he rendered detection impossible. That any motive short of concealment could have induced the substitution of 'Marie, from the French' for 'The Enchanted Lake, by George Sand', the legitimate title of the work, it is difficult to conceive. Either George Sand's production is worthy of being given to the English public, in which case the translator and the editor can have no conceivable right to affect a disguise, or it is not fit to be put before them […]. There is in the act, not only a truckling to prejudice, immoral in itself, but a want of manly straightforwardness in thus parading a gem pilfered from the diadem of another. […] a fraud is committed upon every reader not knowing it to be the production of George Sand. (1847: 88, my emphasis)

Accusations of concealment, illegitimacy, immorality, theft, fraudulence and even an attack on manliness firmly inscribe this particular translation into the literary field of battle. What appears to be at stake here is, once more, 'the monopoly of literary legitimacy' (Bourdieu 1996: 224): on one level, Hays appears to be asserting her own authority to define Sand's right to visibility in the translation process, but behind this seemingly selfless challenge lies another level of rivalry, namely struggles which 'aim to delimit the population of those who possess the right to participate in the struggle over the definition of the writer' (Bourdieu 1996: 224) in the very first instance. Let us not forget that Hays has a vested interest in *La Mare au diable* since the text would undoubtedly be an integral part of her translation project, and so the denunciation of the initial version paves the way for her to redefine how Sand translations should be undertaken, and thereby legitimize her own efforts. As such, Hays's challenge occurs pre-emptively, as opposed to being encoded retrospectively in an existing retranslation.

TT2 Anon

Hays's plans are further thwarted by the publishers Simms & M'Intyre who, in the October of the same year, bring out the first retranslation, *The Haunted Marsh*, as part of their Parlour Library series. Although there is no reaction to this particular publication, Hays had previously made her feelings explicit as regards their translation of *Consuelo* in July. In this case, the battle is fought not on the grounds of any perceived threat to Sand, rather on the perceived threat to Hays's translation project. Her willing ally is, once again, *Howitt's Journal*, where it is noted (with more than a hint of chauvinism) that:

> We regret to see anyone entering the field against the spirited projector of a translation of George Sand's works. Miss Hays, with an enterprise of no ordinary daring, especially for a young lady, having announced and being steadily in progress with a translation every way worthy of the author, we should much have preferred to see the gallantry of publishers giving her a fair chance. (Anon 1847d: 119)

Similarly, they highlight what they regard to be the publisher's attempts to 'swamp Miss Hayes's [sic] translations of George Sand's works by a cheaper introduction of American translations' which 'they had paid a lady for altering' (Anon 1847d: 317), while Francis George Shaw, the American translator of TT3, is also brought into the debate to verify that 'the London edition [of *Consuelo*] is not a copy of my translation, although this has been copiously made use of in its preparation' (Anon 1847d: 318), without his prior consent or knowledge. As such, serious aspersions are cast on the quality and the ethics of the Simms & M'Intyre translation policy, and the challenge to the Parlour Library series is played out along the axes of both symbolic and economic capital. Hays is championed as a creditable and a valiant translator of Sand whose efforts are undermined by unchivalrous, suspect and cut-rate publishers. But the outcome does not go in favour of Miss Hays who 'confess[es] in a preface that they had overestimated the amount of interest they could depend on' (Thomson 1977: 24) for the translation project which is eventually abandoned.

Given that, 'the internal struggles [of the literary field] always depend, *in outcome*, on the correspondence that they maintain with the external struggles' (Bourdieu 1996: 127, original emphasis), it is reasonable to assume that little support was to be gleaned for well-produced translations, in terms of either skill or formatting. Instead, as was also the case with Flaubert, the law of supply and demand leads to a 'rise in the number of producers who can live by their pen' (Bourdieu 1996: 127), meeting the requirements of this 'new popular audience [which] was the chief beneficiary of the educational reforms of the second half of the century' (Hale 2006: 35). A ready acceptance of cheap literature is evidenced in *The Examiner* who maintains that '[its] diffusion [...] cannot be too gratefully welcomed, nor too widely acknowledged', and who acknowledges in particular that, 'entitled to a leading place amongst the remarkable publications of the present time – remarkable even amongst cheap books for its cheapness – must undoubtedly be reckoned The Parlour Library' (Anon 1848d: 51). Even *Howitt's Journal* begrudgingly acknowledges that, sold at one shilling, the Parlour Library is 'not only one of the cheapest, but the most popular series of the time, and calculated to enable the working classes in particular to possess themselves of a great number of standard and elevating works' (Anon 1847g: 318). No doubt Sand would have approved. In this sense, it is the momentum of the cheap press within the British literary system which gives rise to the first retranslation of the ST.

Of further note is the fact that TT2 Anon does not appear alone, but is actually published with *The Old Convents of Paris* by Madame Charles Reybaud; as it follows after this translation, it consequently undergoes somewhat of a reduction in visibility, having to assume a secondary position. The presence of the retranslation is obscured even further by a review in *The Athenaeum* which goes to great lengths to discuss the first title of the volume, while TT2 Anon is dismissed with the hasty statement that 'Of the charming tale by George Sand, which is added, we have elsewhere spoken [ante, p.762]' (Anon 1847i: 1297). Worse still, the reference provided actually alludes to their review of TT1 Anon, *Marie*; this conflation of the two versions ironically raises the profile of the latter, whilst obscuring that of the former. Nonetheless, *The Critic* responds to the Parlour Library edition as follows:

> We are glad to see the works of George Sand at length making their way to popularity in this country, in spite of the prejudices raised against them by the shameless misrepresentations of the *Quarterly Review*. We recommend this volume to all readers weary of the namby-pamby of our own novelists. (Anon 1847h: 230)

Here, the focus is squarely on Sand's text, with no mention being accorded to the other work, thereby restoring the balance, both with regard to the visibility of TT2 Anon and to the reputation of the author.

The appearance of TT1 Anon and TT2 Anon in quick succession begs the question as to whether they may pose a challenge to each other. However, there is no paratextual evidence to suggest that either translation adopts a hostile approach to the other. This lack of rivalry may primarily be explained by the dissimulating strategies of TT1 Anon: to enter into competition with TT2 Anon would then be to divulge the true identity of the source text. Secondly, whether Simms & M'Intyre were aware of TT1 Anon or not, the threat it poses to economic capital is minimal as the format of the two versions points to different target audiences: TT1 Anon cost 5 shillings, while TT2 Anon was sold for the modest price of one shilling, therefore making it more widely available. Also, TT1 Anon makes an obvious show of symbolic capital by naming the French noble, Count d'Orsay as editor; this evidently has the desired effect on *The Athenaeum* who notes that 'the name of the Editor is warrant that both French and English are understood by the translator; – this double qualification being by no means constant among those undertaking the task in these manufacturing days' (Anon 1847f: 763). Thus, the cost and symbolic posturing of TT1 Anon seem to indicate that the publishers have a more élite, discerning reader in their sights, while TT2 Anon has increased appeal for the mass market in light of both its pricing and the entertainment value of the double volume. Consequently, the hierarchical conditions inherent in the literary system, that is the existence of stratified audiences, allowed for the production of two co-existing versions of the ST without any overlap or direct conflict.

However, the Count d'Orsay edition is issued only once, and effectively fails to convert its projected symbolic capital into economic capital, not least because its disguise prevents it from exploiting the ever-growing acceptance of Sand and her pastoral tales towards the end of the nineteenth century. Conversely, the Parlour Library flourishes: according to Adams, the series comprised 101 volumes by 1853, and after its sale in the same year, continued to be published by other houses (1987: 13), including Weldon & Co., who bring out *The Haunted*

Marsh once again in 1884. Thus, the cheaper versions, while poor in symbolic capital, are in a position to profit from the supply and demand generated by the new reading public.

TT3 Shaw

The third version of Sand's pastoral tale is an import which initially appeared in the United States in the same year as the ST (1846) under the title of *The Devil's Pool* and was published in Britain in 1848 by H.G. Clarke in London. Of particular interest is the translator, Francis George Shaw, whose translation of *Consuelo* was, as aforementioned, published in a revised version without his consent. It is highly probable that the same commandeering is also behind this edition, as is also the case with the W. Tweedie version of 1855.

This edition is significant on two counts: firstly, it is the first not to shy away from a literal translation of the source text title and the potentially detrimental associations it creates between Sand and the demonic; secondly, it includes a 'Memoir of George Sand' which serves as a preface to the pastoral tale. This lengthy (and somewhat improbable) anecdote is recounted by a biographer who, having been mistaken for a chimney sweep, receives an invitation to Sand's Parisian residence. Despite realizing the confusion himself, the biographer takes up the invitation, posing as the chimney sweep to gain entrance, before admitting his real identity and being granted an audience with the author herself. The ensuing recollections engage with the stereotypical reports of Sand:

> three-fourths of those who chatter about George Sand amuse themselves at her expense. It is true that the prophetess smokes a cigar, or perhaps more than one; and that she condescends, now and then, to wear a great coat; that amongst her intimate acquaintances they call her George for brevity; but all that is not forbidden by our laws. (Anon 1848c: xx)

The biographer thus confirms the stereotypes expected by the reader but renders them more palatable by stressing their permissibility. He then undertakes a survey of Sand's life, or more precisely, 'by what concatenation of circumstances the poetess came to purchase glory at the price of her mind' (Anon 1848c: xxi), commencing with her childhood in Berry, glossing over her marriage with the caveat that the 'period which we now enter is a delicate one, and one on which it is not easy to obtain facts' (Anon 1848c: xxvii), before providing an overview of Sand's works to date and concluding (perhaps in response to Croker's accusations) that 'if there is poison on one side, you only have to turn the leaf to find the antidote' (Anon 1848c: xxxviii). This final observation suggests that the vestiges of Sand's reputation as morally corrupt still remain and are potentially damaging, symbolically and economically, to a publisher. It follows that this memoir, 'translated from the French' is perhaps no more than a pseudo-translation, that is 'a text which is overtly published as a translation but for which there is no source text, sometimes to avoid censorship or to increase acceptability' (Munday 2009: 217): here, the memoir serves as a means, not of increasing its own acceptability as a text, but rather the acceptability of Sand as an author suitable for British readers by arguing her case at a human level.

At the same time, the inclusion of the memoir, not to mention the exclusion of the Appendix, points to the privileging of entertainment over erudition. One reviewer from *The Critic* responds to its appeal, stating that 'What has most attracted our notice is a short memoir of the authoress prefixed to the tale' (Anon 1848b: 382). While they see through its artifice – 'It is pretended to be written by a curiosity seeker' (Anon 1848b: 382) – the memoir actually eclipses the tale itself, since 'not the least acceptable portion of the brochure is the account of her life' (Anon 1848b: 382). In this respect, the primacy of the retranslation comes under attack not from co-existing versions, but from the peritextual material of the edition itself.

Both the US translation by Shaw and the memoir make a reappearance in 1850, having been reissued by George Slater as part of his Universal series which 'will embrace a more extended range of English and Foreign Literature than Slater's Shilling Series, being at once of a more popular, amusing and instructive tendency' (*The Examiner* 1849: 672, original emphasis). In reality, the scope of this series is less expansive than the advertisement implies, with Sand becoming an integral part of their catalogue. Interestingly, Shaw's translation is issued as *The Enchanted Lake*, which is perhaps no coincidence given Hays's public debate and her legitimization of this very title a few years before: it may well be the case that Shaw, who was personally involved in the dispute, sanctioned the project himself under the title warranted by Hays, or that the publisher seized an opportunity to acquire symbolic capital through this appropriation of an existing, accredited title.

Furthermore, the decision to base one's catalogue on Sand may, on the surface, attest to the dissipation of the author's dubious reputation in Britain as she now falls under the rubrics of 'popular, amusing and instructive' as opposed to maligned and morally corrupt. This growing acceptance of the author is intimated in *Reynold's Miscellany* in 1850, where it is stated that 'Most of George Sand's writings having been translated into English, are more or less familiar to our readers' (Anon: 317), and by 1853 it is clearly declared that the 'enemy has now penetrated to the very heart of the kingdom. George Sand is read, admired and loved' (Anon: 261). However, a closer examination of the titles which make up the series points to additional commercial interests: it would seem that the publishers have acquired the back catalogue of H.G. Clarke and E. Churton, who had first issued the above works in translation, and in so doing, avert the financial burden of having to commission new TL versions to supplement their series. As such, the quest for economic capital within the literary system puts a halt to retranslation proper, and instead encourages repackaging.

Slater's one shilling edition of TT3 Shaw can also be placed in direct commercial competition with TT2 Anon, issued by the Parlour Library. However, in order to stand out from their rivals, the publisher attempts to carve out 'a distinct and distinctive position' within the literary field, where 'to exist is to be different' (Bourdieu 1996: 239). In physical terms, this difference is realized through the format of the translation: while the Parlour Library produced cheap, yet distinctive 'green glazed paper covers' (Adams 1987: 13), Slater's Universal series retained the one shilling price point, but offered a book whose 'size will be a little larger than the shilling series, neatly printed, and elegantly bound in crimson cloth, gilt' (Anon 1849: 672). Thus, TT3 is set apart from all other cheap shilling series by its size, its typesetting as well as the nature, colour and material of its binding. The emphasis is on greater quality for the same price, with the aim that symbolic capital may be converted into economic capital. Here, challenge is contingent not on translation strategy, but rather on format.

The Shaw translation appears once more in 1855 under the W. Tweedie imprint, and again in 1861 as part of the Lea's Sixpenny Library series, but, to the best of my knowledge, no critical reaction to their publication exists. Such silence is far removed from the moral outcry provoked only a few years beforehand, and may be interpreted as a tacit admission of Sand into the literary system.

Presence and absence: 1895–2005

Contrary to the quick succession of the first three TTs, there is a significant gap of almost fifty years before a new retranslation becomes available as part of the J.M. Dent imprint in 1895. In point of fact, this pattern of extended hiatus interspersed by translation comes to characterize the treatment of the ST in Britain to date, but is also indicative of the author's tenuous and vacillating position with the literary canon: as Massardier-Kenney notes, the 'simultaneous blend of [Sand's] presence and absence in the critical landscape is [...] just as apparent when it comes to the English translations' (2004: 71), especially in the twentieth century.

The symbolic significance of Sand in Britain begins to decline in the latter half of the nineteenth century in tandem with the dissipation of the controversy surrounding the author, or at least, with a foregrounding of her pastoral novels above and beyond other more 'suspect' works. As conservative journal *The National Review* notes in 1858:

> George Sand seems to get strength by touching the soil. Her tales of country life, and especially *La Mare au Diable*, are the most perfect [...]. They are free from all that provokes censure in her other writings – from theories, from declamations, from indelicacy. They move as with a quiet flow that is irresistibly fascinating, and are full of beauties of language to which it is impossible to do full justice. (Anon: 68)

The rustic tales are held up as the crowning point of Sand's literary career, with the implication that the author has been quieted, tamed. Divested of her power to subvert, Sand's place within the literary field necessarily shifts; the acceptance of her Berry works leads to a transformation which risks pushing her 'towards the *déclassé*' (Bourdieu 1996: 254, original emphasis), in other words, towards the common and the unchallenging. Yet another factor within the literary field contributes to this marginalization, namely the emergence of new and indigenous literary talent. Thomson points out that 'part of the great effect of George Sand, and to a lesser extent of Balzac, derived from their impact at a time when English fiction was at a low ebb' (1972: 507), and her work therefore responds to what Bourdieu defines as '*structural lacunae* which appear to wait for and call for fulfilment' (1996: 235, original emphasis). But along come Dickens, Eliot, the Brontës, Gaskell, Trollope and others to turn the tide of British fiction, superseding Sand and pushing her out of any prominent position she may once have occupied.

Nevertheless, the press continue to write about Sand in the 1860s and 1870s, and it is within this period that *La Mare au diable* is consolidated as a representation of all that is good and laudable about the author. This is especially true in the months following Sand's death in June 1876; unsurprisingly, the many articles paint a positive portrait of the deceased, but it is the pastoral tale which attracts the greatest degree of acclaim. Take for example *Blackwood's Edinburgh Magazine* which attests that 'in point of genius, and perhaps of interest, we must give the palm [...] to "*La Mare au Diable*"' (Anon 1877: 89). Notwithstanding, *The Pall Mall Gazette* introduces a note of dissention, claiming that

> George Sand's dramas of peasant life were too simple, too idyllic to succeed in England. In their passage, moreover, across the Channel the rustic personages lost none of their unreality, but all of their grace. Nor could their quaint if not precisely characteristic diction bear the process of translation. (Anon 1876: 72)

In this sense, the writer is alone in his estimation of the pastoral novels, but such exposure of perceived inadequacies may well have highlighted a gap in the literary system that, as above, calls to be filled by subsequent retranslation attempts.

TT4 Sedgwick

By the 1880s, Sand's presence in Britain seems to have waned, and as Ponsonby notes, it takes the publication of the *Lettres de Gustave Flaubert à George Sand* in 1884 to 'inaugurate […] the rehabilitation of one whom the man occupying Flaubert's unique place in French literature called mon cher maître' (1901: 609). As such, the symbolic capital of the former is conferred to the latter, bringing her into view once more as an author. But despite this apparent peak in interest, another decade passes before the appearance of TT4 Sedgwick in 1895. Published by J.M. Dent, *The Devil's Pool* forms part of a series, 'The Choice Works of George Sand', comprising *François the Waif* which accompanies TT4 in the same volume, *Fadette* and *The Master Mosaic Workers*. The first three titles underscore the continued privileging of the pastoral tales, and an advertisement for the works in 1895 contains a telling entry from *Encyclopaedia Britannica*: 'No description is needed of works so well known as *La Petite Fadette*, *La Mare au Diable*, and *François le Champi*' (cited in *The Pall Mall Magazine*, Anon 1895: 14). This observation is significant in a number of respects. Firstly, it demonstrates the facility with which the French source texts circulate within the literary system. Secondly, it may also point to the reason behind Dent's decision to specifically include the above as 'choice works': familiarity with the originals sets a precedent for their publication in English for a more popular market, and although the late 1840s onwards had given rise to several cheap, one shilling translations and re-editions of *La Mare au diable*, these were not manufactured with durability in mind. Consequently, their physical presence by the end of the century would have been much reduced, providing a tangible gap for Dent to fill. Thirdly, the British reading public's apparent acquaintance with Sand does not equate to symbolic capital; the author is both present and absent, recognized but marginalized. The appearance of a new retranslation may then serve as a means of rupturing the existing configuration of the system, bringing Sand to the fore once again in an alternative format.

However, the continued visibility of Sand in Britain is inextricably linked to a certain revolution in the publishing world, namely J.M. Dent's creation of the Everyman's Library in 1906, its ethos being that 'for a few shillings the reader may have a whole bookshelf of the immortals; for five pounds (which will procure him with a hundred volumes) a man may be intellectually rich for life'. The reissuing of the now anonymized Sedgwick translation in 1911 forms part of the publication of fifty new volumes in the series, and is met with a positive reaction in the *Times Literary Supplement*: 'George Sand has only newly begun with "The Devil's Pool" and "François the Waif"', while the 'little bibliographies in each volume are much to be commended, and the introductions show sound sense' (Child 1911: 339).

The accompanying peritextual information is in itself another form of newness; moving beyond the entertaining biography of TT3 Shaw, the Everyman's Library includes an introduction, signed E.R. (and presumably written by the series editor, Ernest Rhys), along with a comprehensive list of Sand's works and a brief biography. The introduction is framed by the claims that '*La Mare au Diable* and *François le Champi* belong to the work of George Sand that is destined to live' (Rhys 1911: vii) and that in conjunction with *La Petite Fadette* and *Les Maîtres Sonneurs* 'have the best chance of keeping her name fresh in the over-burdened memory of the present day and the days still to come' (Rhys 1911: x). While retranslation is thus implicated in the rejuvenation of Sand, it is not explicitly so since the direct allusion to the ST attests to the still prevalent synergy between the two literary systems. The introduction further addresses the supposed shift in Sand's writing marked by the pastoral tales, whereby her 'narrative art gained the weight of conviction and the verisimilitude it had lacked in its fantasias and revolt romances' (Rhys 1911: vi), and as such continues in the same vein as the late nineteenth century.

Interestingly, the bibliography provides the reader not only with a list of original fictional works, miscellany, biographies and letters, but also translations – including '*The Haunted Marsh* (*The Enchanted Lake, The Devil's Pool*), 1848, 1850, 1861, by J.M. and E. Sedgwick, 1895' (Rhys 1911: ix). So, while the translators of the present edition are excluded from the title pages, they are nevertheless given a veiled acknowledgement in this list. However, notable by its absence is *Marie*, whose dissimulating title has succeeded in severing the link between source and target text. But overall, this patent acknowledgement of the existence of previous (re)translations would suggest that the publisher is untroubled by the potential of these versions to challenge the symbolic or economic capital of their own. Such a stance may be linked to the publisher's philosophy of knowledge for all. It may also be indicative of an assured confidence either in the superiority of their particular product, or in the fact that these former editions are now hard to find.

The biography in the Everyman's Library edition is remarkable in its brevity: Sand's life is condensed to a list of her dates of birth, marriage and death, and that 'in 1830 [she] went to Paris to earn her living by writing' (1911: n.p.). Rather than focus on her literary output, it is also noted that Sand 'is famous for her association with Alfred de Musset and Chopin' (Anon 1911: n.p.). Little seems to have changed from the nineteenth century, where, as Thomson remarks, 'it is typical that rumours of her life should have preceded any account of her works' (1972: 501). However, on another level, Sand's association with great literary and musical figures may be exploited for the prestige which they then bestow on her, and it is a ready shortcut to increasing the author's own symbolic capital in a period whose memory, as Rhys claims, is 'overburdened' (1911: x). Moreover, the Everyman's Library edition is reissued a further three times in 1923, 1930 and 1933; this in turn begs the question as to whether it is simply the inherent quality of the pastoral tale which keeps Sand's circulating in the literary system, or whether it is the vehicle itself which helps stave off invisibility for the first three decades of the twentieth century.

TT5 Miles

Issued in 1929 by the Scholartis Press, Hamish Miles's *The Devil's Pool* belongs to a series, The Select Novels and Tales of George Sand, and is bordered temporally on both sides by the Everyman's Library reprints which also bear the same TL title. However, Scholartis Press was a private press which 'specialized in sumptuously produced limited editions' (Mumby 1974: 363); as such, the target audience of the publisher was more exclusive than that of the all-embracing Everyman's Library, as is reflected in the limited run of 1,300 copies, costing 8s. 6d. each. According to Mumby, the 'price of novels was a perennial source of dissatisfaction to all concerned' (1974: 308) in the first four decades of the twentieth century, and this is certainly evidenced in a review of Miles's first translation for the series, *Little Fadette*, with the comment that a 'lower-priced edition would probably have been justified' (Ould 1929: 222). Thus, the appeal of the cheap press shows no signs of subsiding in 1929 which explains the continuation of the Everyman's Library reprints in 1930 and 1933.

One feature that both editions have in common is the inclusion of peritextual material, which in TT5 Miles appears as 'A Note on "The Devil's Pool"' by the translator. Also constant is the fact that Sand's 'famous rustic idylls' (Miles 1929: 11) are championed above and beyond all other works by the author, whose 'turbulent and disquieting spirit had taken a new and unexpected turn' (Miles 1929: 11) with their production. And so, the pastoral tales are reinforced once again as a watershed in Sand's literary output, with *La Mare au diable* taking pride of place as a 'small masterpiece' (Miles 1929: 11). But where TT5 Miles sets itself apart from all previous versions is the attention it draws to 'the curious "Appendix" which widens the whole significance of the simple tale' (Miles 1929: 11), emphasizing that 'There is much in its closing chapters with a special appeal to the student of folklore' (Miles 1929: 13) and providing a reference to Sand's articles on Berrichon customs in *L'Illustration*. While TT4 Sedgwick is the initial translation of the Appendix, TT5 Miles is the first version to explicitly underscore the foreignness of the region and the anthropological merits of the work in the accompanying paratextual material.

Yet another first for TT5 Miles is the increased visibility of the translator: Miles features prominently in the peritextual material, that is in the aforementioned note on the text, but also in the notice that the 'first 10 copies of each volume, numbered and signed by the translator, are for sale at 21s' (1929: n.p.). Evidently, Miles's symbolic capital is such that his signature can be converted into economic capital, commanding an even heftier price tag. The translator's prestige also comes to the fore in epitextual material, with one reviewer stating that 'Mr. Hamish Miles [...] is responsible, presumably, for the choice as well as the translation of the stories [in the series], and the task could fall to no better hands' (Cook 1928: 828); *The Bookman* praises his translation of Paul Morand's *Magie noire* as 'a remarkable piece of work', while 'The same translator's version of "*La Mare au Diable*" [...] – one of George Sand's most delightful stories is equally fine' (Anon 1930: 67). *The Bookman* also makes one of the few challenges to the legitimacy of previous versions: 'It is remarkable that the works of George Sand should have to wait until 1928 before receiving an adequate English dress' (Ould 1929: 222). As such, this is one of only a handful of incidences when the Sand translations become implicated in rivalry; Hays's accusations of literary fraud had more to do with the manipulation of the TT title, but here is the first time that a retranslation of the pastoral tale is offset against the implied inadequacies of its former instantiations.

Of note though is the fact that we have already encountered this particular strategy of antagonistic comparison in the same publication, at around the same time, and with the same tropes in reference to J. Lewis May's retranslation of *Madame Bovary*. As was noted in Chapter 2, *The Bookman* applauds the translator for having presented Flaubert's work 'in a more becoming *English dress* that any of those who have hitherto attempted the "insurmountable" task', and this contribution is all the more significant 'since we have scarcely any translations […] which begin to give him *adequate* representation in our language' (Holbrook 1928: 202, my italic emphasis). The seemingly formulaic approach of the two critics may simply be coincidental, or it may signal a watershed moment in the British literary system where agents in the field begin to exploit the perceived correlation between time and progress in the interests of differentiation and position-taking.

But, in spite of the symbolic capital accrued through both the luxury format and the translator, TT5 Miles is a prime illustration of how the literary field and the external economic field intersect. In 1930, the Scholartis Press is lauded for having accomplished 'three years […] of distinguished achievement, which abounds in honourable promise for the future' (Waugh 1930: 715), but this promise is never fulfilled as 'the bottom fell out of [the] market with the Wall Street slump and the private presses never thereafter regained their former buoyancy' (Mumby 1974: 363). The economic depression forced the closure of the press in 1931, putting an end to the distribution of TT5 Miles, and around the same time, TT4 Sedgwick ceased to be reissued as part of the Everyman's catalogue. In light of the fact that a 'work of art does not exist as a symbolic object endowed with value unless it is known and recognized' (Bourdieu 1996: 229), the physical disappearance of the retranslations demonstrates once more to what extent the fate of Sand's translations in English are tied to reconfigurations of the literary system, above and beyond any inherent textual qualities.

TT6 Cowan

After WWII, the next significant event in the publishing world is undoubtedly the paperback revolution, spearheaded by Penguin. But translations of Sand's pastoral tale are nowhere to be found in this remodelling of the literary system; as *The Encyclopedia of Literary Translation into English* notes, 'Sand was bypassed by most mainstream collections of modern literary classics, and notably by Penguin Classics' (Classe 2000: 1226). This eschewal can readily be mapped on to what Schor terms the 'steady decline of Sand's artistic stock during the twentieth century' (1993: 27), or, as Bourdieu would have it, the decline of her symbolic capital which culminates in her trivialized reputation as a children's author. Schor argues that the author's removal from the French canon cannot be dissociated from the fact that 'Sand's works are classified under a rubric that has since disappeared, seemingly without leaving a trace: the idealist novel' (1993: 27), and it is indicative of the connections between the two literary systems that Sand should likewise disappear from view in Britain. Nevertheless, the continually shifting dynamics of a given literary system allows new constellations to form, and the early 1960s bring 'a renaissance of interest in Sand and her work' (Jurgrau 1991: 1). Writing in 1998, Didier also notes that

> for the last twenty years or so, academic work on George Sand has multiplied, with undeserved scorn being replaced by an adoration that is sometimes fanatical. The ignorance of the university critic has given way to an overabundance of studies, especially in France and North America. (6, my translation)

The conditions therefore appear ripe for TT6, translated by Antonia Cowan and issued by Blackie & Co. in 1966, to participate in and benefit from this restitution of Sand.

Unarguably, the choice to issue a new retranslation of *La Mare au diable* goes some way to restoring the presence of Sand within the British literary system, but its success is limited. Firstly, the peritextual material – which amounts to a blurb on the dustcover (Sand still has a time to go before she appears in paperback) and a short biography – marks a further return to the stereotypes which had previously distorted Sand's literary reputation. So, the pastoral novels are upheld as 'the best of her literary output' (Anon 1966: n.p.), and, by noting that '*The Devil's Pool* is a quiet, simple story [...]. A young child will enjoy it, while an adult will marvel at the cunning art of simplicity' (Anon 1966: n.p.), the trope of Sand as a children's author finds expression once again. Furthermore, it is rightly acknowledged that Sand 'does not see pastoral life as a literary mirage of the golden age', but this is preceded by the declaration that she 'is a realist' (Anon 1966: n.p.); in this sense, Sand's specific conception of idealism is denied and an ironic and erroneous link is established to the very movement which forced the author from the literary canon in the first instance. An ongoing fascination with the author's personal life and loves is evidenced in the biography which does not fail to mention Sand's 'numerous love affairs, the most famous being with the poet Musset and with Chopin' (Anon 1966: n.p.), and the pastoral novels are again highlighted as a decisive change of direction. Secondly, the Blackie & Co. publication appears to go unnoticed on an epitextual level given the absence of reviews or advertisements. Bourdieu notes that 'there is no place for those who do not know the history of the field' (1996: 244); the comparative invisibility of TT6 Cowan within the literary system at large may then be explained by its failure to engage with the rehabilitation of Sand. Thus, the importance of the vehicle of retranslation comes into play again: while Sand may have been experiencing a renaissance elsewhere, this TL version serves only to compound the stereotypes which instigated her previous vanishing act. Furthermore, TT6 Cowan demonstrates that not all (re)translations are necessarily aligned to the dominant trends of a given literary system, and it is perhaps this misalignment which arrests the process of retranslation for some forty years.

TT7 Brown

The rehabilitation of Sand appears to find wide-scale expression in the 1990s when the Oxford University Press issue *The Master Pipers* (1993), *Indiana* (1994), *The Miller of Angibault* (1995) and *Mauprat* (1997) as part of The World's Classics series. Not only does this validate Sand's return to the canon as an important nineteenth century figure, it further indicates a shift away from the peasant novels as the sole representations of her oeuvre. Ironically, it is this deviation away from Sand's rustic works which creates the conditions for the return of *The Devil's Pool* in 2005 when TT7 Brown is published (for the first time in paperback) by Hesperus Press. Their motto, *et remotissima prope* – bringing near what is far – speaks volumes, and their publishing policy is clearly expressed in the back pages of each edition:

> Works written by the greatest authors, and unjustly neglected or simply little known in the English-speaking world, are made accessible through new translations and a completely fresh editorial approach. Through these classic works, the reader is introduced to the greatest writers from all times and all cultures. (Anon 2005b: n.p.)

The changing fortunes of the pastoral tales, from privileged to peripheral, in conjunction with the deliberate emphasis by both scholars and publishers on Sand's other works does relegate the ST to a side-lined position: but, it is precisely this positioning which then brings the work into the sights of the publisher. While TT7 Brown certainly serves to reinforce both the presence and the symbolic capital of Sand as a great, canonized writer, it is also the case that its very existence stems from ongoing struggles in the literary system. As Bourdieu states, those agents who 'manage to assert their identity (that is, their difference) and get it known and recognized ("make a name for oneself") by imposing new modes of thought and expression are [...] destined to disconcert', (1996: 239–40), and potentially rupture the existing constellation. By opting to publish works which have long been overlooked, Hesperus Press is essentially defining itself in opposition to series such as The World's Classics; although this latter also adopts lesser-known works, their very inclusion in the series crowns them with a classic status, and it is against this classic symbolic capital that Hesperus Press is making its challenge. In this sense, TT7 Brown becomes not so much a retranslation which vies with previous versions of itself, but a translation which is competing against other TTs from Sand's overall body of work. The stakes of the retranslation game then shift away from Venuti's (2004) conceptualization of challenge as premised on individual textual interpretation, and towards the notion of challenge on the level of the oeuvre.

Given that the symbolic capital of the author becomes interlinked with the symbolic capital of the publisher, attempts to consolidate the latter are in no short supply. Firstly, the publishing policy mentioned earlier echoes the logic, or propaganda, evinced in abundance by the different versions of *Madame Bovary*, namely that new and fresh equals improved. Secondly, the accompanying peritextual material is substantial and boasts an introduction by the translator, Andrew Brown, whose visibility and prestige is further reinforced by the inclusion of a biographical note which outlines his credentials, namely that he 'studied at the University of Cambridge, where he taught French for many years' (Anon 2005a: 121) and that his translation activity encompasses a wide array of other nineteenth-century French authors, 'all published by Hesperus Press' (Anon 2005a: 121). Thus, Brown's symbolic capital, his status as a 'consecrating consecrator' (Casanova 2002: 18), resides in his position as an academic translator and his extensive experience, while this capital is, in turn, reflected back on to the publishers given their monopoly on the translator's proposed skill. Likewise, the edition draws on the more obvious symbolic capital of Victoria Glendinning: 'Biographer, critic, novelist and broadcaster […] former President of English PEN, […] awarded a CBE in 1998' (Anon 2005c: n.p.), she contributes a foreword to the translation and in so doing invests TT7 Brown with a substantial measure of repute.

But it is not simply the visibility of the translator and the contributor which is underscored in the peritextual material; there is also a definite rehabilitation of Sand's pastoral tale which seeks to sever its former associations with the banal and the infantine. In a very Proustian act of remembrance, Glendinning remarks that reading *La Mare au diable* 'takes me back to a stuffy little book room in my convent boarding school' (2005: vii), but it is there that the childhood connections end. Rather, Glendinning attempts to divest the pastoral tale of its innocence and naivety, claiming that 'Reading it now, I see that it is not so simple, and that there is a great deal in it about the sexual imperative' (2005: vii), and concluding that 'it seems to me a book for grown-ups, and worth reading more than once' (2005: ix). While not the first version to engage with the ethnographic merits of the Appendix, Glendinning goes beyond Sand's conservation of rural customs to highlight the author's conceptual aims, namely that the ST should engender 'some better understanding of the value of that life' and acts as 'a riposte to intellectual arrogance' (2005: ix). This reappraising vein continues into the translator's introduction, where it is proposed that 'maybe *The Devil's Pool* is in fact less innocent than it at first seems' (2005: xi), given the portentous and unsettling role played by nature in the tale, but more significantly, as a consequence of Sand's socially motivated portrayal of the peasants which serves to 'extol the provincial […] and apparently deplore the corruptions of city life, the inroads of technology and the loss of peasant traditions' (2005: xii). Likewise, Brown also addresses the Appendix as an ethnographic work, but further underscores the complexity of its creation, being 'a view of peasant life from the perspective of an insider/outsider: a sophisticate's evocation of a certain simplicity' (2005: xv). Together, Glendinning and Brown recast the pastoral tale in a new light, renouncing its perceived harmlessness, and emphasizing the unsettling ambivalences and the artfulness of the ST. In this respect, the restoration of the source text is achieved not necessarily in terms of textual closeness, but rather is played out within the translatorial and allographic peritext.

Multiples of one

According to Bourdieu, symbolic capital can be 'accumulated over the course of time by the action of successive generations' (1996: 221), and in the case of the *Madame Bovary* retranslations, this collective effort ensured the continued rejuvenation and canonization of Flaubert's work. However, the hierarchical structure of the literary field means that the potential exists for successive generations to bring about a reversal of this dynamic, effecting instead the dissolution of symbolic capital and forcing the given work or author towards the position of the *déclassé*. As far as Sand is concerned, the cumulative impact of the retranslations of *La Mare au diable* may well be understood in reference to this latter, extenuating movement. For the prevalence of this particular work in retranslation is perhaps to the detriment of Sand's other works and their visibility, inscribing a one-dimensional portrait of the author into the British literary system as a writer of the bucolic and the idealistic. As such, the retranslations attain a critical mass which debilitates, rather than rehabilitates; Sand's alignment with the outmoded form of writing arrests her in a de-canonized position, as Schor (1993) has pointed out, while the frequent paratextual emphasis in the retranslations first on her lovers and then on her supposed 'taming' serves only to consolidate her trivialization further still. Despite the efforts of Hesperus Press and OUP to re-establish Sand's symbolic capital, the former by creating a rupture with her reputation as a children's writer and the latter by revealing the breadth of her oeuvre, the body of retranslations bear down significantly on her position. It follows that the potential for future struggles over the literary survival of the author is high, and that retranslation may still play a key role in counterbalancing the process of wearing out which was compounded in the bulk of the former instantiations of *La Mare au diable.*

Conclusion

By piecing together the various and varied positions occupied by the (re) translations of *La Mare au diable*, as recoverable from para- and extratextual material, it becomes clear that the vicissitudes of the English versions cannot be dissociated from internal issues of symbolic and economic capital, nor from the external field of power. Victorian morality, the rise of the cheap press, the economic downturn in the 1930s and the critical rehabilitation of Sand, all have an impact on the presence and absence of retranslation in the literary field.

While the retranslations are certainly implicated in acts of rivalry, the scope of this rivalry reaches beyond that of textual interpretation, as anticipated by Venuti, and beyond that of the influence exerted on each other per se, as forecast by Pym. The legitimacy of the initial translation is challenged for the threat which it poses to a larger translation project; the publication of TT2 Anon and TT3 Shaw alongside another translation and a fictional memoir, respectively, introduces a certain struggle for visibility within the confines of a single volume; the challenged launched by TT3 Shaw against TT2 Anon is premised on format, not content; lastly, the diversity of Sand's own oeuvre instigates a vying for position between her pastoral and more neglected works.

In other instances, there is a deliberate absence of rivalry. The initial translation renounces any evident outward link to its true heritage for fear of moral censure; in so doing, it effectively removes itself from the game of legitimization, but ensures that it still has a stake in the accrual of economic capital. In addition, TT4 Sedgwick shows no signs of reticence in its naming of previous retranslations; while this may be attributed to a certain posturing which suggests assuredness in the authority of the translation, it may also point to the physical reality that these former versions are innocuous given the wearing out, not of their symbolic capital, but of their material form. It would also appear that the fate of TT6 Cowan is one of obscurity, having failed to identify the sea-change in the field with regard to Sand and, subsequently, to maximize on the renewed potential for symbolic capital within the field.

Evidently, the most recent retranslation strives towards a reconfiguration of the field by asserting the value of the source text. However, the corpus of (re)translations as a whole are implicated in the accumulated depreciation of Sand's symbolic capital, in the sense that their singular emphasis on the pastoral landscape of the author's oeuvre eclipses the true breadth of her writing, and with it, the potential for increased symbolic capital. Nevertheless, the contrast between the devitalizing behaviour of the Sand (re)translations and the revitalizing behaviour of their Flaubert counterparts does signal the importance of exploring a given body of retranslated works as a cumulative entity, and not simply as a series of distinct interpretations.

4

Flaubert and Sand: Narrative Touchstones

As the preceding chapters have shown, the emergence, format and status of retranslations in the literary field are all contingent on a tangle of ideological, commercial and symbolic variables. Attention will now turn from the external to the internal in order to investigate Berman's progressive trajectory of increased closeness to the ST. However, the methodological challenges of attempting to plot the specific textual bearings of a given retranslation, and the ways in which these vectors alter from one text to the next, are many and varied. As Paloposki and Koskinen have pointed out, 'measuring concepts such as improvement, closeness or accuracy in translations is singularly difficult. [...] theoretical writings on retranslations show a variety of starting points and methods of inquiry, and employ different units of comparison with which to study texts' (2010: 30). The heterogeneity of approaches to what is being measured and how it is being measured thus frustrates the emergence of a single, unified picture of retranslation behaviour. An even greater obstacle is posed by those cases which do not clearly define their standards and specific units of comparison. Accordingly, this chapter sets out to propose transparent and flexible lines of enquiry which take into account the specificities of the source texts, define closeness in accordance with these specificities, before suggesting concrete and replicable benchmarks of comparison.

It is important to note that there are some overlaps between this present study and Lance Hewson's (2011) development of *An Approach to Translation Criticism* where he explores selected retranslations of *Madame Bovary* in conjunction with those of Austen's *Emma*: any engagement with Flaubert will necessarily invite reflections on the uncertainty of meaning and Free Indirect Style (FIS). In the course of his critical comparisons, Hewson also elaborates an evaluative typology which allows the relationship between source and target text to be positioned along the cline of 'divergent similarity', 'relative divergence', 'radical divergence' and 'adaptation'; according to its positioning, the translation will then be categorized as either a 'just' or a 'false' interpretation of the original (2011: 27). However, although Hewson tests his approach against a corpus of *Madame Bovary* retranslations, his sole focus is on the classification of individual translations; there is no attempt to position the retranslations in relation to each other, and therefore no attempt to weigh the findings against existing assumptions on retranslation behaviour. The method advanced is also somewhat unwieldy, demanding a series of complex interpretative manoeuvres which include additional layers of classification and percentage calculations, and it will subsequently not be incorporated into this study. Instead, degrees of divergence from or proximity to the source text will be measured here in a way which eschews formulary methods in favour of a more malleable toolkit.

On a first level of analysis, the case study on *Madame Bovary* and *La Mare au diable* will be framed in reference to narrative theory (Baker 2006); working through the typology of narratives and their features will bring to light the specific characteristics of each work, on the basis of which a comparative checklist for closeness can be established. The equivocality of Flaubert's Free Indirect Style, especially the merger of narrator with protagonist, further poses its own methodological problems. Accordingly, a systemic functional approach will be proposed which should help to explore this narrative device from a more stable footing. This particular method will differ from existing Translation Studies approaches to the closely related narrative concept of point of view, following instead in the footsteps of narratologists who advance alternative paradigms for the study of narrative construction. Finally, this chapter will reflect on the questions of representativeness and replicability which necessarily attend any in-exhaustive and text-specific case study.

Narrative theory

Although the works of Flaubert and Sand differ significantly in terms of style, thematic content and humanitarian outlook, the one point at which both *Madame Bovary* and *La Mare au diable* do converge is in the extent to which their stories are embedded in and derive much of their meanings from their respective social settings; the former is firmly located within the oppressive and mediocre confines of French provincial bourgeoisie; the latter within the more positively drawn surroundings of the rural Berry region. In this respect, the source and target texts lend themselves to an exploration through the lens of narrative theory, a social and communicative theory which understands narratives broadly as '*the* principal and inescapable mode by which we experience the world' (Baker 2006: 9, original emphasis). Whereas literary and linguistic approaches have traditionally viewed narrative as 'an optional mode of communication' (Baker 2006: 9), this broader approach deems narratives be a fundamental and constitutive part of people's everyday lives, having the power to shape memories, identities, beliefs and relations with others. The texts under investigation here can in turn be recognized as stories which observe, record and mediate particular experiences of provincial and rural ways of life, and which then elicit particular responses from the reader. As Baker's work has shown, the typologies, features and framing devices of narrative theory have immense explanatory power when it comes to distinguishing how and to what effect source narratives are reconstructed through translation. Although Baker's focus is squarely on the translator's role in the transmission of those narratives which can provoke, perpetuate or curtail conflict, this explanatory power is not necessarily diminished in a literary context. The key concepts of narrative theory will be outlined next, and their significance to the present study will be discussed in more detail.

Types of narrative

Following the work of Somers and Gibson (1994), Baker (2006) outlines four distinct narrative types: ontological (personal), public, conceptual and meta narratives. First, ontological narratives are the 'personal stories we tell ourselves about our place in the world and our own personal history. These stories both constitute and make sense of our lives' (Baker 2006: 28). Within the context of literature in general, these personal stories can be attributed to the characters who exist within the fictional world, and within the context of this case study in particular, it is the ontological narratives of Emma in *Madame Bovary* and of the anonymous Berrichon narrator in the Appendix to *La Mare au diable* which will be brought into relief. However, where this category loses some of its tenability is in the assumption that personal stories help the teller 'make sense of their lives', for neither ontological narratives explored in this case study can be classified as particularly coherent. This is especially true of Emma's story, which is marked by self-delusion and fantasizing, by her attempt to build an alternative self, and so to flee the banality of her real-life provincial existence. The extent of her dissimulation was such that it was given its own psychopathological classification, *le bovarysme*, by French philosopher Jules Gaultier: in Emma, 'the need to see herself as something she is not forms the basis of her personality, reaching there an incomparable level of violence and manifesting itself as the refusal to ever accept reality' (1921: 30–1, my translation). In Emma's case, her personal stories are anchored in the illusory, and serve to tear down, as opposed to constitute, her existence.

To a less dramatic degree, the ontological narrative of the Berrichon narrator is also the site of tension. Although he speaks of a childhood spent in the Berry and establishes his knowledge of the village customs, the narrator's philosophical reflections in the preface to the ST, not to mention the written medium in which he expresses himself, attest to an education and a social standing which then distance him from the peasants of the region. Whitebrook argues that 'a person has to exist, to tell their story, in a social world – they are a situated, located self' (2001: 24, cited in Baker 2006: 28), but the narrator simultaneously occupies two distinct social worlds, the rural and the urban, and his sense of belonging is subsequently strained.

But fractured or otherwise, these personal stories become public the moment they are 'elaborated by and circulating among social and institutional formations larger than the individual' (Baker 2006: 4), including the literary system. It is within this context that the reader, the translator, the reviewer, the critic and so on all gain access to the ontological narratives embedded within the (semi)-fictional worlds of the novels. And it is thus from this public standpoint that it becomes possible to ascertain how the individual narratives are told and retold across the successive (re)translations.

Additionally, *Madame Bovary* and *La Mare au diable* are very much the products of the conceptual narratives of their respective authors. Baker defines these particular narratives as 'the stories and explanations that scholars in any field elaborate for themselves and others about their object of enquiry' (2006: 39); but for the purposes of this study, it is possible to expand the definition further to encompass the stories and explanations elaborated by the *writer* in reference to his or her creation. Outlining the conceptual narratives of Flaubert and Sand will demonstrate the striking disparity between what each author believes literature can (or should not) do while showing how their stories intersect with the final narrative type, the meta narrative, defined as those public narratives 'in which we are embedded as contemporary actors in history… Progress, Decadence, Industrialization, Enlightenment, etc.' (Somers and Gibson 1994: 61).

But again, Flaubert poses something of a problem within this paradigm since he famously conceptualizes the role of the author as follows: 'The artist in his work must be like God in the universe, present everywhere and visible nowhere' (1927b: 164, my translation). In so doing, he privileges the impersonality of the author and, as Culler puts it, 'call[s] into question the notion that made literature a communication between author and reader' (1974: 13). The reader of the public narrative can then experience the literary world, but there will be no overt guidance as to what their response should be. In this respect, Flaubert is much less an embedded actor, but rather a deliberately evasive and dispassionate one. His emphasis on impersonality can be read in its relation to the meta narrative *l'art pour l'art*, which rejected the didactic in favour of the aesthetic: 'the morality of art lies in its very beauty' (Flaubert 1927b: 136, my translation). In other words, if Flaubert is to be framed as an engaged writer, it is his engagement with style that matters – with how stories are told, and not which stories are told in his 'livre sur rien' [book about nothing] (1927a: 31).

Conversely, Sand is every inch the embedded actor, holding firm the belief that 'the duty of the writer is to work towards the transformation of mentalities' (Didier 1998: 823, my translation). What emerges from *La Mare au diable* is the desire to open the eyes of the Parisian reader to the charms and merits of the Berrichon countryside, people and dialect, so that they might better understand their peasant neighbours and move towards social reform which would see the breaking down of class barriers between town and country. The source text is charged with what Naginski terms Sand's 'eudaemonistic mission of art, and its duty to construct the utopian possibilities of the future' (1991: 229), and the author's idealistic belief in the capacity of humanity to move towards this utopia thus feeds into several meta narratives of her time, namely fraternity and progress. As Schor notes, '*Sandian idealism is a politics at least as much as an aesthetics*' (1993: 14, original emphasis), an idealism which relies heavily on the communication between author and reader that Flaubert renounces.

Features of narrative

While the typology just discussed affords broad insights into the compositional context of the two source texts, a more nuanced comparative account of (re) translation behaviour can be achieved by exploring the narrative features – the general mechanisms through which narratives are constructed. Continuing to draw on Somers and Gibson (1994), Baker sets out the four key features which are discernible in narrative: temporality, relationality, casual emplotment and selective appropriation (2006: 50–77). Each of these features will serve as a means of ascertaining the specificities of the source texts and, subsequently, as a benchmark for comparison across the (re)translations. But these categories are not particularly sensitive to the very *textual* mechanisms through which given narratives are constructed. Baker does consider translation as a process of narrative (re)framing which can exploit

> practically any linguistic or non-linguistic resource, from paralinguistic devices such as intonation and typography to visual resources such as colour and image, to numerous linguistic devices such as tense shifts, deixis, code switching, use of euphemisms, and many more. (2006: 111)

Within the context of this study, a more focused and definite checklist must be elaborated, one which allows an incisive analysis of how narrative features have been framed in the ST and then reframed in the (re)translations. To this end, the definition of narrative features and their relevance to each source text will be supplemented by a discussion of the specific narratological and/or stylistic devices which underpin the features and which will be integrated into a better refined comparison between originals and (re)translations.

To begin with **temporality**, this feature recognizes that 'the elements of a narrative are always placed in *some* sequence, and that the order in which they are placed carries meaning' (Baker 2006: 50–1, original emphasis). That sequencing may or may not be chronological, but the narrative flow of events and people will ultimately impact on how the story is interpreted and understood. As far as Flaubert is concerned, cohesion becomes a particularly illuminating benchmark given the author's architectural conception of writing which compares prose to a wall with invisible joints and straight lines of continuity (1927a: 264). This simile attests to the author's preoccupation with the fundamental 'internal force' (1927a: 345) of style; if form and content are to be inseparable, then one must be bound to the other in an invisible yet enduring manner. No cracks, no buckling can appear in the prose which might suggest a cleaving of the two. Thus, in order for a (re)translation to preserve the temporality of original, there must be no interruption in Flaubert's coherent sequencing of narrative events, accomplished primarily through an unusual use of conjunctions as well as through lexical cohesion.

The feature of temporality can further be examined in reference to the macro-structure of Sand's pastoral tale. The Appendix was initially 'destined to flesh out an overly slender novel' (Cellier 1999: 23, my translation) and therefore follows on from the main fictional tale. The two parts remain connected by the protagonists, Germaine and Marie, whose wedding serves as a premise for charting Berrichon traditions. However, despite the sequential relation between the main story and the ethnographic study, the secondary position of the Appendix leaves it open to non-translation, and this process of omission will evidently have an impact on how cultural identity and meaning is revealed or concealed in the (re)translations.

Another interpretative resource is the feature of **relationality** which allows narrative events to be understood in reference to their spatial, temporal social and cultural settings. Without this constitutive feature, it would be 'impossible for the human mind to make sense of isolated events or a patchwork of events' (Baker 2006: 61). This narrative feature is particularly significant to *Madame Bovary* since the work can be read as Flaubert's caustic reaction against what he deemed to be the mediocrity, stupidity and greed of the middle classes in mid-nineteenth century France. The work can also be read in an antagonist relation to the literary movement of romanticism, which Flaubert rejects on the basis of its propagation of unattainable ideals through works rife with clichés and excessive lyricism. Heavy use of is made of irony throughout *Madame Bovary* as a means of undercutting the fantasies and fallacies of romanticism, especially with regard to Emma and the dream worlds she creates, which are fuelled by the sentimental, melodramatic reading material of her youth. The subjectivity and dissimulation of romanticism is further attenuated in the novel by the detachment and the scientific observations of realism which serve to depict the minutiae of everyday life. For Flaubert, 'realism becomes impartial, impersonal, and objective' (Auerbach 1953: 482); it is a mode of writing which allows the author to lay bare the shortcomings of the bourgeoisie without any explicit comment or opinion to guide the reader. But this is tempered, as Heath has noted, by the fact that realism for Flaubert is also 'as execrable as the reality it knows and depicts, [...] caught in the surrounding stupidity, the general fetidness' (1992: 32). It follows that *Madame Bovary* is both anchored in and a reaction against the social and cultural backdrop to its writing. But it is also important to remember that this critique, this sardonic 'book about nothing', is ultimately a stylistic feat, a tribute to *le Beau* which transcends its immediate context. Consequently, the (re)translations can be explored in relation to whether or not they preserve the author's ironic treatment of the bourgeoisie and their penchant for the excesses of romanticism, and the extent to which the detached impersonality of the narrator is retained.

The events in the Appendix to Sand's *La Mare au diable* are located squarely in the Berry region and derive much of their significance from this spatial relationality. The Appendix is also marked by a certain 'unease in narrative point of view' (Brown 2005: xiv) which mirrors the narrator's dual belonging to both town and country, but in this instance, the tension is central to the transmission of Berrichon identity. The bourgeois narrator points himself in the direction of an educated Parisian readership, but has his feet planted in the soil of the Berry, purporting to know the protagonist, Germain, and his stories on a personal level. While in the Berry, the narrator is no longer fully of the Berry, and it is precisely this position which allows him to mediate the bucolic to his audience and ultimately foster understanding of the other as a basis for progress. In addition to this spatial dimension of relationality are the significant temporal bearings of the Appendix which emphasize the age-old traditions of the Berry. Although many of these traditions have fallen into disuse as a consequence of industrial progress, this focus on value and the richness of the Berry way of life nevertheless serves as a foundation for mutual understanding and recognition, and therefore of progress in the fraternal sense. Or, as Powell puts it, Sand 'look[s] to the future of France from the ironically conservative point of view of the provinces' (1990: 64). The narrative device which will be of most significance in the analysis of relationality will be deixis, that is 'those features of language which refer to the personal, temporal or locational characteristics of the situation within which the utterance takes place, whose meaning is thus relevant to that situation' (Crystal 2005: 127). More specifically, social deixis will be examined in the context of the complex relationship between narrator and reader; place deixis will be investigated as a means of discerning how the narrator negotiates his position of dual belonging; and time deixis will highlight the specificities of the Berrichon calendar as well as the ravages of industrialization on tradition.

A third narrative feature is **causal emplotment** which is concerned with how events are arranged into sequences of causality within the boundaries of a given narrative itself, rather than in relation to its context. This feature is fundamental to the meaning of a given narrative, since it 'allows us to *weight* and *explain* events rather than simply list them, to turn a set of propositions into an intelligible sequence about which we can form an opinion. It thus charges the events depicted with moral and ethical significance' (Baker 2006: 67, original emphasis). But Flaubert's narrative has been constructed precisely so as to avoid emplotment that is explicitly 'charged'; indeed, one of the reasons it was brought to trial in France in 1857 was the work's purported failure to categorically denounce the adulterous behaviour of its protagonist. That is not to say the work is devoid of moral significance, but rather that significance is latent, there for the finding by an astute reader. For as far as Flaubert is concerned, 'If the reader does not derive from a book the moral that should be there, it is because the reader is an imbecile' (1930a: 285, my translation).

One of the defining narratological devices of *Madame Bovary* is Flaubert's use of Style Indirect Libre, or Free Indirect Style, which simultaneously occasions and dissimulates the author's critique of bourgeois values and Emma's romanticized self-deception. FIS is generally accepted as an intertwining of the voice of the narrator with that of the protagonist; the bivocal hybridity of the style, which fuses direct and indirect speech or thought and omits discourse markers, consequently creates a high degree of incertitude as to 'who speaks', in Genette's (1980: 203) terms, and this incertitude is keenly felt in 'a large number of ambiguous and polysemous cases, and often in passages that are wholly equivocal' (Perruchot 1975: 268, my translation). As a result, the reader is left without any clear markers of orientation as to who is speaking and when which might help them understand the event. To complicate matters further, this 'problem of unconfirmability' (Toolan 1988: 125) inherent in FIS can equally be extended to the question of 'who sees'. For Flaubert blends not only voices, but also focalizations, a merger which then frustrates any attempt to isolate one particular set of eyes through which the fictional world is portrayed. It becomes impossible for the reader to ascertain whether the vista presented is to be related back to one perspective or the other. As LaCapra explains, the 'effect is in one sense that of language writing or speaking itself but not emanating from a secure or fixed source and not communicating a precise message or evaluative position with respect to characters and events' (1982: 147). The causal emplotment of this particular narrative is thus thwarted by a narratological device which splinters the unity of the speaking and of the seeing subject into a cacophony and a kaleidoscope of different interpretative possibilities.

As Baker notes, narrative features 'overlap and are highly interdependent. Temporal and spatial sequences participate in elaborating patterns of causal emplotment, and causal emplotment in turn is partly realized through selective appropriation, and so on' (Baker 2006: 5). This is certainly the case in *Madame Bovary*, where Flaubert's ironic and impersonal critique of the bourgeoisie and romanticism (relationality) is closely intertwined with the author's uncertain use of FIS (causal emplotment), not least since 'the Idea exists only by virtue of its form' (Flaubert 1926b: 321). As a result, these two features will be explored in conjunction with each other in respect of this particular work. In Sand's Appendix to *La Mare au diable,* the causal emplotment of the narrative has been designed according to the age-old precept of *instruire en amusant*, of educating the reader while entertaining them. It penetrates every facet of the narrative, and will subsequently not be considered in isolation from the other features.

The feature of **selective appropriation**, the process whereby 'some elements of experience are excluded and others privileged' (Baker 2006: 71), is less illuminating as far as *Madame Bovary* is concerned. Although the narrative world can be interpreted as a realistic depiction of life in the provinces, it is nevertheless entirely founded on an act of invention. Each and every element of experience, from the characters' physical surroundings to their psychological make-up, is one instantiation of an almost limitless configuration of possible scenarios. Consequently, there is no solid basis of experience that would allow a meaningful consideration of which experiential components were appropriated as opposed to others. On the other hand, Flaubert's search for *le mot juste* has become the stuff of legends, and it is this act of selective appropriation from the arsenal of language which is significant: 'After all, the whole talent for writing lies simply in the choice of words' (Flaubert 1926b: 471, my translation). The issue of word choice effectively extends across all other constitutive features of the narrative and will therefore not be treated independently.

As far as *La Mare au diable* is concerned, the Appendix does paint a detailed, multifaceted portrait of the Berry region, but this portrait is by no means comprehensive. Instead, Sand singles out which people, events, characteristics and traditions will be tasked with charming and instructing, and in so doing, implements the narrative feature of selective appropriation. In other words, the narrative has been 'constructed according to evaluative criteria that enable and guide selective appropriation of a set of events or elements from the vast array of open-ended and overlapping events that constitute experience' (Baker 2006: 71). Sand thus constitutes her narrative world by charting certain facets of an extant but threatened way of life: wedding traditions, Berrichon dialect, the vocal qualities of the peasants and the material objects of the region are all selected as a means of engaging the Parisian reader and fostering their understanding of the Other. The (re)translations can thus be compared according to how these markers of Berrichon identity have been affected by their move abroad.

Narratology and Systemic Functional Grammar: Foundations and changes in direction

In view of the fact that Free Indirect Style brings about 'a discoursal chafing at the bounds of normal grammar' (Toolan 2006: 261), the comparative analysis of the *Madame Bovary* (re)translations will further be informed by insights and paradigms from narratology and Halliday's Systemic Functional Grammar (SFG). This dual approach should pave the way towards a better understanding of how this ambiguating device functions and how it has been treated in the (re)translations. Indeed, there is a strong precedent in Translation

Studies for drawing on narratological and/or systemic functional approaches in the analysis of literary texts. The details of this interpretative background will be outlined next, starting with the explorations of voice in translation and then moving on to a summary of the precepts of Systemic Functional Grammar and how they have been applied by various translation scholars. Particular focus will be placed on those studies which investigate point of view in this manner, a narratological feature which can be constructed through FIS. However, there has been some debate in narratology as to the applicability of point of view as a concept; this will be discussed in the following sections, where a new schema for a systemic functionalist study of Free Indirect Style will also be delineated.

Voice

In narratology, it is generally the work of Genette (1980: 212–62) that serves as the most prominent and enduring point of reference for voice. In his theory of narrative, Genette defines voice according to who is narrating, when the narration occurs and where it occurs. More specifically, Genette's model distinguishes between whether the narrating person is absent from the story they recount (as a heterodiegetic narrator), or present in that story (as a homodiegetic narrator). Additionally, Genette draws a distinction between narration that takes place outside of the story word (extradiegetic narration) and narration that emerges from inside the story world (intradiegetic narration).

In turn, the complementary articles of Schiavi (1996) and Hermans (1996) have brought the category of the translator's voice to the fore in Translation Studies, reacting simultaneously against the ideological relegation of the translator to a secondary, 'invisible' (Venuti 1995) position and against the failure of narratology to 'distinguish between original and translated fiction' (Hermans 1996: 198). While Schiavi (1996) reworks Chatman's (1978) scheme of narrative communication in order to incorporate the 'implied translator' and 'narrator of translation' into the chain, thereby reinforcing the agency of the translator in the communicative process, Hermans sets out to reveal 'those instances where the translated text itself shows visible traces of a discursive presence other than the ostensible Narrator' (1996: 198–9). This discursive presence is that of the 'other' voice, the Translator's Voice. Although sometimes irrecoverable, hidden behind the voice of the narrator, Hermans argues that the Translator's Voice makes itself heard in three distinct scenarios: (i) where the translator intervenes in the text to explain cultural or historical references that would be otherwise inaccessible to the new target readership; (ii) where the translator has recourse to paratextual material, especially notes, in order to resolve incongruities which emerge in translation from 'self-referential' uses of the source language (e.g. puns, direct statements that reveal the original language of communication); and (iii) where the translator is confronted with what Hermans calls 'contextual overdetermination', that is where the link between what is being said, how it is being said and where it is being said is so strong as to forestall translation into another mode and place of saying. In all three cases, the Translator's Voice resounds, more or less discernibly, from the text or the paratext, attesting to 'more than one voice in the narrative, more than one discursive presence' (Hermans 1996: 198).

However, Hermans' question, 'Whose voice comes to us when we read translated discourse?' (1996: 197) seems to lead on from the assumption that the voice coming to us from the source text is that of the author, 'the authoritative originary voice' (1996: 197). This approach is problematic since it proceeds from the conflation of text author with text narrator, thereby negating a critical distinction in narratology between the agency of the one 'who writes' and the one 'who speaks', to borrow Bal's terms (2006: 13). Nowhere is this distinction more pertinent than in the narration of *Madame Bovary* from which the author deliberately and wholly withdraws, for 'the novelist does *not have the right to express his opinion* on anything at all' (Flaubert 1929: 253, original emphasis, my translation). The univocality of a given source narrative can be called into question if we consider Bal's observation that a narrator 'can yield the floor to a character' (2006: 16) at any given moment, as exemplified by direct speech. The narrative texture is thus interwoven with and articulated by voices which stem from numerous sources. Similarly, in cases of Free Indirect Style, what Pascal terms a 'dual voice' can be heard, one 'which through vocabulary, sentence structure, and intonation subtly fuses the two voices of the character and the narrator' (1977: 26). In *Madame Bovary*, the impersonal voice of the narrator runs together with the melodramatic voice of the protagonist. The detachment of one resounds alongside the self-delusion of the other, creating a discordance in which irony is to be found. In contrast to Hermans, my concern when exploring the treatment of FIS in the *Madame Bovary* (re)translations is not whether translation '*creates the prospect* of a runaway inflation of voices and meanings' (Hermans 1996: 210, my emphasis), but whether it preserves or reduces the polyvocality already inherent in the source text.

Systemic Functional Grammar and Translation Studies

This study will integrate Systemic Functional Grammar (Halliday 1994; further developed by Halliday and Matthiessen 2004) as an additional navigational aid in its investigation of Flaubert's often equivocal and disorientating use of FIS. It will serve as a more detailed map, an 'overview of language that will enable us to locate exactly where we are at any point along the route' (Halliday and Matthiessen 2004: 19); the key reference points of that map are the lexicogrammatical choices made in the source text, which can then be overlaid with and compared against the choices made in the respective target texts. In the terminology of Halliday's model, *Systemic* signals the fact that 'the grammar of a language is represented in the form of system networks' (Halliday and Matthiessen 2004: 23), that is of paradigmatic choice, and *functional* refers to the way in which language choice allows us, fundamentally, 'to make sense of our experience, and to carry out interactions with other people' (Halliday and Matthiessen 2004: 24). Halliday's map is also a multidimensional one. If lexicogrammatical choice is at the heart of meaning making, the fact that 'texts are typically making not just one, but a number of meanings simultaneously' (Eggins 2004: 11), must be accounted for. These multiple meanings have been categorized by Halliday into a tripartite of 'metafunctions' of language which are realized on the level of the clause: the ideational metafunction (clause as representation) which is construed through Transitivity[1]; the interpersonal metafunction (clause as exchange), construed through Mood; and the textual metafunction (clause as message), construed through Thematic structure.

Halliday has himself shown the value of approaching a literary work from a systemic functional perspective. Considered by Carter and Stockwell to be 'one of the most groundbreaking analyses in stylistics' (2008: 19), Halliday's (1971) inquiry into William Golding's *The Inheritors* documents the ways in which lexicogrammatical choices have direct bearing on the creation of meaning and, in particular, on the portrayal of the 'people' (Neanderthal man) in contrast to the 'new people' (homo sapiens). Halliday focuses on Transitivity, 'the cornerstone of the semantic organization of experience' (1971: 359), in order to demonstrate that the different ways in which the two peoples understand and engage with the world also 'appear as differences within the text itself between what we have called "Language A" and Language C"' (1971: 358). Whereas the former is marked by an absence of cause and effect and the subject has no direct impact on their surroundings, the latter is characterized by an active agency that alters the external world. In this sense, the transitivity patterns contribute to the drawing of a key thematic distinction at the centre of the literary work.

The analytical value of Halliday's model of language has been carried over into Translation Studies by a number of scholars. Moving one level above textual issues of lexicogrammatical choice, House builds the 'Hallidayan "trinity" [of] Field, Tenor, Mode' (1997: 107) into her model for the comparative analysis between the contextual situation of a ST and that of a TT. These three benchmarks of register – subject matter, the relationship between the communication participants and vehicle of communication – thus serve as the basis for House's assessment of functional equivalence. Hatim and Mason (1990) also integrate this Hallidayan approach to register into their three-dimensional model for the study of translation in context; what is communicated, between who and how, forms the basis of the communicative dimension of context, which is further aligned with the pragmatic and semiotic dimensions of context. Their subsequent work, *The Translator as Communicator* (Hatim and Mason 1997), shows further evidence of a systemic functional approach on a textual level, where patterns of transitivity and modality are analysed in relation to their construal of a particular ideology or world view. Turning then towards questions of theme–rheme distribution, markedness and cohesion, Baker (1992) too makes illuminating use of Halliday's systemic functional model. Furthermore, all three metafunctions of SFG have been employed by van Leuven-Zwart (1989; 1990) in her elaborate exploration of translation shifts in fictional narratives. A comparative model is first used in order to identify microstructural shifts between the ST and TT; the impact of these shifts on the macrostructural level of the text is then determined by means of a descriptive model organized around the ideational, interpersonal and textual levels of meaning. The categories of segmentation (i.e. word order) and cohesion subsequently emerge as particularly susceptible to alteration in translation, and were taken up by Munday (1998) in his corpus-based comparative analysis of a short story in Spanish by Gabriel García Márquez and its English translation, where they are determined to be 'useful in identifying changes in the narrative viewpoint' (1998: 15) that is presented to the readers of the TT.

Clearly, those studies which underpin their analyses of narrative viewpoint with a systemic functional approach are of particular pertinence to this present investigation of Flaubert's Free Indirect Style which blurs the lines between narrator and protagonist. In this respect, the works of Bosseaux (2007) and Munday (2008) are further important points of reference, drawing as they both do on stylistician Paul Simpson's (1993) model of point of view, which is itself premised on Halliday's systemic functional classifications. Simpson, building also on the works of Uspensky (1973) and Fowler (1996), establishes four categories of point of view: *spatial* and *temporal* point of view refer to how a given narrative is framed in terms of the visual perspective of the narrator and the unfolding of the events across time; *psychological* point of view 'refers to the ways in which narrative events are mediated through the consciousness of the "teller" of the story' (Simpson 1993: 10); and *ideological* point of view serves to encode evaluative worldviews. For Bosseaux (2007: 27–8), 'Simpon's model offers elements that are particularly relevant to the elaboration of a comparative model by which to analyse originals and their respective translations.' In her corpus-based analysis of the French (re)translations of Virginia Woolf's (1927) *To the Lighthouse* and (1931) *The Waves*, Bosseaux employs several of the linguistic components which realize the various planes of point of view as her comparative starting point. More specifically, deixis, modality, transitivity and free indirect discourse are all used as a means of assessing the impact which translation exerts on narrative point of view, and subsequently on characterization. In Munday's investigation into the translation of ideology in a Latin American context (2007), the textual analysis rests on a modified version of Simpson's model. Uspensky's (1973) category of *phraselogical* point of view, concerned with the representation of speech, is brought in as an additional comparative benchmark. Accordingly, Munday shows how shifts in naming strategies can 'affect the phraseological plane of point of view' (2007: 204), and also how shifts in tense can 'affect the spatio-temporal point of view of the narrator' (2007: 211). A more comprehensive application of this revised model comes to the fore in Munday's (2008) work *Style and Ideology in Translation* where lexical, semantic and syntactic shifts in the translation of Latin American fiction are correlated to the impact which they have on the overarching planes of point of view. Munday also provides a valuable schema which shows precisely how Halliday's systemic functional metafunctions and their lexicogrammatical realizations have been mapped on to the different planes of point of view (Table 4.1).

Table 4.1 Planes of point of view

Planes of point of view	Linguistic markers
Psychological ('mind style')	Type of narrator, **ideational function**, transitivity structures, denotational lexical items; cohesion (part of the **textual function**)
Ideological	**Interpersonal function**, modality structures, evaluation, linked to authorial voice and implied author
Spatio-temporal	Textual function, particularly tense, deixis, sequencing
Phraseological	Naming, pronouns, speech representation, use of foreign and non-standard forms

Source: Munday (2008: 24)

Despite the proven expository value of this approach, it is also important to bear in mind that point of view has attracted significant criticism from scholars within narratology. These criticisms will be discussed in more detail next, and, on the basis of the arguably more succinct narrative concepts that have been proposed as an alternative, a new approach to the systemic functional analysis of Flaubert's work will be proposed.

Point of view vs. focalization

The first – and most influential – rebuff to point of view comes from Gérard Genette who draws attention to its 'regrettable confusion between the question *who is the character whose point of view orients the narrative perspective?* and the very different question *who is the narrator?* – or, more simply, the question *who sees?* and the question *who speaks?*' (1980: 186). Genette then goes on to propose a more clear-cut distinction between the categories of 'focalization' (pertinent to the question of seeing) and 'voice' (pertinent to the question of speaking), which not only marks a key point in the development of narratology, but also facilitates a move away from what Toolan terms the 'great and continuing nuisance perpetuated by the term "point of view"', namely the 'conflation and confusion of two distinct narrative practices' (1998: 68).[2] In this new model, the issues central to point of view now fall under different banners; matters of a character's psychological make-up and their spatio-temporal perspective are subsumed under the rubric of focalization, while the category of voice encompasses how narrators convey those perspectives.

Genette's fundamental distinctions allow for a more precise, differentiated approach to the exploration of narrative structure and have gained widespread currency in narratology, to the extent that Nieragden has registered surprise that 'Remarkably, quite a large number of new explorations in theory still favour [point of view] over the more elaborate systematics of focalization' (2002: 688), most notably (for the purposes of our study) the explorations of Simpson (1993), as well as those of Calvo and Weber (1998). However, Genette's model has not gone unchallenged, and the more exacting status of focalization stems as much from subsequent reworkings of the category as it does from its initial conceptualization. In particular, Mieke Bal (1985) has substantially revised and redefined Genette's (1980: 185ff) original threefold typology of focalization which distinguished between: (i) zero focalization which points to the presence of an omniscient all-seeing, all-knowing narrator; (ii) internal focalization whereby the story world is seen through the eyes of one (or more) of the characters; and (iii) external focalization, which presents all but a limited view of events and characters, analogous to the superficial reach of a camera. Bal takes issue with this classification for a number of reasons. Firstly, she cogently points to 'the impossibility of zero focalization' (2006: 132) in a story, since narratives can never be entirely objective and will always be mediated from a particular perspective. Secondly, Genette's approach to internal and external focalization is deemed to be problematic because the distinction is premised on 'a wholly different principle of classification' (2006: 10) in the sense that internal focalization is concerned with who sees, whereas external focalization is a matter of what is seen. In order to resolve this incongruity, Bal (1985: 146) introduces the dual concept of the *focalizer* and the *focalized*, that is the respective subject and objects of focalization, in conjunction with the categories of *internal* and *external* focalizations. Here, the internal–external dichotomy marks a crucial boundary between the inside and the outside of the story world, between an extradiegetically positioned External Focalizer (EF) and an intradiegetically positioned Character Focalizer (CF), and not between open and closed access to a character's internal life, as is the case with Genette.

Bal and Free Indirect Style

According to Jahn, 'One of the questions that every narratologist has to decide for himself or herself is whether to stick to Genette's or Bal's model' (2007: 102). This study will stick with Bal for the primary reason that it lends itself well to the study of *Madame Bovary*, where the prominence of Free Indirect Style demands a model that can both accommodate and differentiate the ambiguity through which this narrative device operates. Bal's notion of the External Focalizer has come under criticism from Fludernik for 'fl[ying] in the face of Genette's binary distinction between "speaking" and "seeing"' (2006: 20–1) since it appears to locate this set of eyes on the same extradiegetic level as the story-telling narrator. Bal has defended her classification by arguing that: 'if I seem to draw together what [Genette] disconnected, I am not invalidating his distinction but, on the contrary, radicalizing it. For to treat agents of focalization and voice in isolation conceals the parallelism of their organization in narrative' (2006: 19). And nowhere does that parallelism function more strikingly and bewilderingly than in Flaubert's use of Free Indirect Style. Although FIS is often framed as a mode of speaking (or thinking), as indicated by the terms 'Free Indirect Discourse' and 'Free Indirect Speech', the uncertainty which pervades the level of voice equally extends to that of focalization in Flaubert's narrative composition. It is therefore not by accident that I have chosen to calque the French term 'Style Indirect Libre' since style does not introduce a bias towards speech or thought, but rather encompasses both a blending of voices, or polyvocality, and a blending of perspectives, or what I will term 'polyfocality'. The model proposed by Bal makes room for acts of speaking and of seeing which emerge simultaneously from both inside and outside the story world, and subsequently offers a workable approach with which to interrogate how Flaubert's tenebrous and unsettling fusion of omniscient narrator with unknowing protagonist has been dealt with in the (re)translations.

A new systemic functional approach to seeing, speaking and sequencing

The move away from point of view and towards the use of focalization and voice presents an opportunity to redraw a new systemic functional approach to the exploration of FIS. For Systemic Functional Grammar itself remains a highly useful tool that allows a momentary suspension of what Genette has called 'the indefinite trembling of things' (1966: 242) in Flaubert's writing. In other words, the relevant metafunctions can be mapped onto and used to untangle the ambiguous merger of focalization and voice, thereby allowing the topography of FIS to be pinpointed in the ST and then serve as a more precise comparative benchmark for the contours of the TTs. A systemic functional approach will be of further value when exploring how Flaubert has employed certain cohesive devices in order to ensure the integrity and polish of his narrative architecture.

Specifically, it is the ideational and interpersonal metafunctions which will prove advantageous in the exploration of Flaubert's FIS, this amalgamation of acts of seeing and speaking. In the first instance, the ideational metafunction is the level on which 'the clause has meaning as a representation of some process in ongoing human experience' (Halliday and Matthiessen 2004: 59). If 'human' is understood as 'fictional character' or 'narrator', then focalization – who sees – essentially becomes a vehicle for construing the experiences played out in the narrative world. Furthermore, it is the system of Transitivity, including participants, processes and circumstances, which serves to realize this construal. The choices made in the source text on this level of meaning can then be scrutinized in parallel with the choices made in the (re)translations so as to plot how Transitivity has been re-construed in translation and how this might impact on Flaubert's impersonality and critique of society.

In the second instance, the interpersonal metafunction allows the clause to become the site of interaction, 'whereby we inform or question, give an order or make an offer, and express our appraisal of and attitude towards whoever we are addressing and what we are talking about' (Halliday and Matthiessen 2004: 29). Hence, interpersonal meaning can serve to illuminate the question of who speaks, how and to whom. In particular, interactions between speaker and addressee are facilitated by the Mood element of the clause which 'carries the burden of the clause as an interactive event' (Halliday and Matthiessen 2004: 120). The primary components of the Mood – the Subject and the Finite elements – will form the backdrop to an investigation of any shifts that take place in (re)translation which have a bearing on focalization. The reference points of SFG will thus function once again as touchstones in Flaubert's unstable landscape of impersonality and irony. The Table 4.2 presents an outline of how the ideational and interpersonal metafunctions have been mapped on to the two key narrative markers of FIS:

Table 4.2 FIS and SFG

Narrative markers of Free Indirect Style	Metafunctions
Focalization	**Ideational** (clause as representation); realized through **Transitivity** (participants, processes, circumstances)
Voice	**Interpersonal** (clause as exchange); realized through **Mood** (Subject, Finite elements)

In addition, Halliday's systemic functional approach can also be used to frame the analysis of temporality in *Madame Bovary*. Here, focus can be extended beyond the level of the clause to consider, first of all, how 'the flow of events is construed as a series of episodes' (Halliday and Matthiessen 2004: 363) through taxis and logico-semantics in clause complexes, and secondly, how meaning is construed and continued across different parts of the text through cohesion. Once again, the categories of SFG can be utilized as a means of mapping the smooth lines of narrative construction in the ST, against which the contours of the (re)translations can be assessed.

Nevertheless, it will be important to resist the temptation to deal in absolutes. For the confidence with which Halliday asserts that 'there is no facet of human experience which cannot be transformed into meaning' (Halliday and Matthiessen 2004: 29) stands in stark contrast to Flaubert's conviction that language is inadequate when it comes to portraying the reality of that very experience. But while language may be inadequate for Flaubert, style is not; as Heath observes, 'To aim at style is to aim at a disengagement from the noise of language in the world, […] which is then to find some possibility of meaning, under and through and against words' (1992: 135). Indeed, this pronouncement is an echo of Flaubert's own reflection that 'style is as much *under* words as it is *in* words' (1927b: 315, my emphasis and translation). It follows that the author's style can function on a substratum of the text which may be obscure to SFG; it is the deferred meanings, the non-meanings, as expressed through style and routed under words which merit an attention that is not integrated into the SFG approach. The comparative analysis will thus be attuned to those specificities of the source text which cannot be mapped using Halliday's topology.

Overview of comparative approaches

Narrative theory facilitates a top-down approach to the comparative analyses of *Madame Bovary* and *La Mare au diable*. On an initial level, the various types of narrative allow a teasing out of the relations between the stories recounted within the body of the texts themselves and their conceptualization by the authors, as well as their intersections with overarching discourses. Refining the analysis further still, the narrative features provide a structured framework which can be used to identify and define the specificities of the source texts, and which will subsequently serve as stable and meaningful points of comparison across the (re)translations.

As far as the *Madame Bovary* (re)translations are concerned, the first line of enquiry will be the work's ambiguous form of causal emplotment, as realized (or obstructed) through FIS. Here, there is significant overlap with the feature of relationality since the impersonality and irony on which this narrative device is premised is also tied to the author's critique of the mores and values of bourgeois society. However, this study will move away from the 'point of view' model that has previously been adopted by Bosseaux (2007) and Munday (2007, 2008) so as to draw a more clear-cut distinction between voice and focalization. Systemic functional categories will continue to inform the comparison; voice will be explored on an interpersonal level, and focalization on an ideational one. The feature of temporality will then be examined, namely how the narrative has been sequenced through the device of coherence. As a consequence of Flaubert's all-pervading enthrallment with choosing *le mot juste*, the narrative feature of selective appropriation will not be isolated as comparative category in its own right.

In turn, the study of the *La Mare au diable* (re)translations will begin with an investigation of temporality which will take into account whether or not the ethnographic Appendix actually follows on from the main tale. Next, the feature of relationality and the narratological tool of deixis will function as a criteria for evaluating how the (re)translations deal with the dual positioning of the narrator and the poignant references to time and tradition. Finally, selective appropriation will be taken as a starting point for an exploration of how those privileged markers of Berrichon identity have been dealt with in the (re) translations, and the subsequent impact on the epistemological representation of the Other. Throughout, emphasis will also be placed on the impact of (re) translation on causal emplotment.

Tables 4.3 and 4.4 provide a schematic representation of the key comparative cornerstones that will be used to analyse the (re)translations of each work.

Table 4.3 Flaubert: Comparative approach

Narrative features	Comparative benchmarks
Relationality and causal emplotment	Free Indirect Style (clause as representation; clause as exchange)
Temporality	Organization of narrative world (taxis and logico-semantics; cohesion)

Table 4.4 Sand: Comparative approach

Narrative features	Comparative benchmarks
Temporality	Presence or absence of Appendix
Relationality	Deixis
Selective appropriation	Berrichon identity

On representativeness and replicability

The decision to explore retranslation behaviour in reference to the two different source texts was motivated by the logic that 'multiple-case studies have considerable advantages over single-case studies in terms of the rigour of the conclusions which can be derived from them' (Susam-Sarajeva 2009: 43–4). The next methodological step is to address the representativeness, and subsequently, the generalizability of these two cases. It is beyond the capacity of this book, and perhaps even that of the researcher, to provide an exhaustive comparative analysis between *Madame Bovary* and *La Mare au diable* and their respective (re)translations. Instead, a process of sampling must be instigated; as Hermans points out, 'If exhaustiveness is beyond reach, shorter extracts will have to do' (1999b: 70). But contrary to many comparative analyses in TS, where samples appear to be randomly generated (see, for example, O'Driscoll 2011) in line with Toury's suggested '(ad hoc) coupled pairs' (1995: 77), these case studies will adopt a more targeted approach to the selection of passages. To this end, the methodology will be informed by Berman's rationale that translation criticism should focus on those areas where the original 'condenses, represents, signifies or symbolizes itself. These passages are *significant zones* wherein a work realizes its own ambitions […] and reaches its own centre of gravity' (1995: 70, original emphasis). Since these 'significant zones' promise a concentration of variables of narratological, stylistic, ethical etc. import, such representativeness allows for a greater degree of generalizability once these zones have been compared with their corresponding TT segments.

The comparative analyses of *Madame Bovary* will converge on an excerpt drawn from Part II, chapter 7 of the work where Emma falls into a melancholic reverie following the departure of Léon. This particular passage certainly accords to the profile of a significant zone; thematically, it represents the nothingness, or the inaction, which stems from Emma's inability to engage with the present, and stylistically, it showcases the author's use of Free Indirect

Style, irony and cohesion. As previously mentioned, the section of *La Mare au diable* under enquiry will be the Appendix to the pastoral tale. Since it comprises four chapters and can be read as a self-contained work in its own right, the analysis will extend over the entire Appendix. Writing to her editor in 1846, Sand describes the Appendix as a 'truthful exposé of a noble part of our ancient, rustic customs that originated with the Gauls', whose merit lies in the interest 'which can be generated by these curious customs' (cited in Cellier 1999: 216, my translation): the centre of gravity in this significant zone is thus the author's ethnographic aims, that is the charting and preservation of Berrichon identity. In short, both textual analyses will hopefully give way to results and generalizations that shed light on the phenomenon of retranslation in a more robust and revelatory manner.

This methodology has also been designed with replicability in mind. Since multiple (re)translations will be explored for each source text, the analysis must be constructed in such a way as to allow each and every target text to be evaluated according to the same criteria. The benchmarks already outlined will facilitate consistency across the exploration of the two corpora, and ensure that the lines of enquiry are as transparent as possible. Although this particular approach has very much been tailored to the specific works under investigation and significant zones, there is nevertheless a high degree of flexibility built into the model which means that it can be adapted and re-tailored to any number of (re)translation studies. Narrative theory can be used to elucidate the type of stories being told in the source text(s) and their particular narrative features, and this exercise will bring into focus those facets of the original work which are worthy of close attention. In order to clarify how the narratives have been constructed in more detail, pertinent narratological and/or stylistic devices can be isolated and employed as repeatable touchstones across the selected target texts. Where ambiguity is an issue, Systemic Functional Grammar can provide an additional level of precision. As the survey in the introduction has shown, there is a definite need both for more empirical studies of retranslation and for a more unified approach to those studies. This method hopes to go some way to responding to that need by offering a replicable framework that can be adapted to a wide number of case studies, both literary and non-literary. In turn, the generalizability of findings on (re)translation might be enhanced.

5

Tales of a 'belle infidèle'

Introduction

Having outlined the hybridized, descriptive methodology in the previous chapter for handing the textual analysis, what follows here is a detailed comparative study between the original *Madame Bovary* and the eight British (re)translations which recount the tale of this 'belle infidèle' in various instantiations. Not only does this study seek to determine whether there is any evidence of a return to the specificities of the source text over time, but it will also facilitate an exploration into how Flaubert's idiosyncratic narration and narrative organization are affected when passed through the filter of translation. Given the relative complexity of the interpretative process carried out here, it is worth restating the methodological underpinnings of this analysis. The first issue that will be explored is how Flaubert's impersonality, and its attendant critique of provincial life, has been remediated in the (re)translations with specific reference to FIS and the resultant ambiguity as to who speaks and who sees. It is at this point that the narrative features of causal emplotment and relationality converge, and the selected source text examples in which voice and focalization also converge will be explored in reference to the more tangible benchmarks offered by the interpersonal and ideational metafunctions of Systemic Functional Grammar (SFG). The analysis will then consider the extent to which the 'internal force' of Flaubert's narrative has been maintained or undermined through (re)translation. In other words, how has the feature of temporality, the forward thrust of the author's 'book about nothing', been reframed? Again, Systemic Functional Grammar offers a framework for the comparison of how texts cohere around and beyond the level of the clause.

All the examples examined below have been taken from the opening paragraphs of *Madame Bovary*, Part II, Chapter 7 (MB 126–7). This extract, or signifying zone in Berman's terms, boasts a concentration of the themes (Emma's daydreams, her romantic illusions/clichés and adulterous desires, all responses to her suffocating lack of fulfilment) and of the stylistic devices (Free Indirect Style, impersonality, irony and cohesion) which drive Flaubert's narrative forwards. Each source text example will be accompanied by a literal back translation for ease of access and the (re)translations will be referenced according to the abbreviations listed at the front of this book and again in Table 1.1.

Free Indirect Style: Reframing causal emplotment and relationality

Before undertaking any descriptive analysis of translation shifts, it is first necessary to consider what a return to or a full revelation of the particularities of FIS in (re)translation might mean. For the grammatical devices on which FIS is premised – the absence of verbum dicendi, the transposition of tense and person, as well as the use of deictic and modal markers – function in much the same way in both the source and target languages, and will therefore not place any great strain on the ability of the latter to reflect the former. However, where the FIS of the source text does prove challenging is on the level of discourse, pervading the narrative with an ambiguity, an evasiveness as to who is speaking and who is seeing; it is within such passages that Flaubertian impersonality and irony prevail. Consequently, in order for a (re)translation to preserve this specificity, it must ensure that its own grammatical foundations provide an analogously unstable basis for voice and focalization. Only in the ensuing incertitude can the ironic, impersonal timbre of the source text be heard, and the inherent denigration of the characters revealed. The following analysis will examine whether the (re)translations maintain the polyvalence set in motion by FIS, or on the contrary, whether they untangle the intermingled strands of voice and focalization, moving the text further away from the fundamental instability of the original.

Voice

The first, and most readily recognized, source of ambiguity which must be considered within the parameters of FIS is that of voice. Systemic Functional Grammar defines a clause as 'an interactive event involving speaker, or writer, and audience' (Halliday and Matthiessen 2004: 106); however, such clarity of definition is thwarted by Flaubert's use of FIS, since the voice of the character cannot be disentangled from the voice of the narrator, to the extent that the question must be posed: 'Is it even possible to assign one speaker – and one addressee – in accordance with the communication model?' (Perruchot 1975: 259, my translation). It is precisely this undecidability, this lack of conformity which confounds any attempt to pinpoint *qui parle*, who speaks, within FIS; rather, the narrative resounds to a polyphony of voices, the sources of which refuse identification. The voice of the narrator blends with that of the character, direct and indirect speech become indistinguishable, giving way to an impersonal space wherein passages of FIS may be, as Culler puts it, 'read with a certain detachment and judged as ironic comments on their various sources' (1974: 198). However, both voices must be present as a condition for this interpretation; should the intermingling be unravelled through translation, irony will no longer have a space in which to prevail. In order to examine how the polyvocality of the key passage is balanced in the (re)translations, the fundamental elements of how the clause functions as an 'interactive event' (Halliday and Matthiessen 2004: 117) will be investigated, including considerations of tense and clause type, as well as the absence of interaction and the impact of additions. Building on Bal's (1985) distinction between the External Focalizer and Character Focalizer, the two voices in FIS will henceforth be differentiated as the External Vocalizer (EV) and Character Vocalizer (CV).

One of the fundamental constituents which allow a clause to function as an interpersonal exchange is its Finite element, that is the verbal operator which conveys tense and modality. Its primary role is to give a statement 'a point of reference', either 'to the time of speaking', or 'to the judgement of the speaker' (Halliday and Matthiessen 2004: 115). In the first case, finite verbs serve to anchor a given statement in the past, present or future, while the latter is expressed by modal verbs as a means of establishing degrees of likelihood or obligation. As such, the Finite element is responsible for framing the speech event, and thus voice, on both a temporal and modal level. However, when examined within the context of FIS, the Finite elements of a given clause become, in essence, less finite: the presence of two indistinct voices, that is two speakers, means that there can be no one point of reference. Rather, the duality and the indefiniteness of each statement must be taken into account.

The present tense is frequently employed in those instances of FIS which make gnomic generalizations. While one voice is sincere in its postulations, the other may undercut this sincerity by insinuating the hackneyed bent of such universalism. To complicate matters even further, Flaubert's particular use of the imperfect tense must also be entered into the equation: in this respect, the author dislocates standard SL patterns of time by substituting the 'singulative' frequency (Genette 1980: 114) and definitiveness of the simple past with the imperfect tense. Thus, the imperfect comes to represent a whole gamut of aspects – in addition to its normal descriptive, habitual or ongoing aspect, the tense has also become a marker of completion, that is of pseudo-iterative narration, defined by Genette as 'scenes presented, particularly by their wording in the imperfect, as iterative, whereas their richness and precision of detail ensure than no reader can seriously believe they occur and reoccur in that manner' (Genette 1980: 121).

It is these complexities of FIS which disrupt standard narrative patterns, and which ultimately serve to stifle the emergence of one solitary voice, and thus the expression of one clearly defined position in terms of tense and modality. As is the case with Flaubertian focalization, it is this very absence of finiteness which destabilizes the narrative and at the same time provides a footing for irony. Therefore, in order for any (re)translation to reflect the specificities of the source text, an analogous degree of disquiet must also prevail.

Present tense

To begin with the issue of generalizations, the following sentence serves as a good example of Flaubert's use of the gnomic present:

> C'était cette rêverie que l'on **a** sur ce qui ne reviendra plus, la lassitude qui vous **prend** après chaque fait accompli, cette douleur enfin que vous **apportent** l'interruption de tout mouvement accoutumé, la cessation brusque d'une vibration prolongée. (MB 126)
>
> [*It was that reverie one* ***has*** *about what will return no more, the listlessness that* ***comes*** *over you after each fait accompli, in a word, this pain that the interruption of all routine movement, the brusque cessation of a lingering vibration,* ***brings*** *to you*]

Here, the present tense expresses an apparently timeless and universal truth, and also marks a moment of rupture in a narrative otherwise constructed in the past tense, thereby setting in motion 'an effect of synchrony between the diegetic time, narrative time and the time of reception' (Laurent 2001: 97, my translation). The temporal distance between character, narrator and reader is momentarily attenuated, placing everyone on an analogous timescale of (supposed) perpetual truth.

This technique is by no means foreign to the target language grammatical system, where the gnomic present is also used in generic utterances; thus, each (re)translation has at its disposal the opportunity to remain close to the ST in terms of both form and content. Indeed, this is what happens in the majority of the versions, with the exception of TT5 Russell. Here, several different aspects are at play in the contracted phrase: 'It was the spell cast by the departed, the lassitude that follows the event, the pain caused by any accustomed motion breaking off or prolonged vibration abruptly ceasing' (TT5 Russell 136). The reformulation is such that the active present tense is outweighed by the prevalence of passive constructions, especially by the two past participles. Certainly, the polyvocality of the ST remains since the utterance could be attributed to the EV or to the CV; nevertheless, the universal dimension as marked by the gnomic present is not fully divulged, with the result that Emma can no longer be heard as an echo of aphorisms drawn from her bourgeois, romantic reading, while the narrator is subsequently denied the opportunity to permeate such echoes with the sour note of irony. In this first example then, the latent criticism of the source text is obstructed by one retranslation alone, that is TT5 Russell, to produce a pattern which does not tally with the history-as-progress modelling of the phenomenon.

Imperfect tense

Central to the ambiguity of the key passage is also the destabilizing use of the imperfect tense, not least in those moments of Emma's reverie where she is transported into another reality. Such is the case in the following sentence which expresses the protagonist's remembrance of time spent with Léon:

> Il **lisait** tout haut, tête nue, posé sur un tabouret de bâtons secs; le vent frais de la prairie **faisait** trembler les pages du livre et les capucines de la tonnelle… (MB 127).
>
> [*He* ***was reading*** *out loud, bare-headed, at repose on a stool of dry sticks; the fresh wind off the meadow* ***was setting*** *atremble the pages of the book and the nasturtiums of the arbour…*]

Here, the finite verbs give way to a number of potential interpretations: since there is no transposition of the imperfect tense in a move from direct to indirect discourse, both the original and reported speech events can be framed retrospectively as iterative (Léon read on a repeated number of occasions), pseudo-iterative (Léon read only once, but the action is represented as habitual) or incomplete (Léon was in the midst of reading). However, when reporting past events, an original statement in the immediate present (Léon is reading) will undergo a backshift to the imperfect, thereby affording another aspect to the voice of the CV, namely one which places her in the moment, reliving the experience in a direct manner.

To begin with the treatment of the finite verb ***lisait*** [*was reading*], the retranslations demonstrate a preference for the habitual past: TT2 Blanchamp (104), TT3 May (149), TT7 Mauldon (110) and TT8 Thorpe (117) all opt for the modal construction 'would read', and TT5 Russell for 'used to read' (136), thereby allowing the aspect to be interpreted as either iterative or pseudo-iterative. The anterior frame of reference in these versions, however, precludes the possibility that Emma's reverie is located in a past which is ongoing in her mind, or that she has positioned herself in that ongoing moment as if it were her present. With TT4 Hopkins, the clause construction is manipulated so that the finite verb is downgraded to a present participle dependent on a matricial verb: 'What lovely afternoons they had spent alone together […], he, reading' (147). In this instance, the participle is bound to the preceding pluperfect verb group, situating the action squarely in the past and also rejecting the continuous aspect. However, this participle, which is essentially non-finite in nature, does go some way to preserving the ambiguity inherent in the ST imperfect aspect; although the action is located in the past, the present participle can nevertheless encapsulate repetitive and incomplete aspects within that temporal framework.

The only version to encase the action in the perfective is the initial translation, TT1 Marx-Aveling, where the statement 'He read' (135) renders the action completed and located within the definite parameters of the past. Not only does this skew the original statement of the CV by clarifying its temporal boundaries, but it also points more clearly towards the presence of a more traditional, omniscient EV. As Huss notes, Flaubert's use of the imperfect 'lends a subjective colouring to an event, where the conventional narrative tense, the past historic, would reflect the unambiguous authority of a narrator firmly established at an organizing distance from events' (1977: 143). Thus, the use of the simple past in TT1 Marx-Aveling drowns out the ambiguity of the ST imperfect, both in terms of aspect and of voice; the definitiveness of the action disallows Emma to deceive herself with illusions of frequency or temporal proximity to Léon, while the use of the customary narrative tense silences any voice other than that of the external, objective narrator.

Perhaps the version which approximates the equivocalness of the ST to the closest degree is TT6 Wall, where Léon 'would be reading' (99); this use of the imperfect in conjunction with the present progressive participle allows both the iterative and the ongoing aspects to come to the fore, thereby encompassing a broader range of possibilities in comparison to the other versions. However, the continuity suppresses the potential for the tense to convey any aspect of (melodramatic) definitiveness, nor could the verbal group have been transposed from the present, thereby silencing the CV who has repositioned herself into an alternative actuality. Nevertheless, this act of combining the habitual and the ongoing aspects into what may be labelled an imperfect progressive aspect is in itself significant: whereas standard TL narrative patterns evince a choice between one or the other, that is the iterative or incomplete aspects, TT6 Wall takes the atypical step of opting for both, in other words, for disrupting the TL to a certain extent. It thus becomes possible to draw a parallel between this non-conformity to TL narrative patterns and Flaubert's own unsettling use of the imperfect tense.

As far as the second instantiation of the imperfect tense in this example is concerned, that is ***faisait*** trembler [*was setting atremble*], it is of note that all the (re)translations deal with the verb in a manner different from that of the first example. TT6 Wall now narrows the aspect presented to that of the habitual: 'breezes would flutter' (99), thereby discontinuing the disruption evinced by the preceding ambiguous construction and restricting the potential temporal locations of the CV. In a move away from the finiteness of the iterative, TT7 Mauldon opts for the present participle with 'the fresh breeze from the meadows ruffling the pages' (110); although the participle is still governed by the matricial use of the habitual aspect in the first clause, it nevertheless captures both the repetitive and unfolding aspects of the imperfect, whilst also allowing the voice of the CV to carry across from an imagined present. The initial translation also evinces a shift away from the use of the preterite in the first clause, albeit a slight one; the incorporation of a present participle in 'the fresh wind of the meadow set trembling the leaves of the book' (TT1 Marx-Aveling 135) relieves the phrase somewhat from the definitiveness of the main verb, allowing strains of incompletion to be heard which point to the CV in her state of reverie. However, the overriding aspect remains that of completion, which once more underscores the presence of an EV.

Of the remaining versions, TT2 Blanchamp, TT3 May, TT5 Russell and TT8 Thorpe convey the iterative in the first clause; in the second clause, they all relegate the finite verb to the definitive preterite in an apparent mismatch of temporal frameworks: rather than an habitual action, the wind 'rustled' (TT2 Blanchamp 104), 'fluttered' (TT3 May 149; TT5 Russell 136) and 'trembled' (TT8 Thorpe 117) the pages of the book. Likewise, although the use of the present participle in TT4 Hopkins had the potential to express the repetitive and ongoing aspects of the imperfect, the second instantiation of the imperfect here too becomes 'the wind […] fluttered' (147). However, on closer inspection, these aspectual shifts do not occur without compensation elsewhere. In three versions, the conjunctions 'whilst' (TT2 Blanchamp 104) and 'while' (TT4 Hopkins 147; TT5 Russell136) now take the place of Flaubert's semicolon and render the second verb simultaneous to that of the first, that is the (pseudo-)iterative action of reading. Indeed, this conforms to a standard pattern of TL usage, where 'with reference to habitual actions in the past [...] English very often uses the preterite in such contexts whereas French does not' (Price 1998: 313). Consequently, the use of the preterite in the TL does not drown out the imperfective aspect of habituality. Even where TT3 May and TT8 Thorpe omit any overt markers of simultaneity in their respective observations that 'The wind blowing in cool from the meadows, fluttered the leaves of the book' (TT3 May 149) and 'the cool wind from the meadows trembled the pages of his book' (TT8 Thorpe 117), their instantiation of this second verb is nonetheless temporally framed by its (pseudo-)iterative precedent. Thus, what at first glance may appear to be a disjunction between the SL imperfect and TL preterite reveals itself to be a partial convergence of aspect.

Ultimately though, none of the (re)translations succeed in fully conveying the ambiguity of voice and the iterative force of Emma's reverie that can be heard and felt in the source text. In this example, it is certainly the initial translation which introduces the greatest tearing apart of FIS through its use of a perfective tense; it is the voice of the narrator which prevails in TT1 Marx-Aveling, but this narrator has been deprived of his power to chide since the object of his censure, the empty romanticism of the bourgeoisie echoed in the voice of Emma, is no longer present as a counterpoint. But the disambiguating, and therefore flawed, strategy in the initial translation does not then open on to a succession of 'corrective' retranslations. On the one hand, it is TT6 Wall, a much later version, which boasts the most uncertain use of aspect and voice, but this is followed chronologically by a regressive motion in TT7 Mauldon and TT8 Thorpe where the full potential of the imperfect tense to intimate Emma's futile escape to the past is disallowed. So, although the starting point of the Retranslation Hypothesis is in place, the trajectory through the retranslations themselves is by no means an uninterrupted move towards improvement.

Absence

To return to the SFG definition of the clause as exchange, it is the Mood structure which is responsible for conveying interpersonal meaning through its Subject and Finite constituents. Thus, the function of the Mood structure is closely linked to the expression of voice. However, in some instances, a clause can be marked by the absence of the Mood elements, which in turn renders the question of who speaks all the more complex. Halliday distinguishes the use of ellipsis as one particular site of absence (Halliday and Matthiessen 2004: 151–4). However, for the purposes of this analysis, it is necessary to go beyond this particular definition of ellipsis, which is tied to the question and answer process and whose 'meaning is "go back and retrieve the missing words"' (Halliday and Matthiessen 2004: 569); instead, the reach of ellipsis will be extended to encompass instances where meaning is beyond retrieval.

Ellipsis is present in the key passage in the unfinished sentence: 'le vent frais de la prairie faisait trembler les pages du livre et les capucines de la tonnelle…' [*the fresh wind off the meadow was setting atremble the pages of the book and the nasturtiums of the arbour...*] (MB 127). Here, the punctuation graphically indicates aposiopesis, that is it 'marks a clear break in the continuity of the syntagmatic chain' (Laurent 2001: 46, my translation). Indeed, as Haig pointed out, 'unpredictable typography' (1986: 11) is one of the characteristics of FIS, and as such, the points of ellipsis are a very visual marker that two different voices are to be heard in this example. As far as the CV is concerned, the reader can hear the thoughts of the protagonist as they unfold, and then trail off. By allowing this discontinuity, the EV rejects his omniscient authority and merges his voice seamlessly with that of Emma; however, the apparent harmony of voices gives way to a certain discordance, whereby the narrator's silence ironically underlines the inadequacy of Emma's imagination since her reserve of romantic clichés appears to have been exhausted.

And yet the first three (re)translations do not include any elliptical punctuation. In TT1 Marx-Aveling, the reverie is expressed as the wind:

> set trembling the leaves of the book and the nasturtiums of the arbour. (135–6)

In TT2 Blanchamp, it merely:

> rustled through the leaves of his book. (104)

In TT3 May, it:

> fluttered the pages of the book and the nasturtiums of the arbour. (149)

Consequently, there is a negation of absence at play in these three versions which obscures the immediacy and subjective discontinuity of the unfolding voice(s). Although the ellipsis points are restored in TT4 Hopkins and TT5 Russell, they do not appear without some alteration, namely the addition of a full stop:

> the pages of his book and the nasturtiums growing on the arbour…. (147)
> the pages of his book and the nasturtiums round the arbour…. (136)

It follows that TT4 Hopkins and TT5 Russell indicate elided meaning, but the position of the full stop in the former restricts the extent to which the discontinuity is permitted, while that of the latter misrepresents the moment at which the pause occurs and introduces a definite disambiguation since the nasturtiums no longer have the potential to function as a subject. Thus, in all of these versions, the potential for subjectivity and inadequacy is lessened, and the voice of the CV becomes endowed with a greater sense of control and competency. In turn, if the voice of the EV is to be teased out from such a merger, it too undergoes a reduction in latent criticism; the gaps in meaning are suppressed or confined, counteracting the instability of the text, and as a result, the basis for irony is eroded.

In contrast, it is TT6 Wall, TT7 Mauldon and TT8 Thorpe which preserve the ambiguity inherent in the ST blend of voices. In TT6 Wall where 'breezes would flutter in the pages of his book and among the nasturtiums of the arbour ... ' (99), and in TT8 Thorpe where 'the cool wind from the meadows trembled the pages of his book and the arbour's nasturtiums ... ' (117), the lack of any additional punctuation to qualify the ellipsis allows the full potential of the ST uncertainty to be realized. With TT7 Mauldon, the ambiguity is taken even further: the inclusion of a comma in 'the fresh breeze ruffling the pages of his book, and the nasturtiums growing round the arbour ... ' (110) now isolates the latter noun group, with the result that this may be interpreted as either a direct object of the main verb, or a new subject which is left unqualified. In conjunction with its preservation of the ellipsis points, TT7 Mauldon thus facilitates both the faltering voice of the CV and the scathing voice of the EV. Consequently, there is a notable progressive restoration at play in this one example since the more recent retranslations do appear to exhibit a more attentive reading of the source text.

Addition

In other passages of FIS, it is certainly the case that Flaubert was prone to what the narratologist Toolan would term 'narratorial tinkering' (1988: 121), that is the revision of the phraseology of the original utterance or thought which, in the particular instance of the ST, leads to 'evident moments at which the writing outruns her [Emma's] own formulations' (Heath 1992: 123). It follows that the double vocalization of FIS allows access to the inner workings of the protagonist's mind, but this access has been modulated by a narrator who makes his voice heard in a stylized and sophisticated language and reveals himself as a simultaneous vocalizer, or perhaps more specifically, as Emma's ventriloquist.

One particular characteristic of this overt tinkering is the way in which Emma's thoughts are conveyed; rather than always reproduce the inner workings of her mind as they may have been realized by the protagonist herself (as was the ironic case in the earlier example), a certain degree of deviation occurs when the utterances pass through the lyrical filter of the EV. More precisely, the polyvocality which emerges from the ST is attuned to the impressionistic and to the abstract, as opposed to the materiality of the narrative world, thereby representing Emma's frustrated relationship to what is concrete. Not only does this stylistic modulation serve as means of ironic distancing, but it also allows the narrator to demonstrate the extent to which the character's consciousness, nourished by romantic illusions, remains unanchored in reality.

A case in point is Emma's reminiscence that:

> Ils s'y **étaient promenés** bien des fois, **à** ce même murmure des ondes, **sur** les cailloux couverts de mousse (MB 126)
>
> [*They had* **walked** *there many a time,* **to** *this same murmur of the waters,* **on** *the pebbles topped with moss*]

The sentence comprises only one material verb and two fragmented prepositional phrases which are undoubtedly marked by the author's concern for cadence and sound, as well as by his scorn for literary clichés. These prepositions are also significant in that the aural and tactile sensations which they express remain unanchored by what Halliday would term a 'perceptive mental process' (Halliday and Matthiessen 2004: 199). In other words, the memories and emotions of the protagonist flicker in and out of the narrative, unfettered and imprecise in their non-finite clauses; the indeterminate relationship between Emma's consciousness and the reality of her situation is thus emphasized, while the author reveals the powerful thrust of his style against the banality of the subject matter.

However, this clause complex is susceptible to alteration in the majority of the versions: TT2 Blanchamp, TT3 May, TT4 Hopkins, TT5 Russell and TT7 Mauldon enhance the dependent clauses with finite verbal groups or present participles. Emma and Léon thus '**listened** to the murmuring of the waves over the moss-covered stones' (TT2 Blanchamp 104); '**listened** to the murmur of the water foaming over the pebbles' (TT3 May 149); 'had walked beside it, **hearing** the murmur of its waters, **watching** the mossy stones' (TT4 Hopkins 147); they were '**listening** to that same murmuring of the water over the mossy pebbles' (TT5 Russell 136) or '**listening** to that same water murmuring over those same moss-covered stones' (TT7 Mauldon 110). It follows that the addition of cognitive verbs of aural perception adds an element of stability, thereby tethering Emma's flight of fancy more firmly to the real and closing the ironic gap between her immediate and her imagined existence. Indeed, most of these versions disambiguate the second prepositional phrase by tying it explicitly to the action of the water, while TT4 Hopkins alters the dynamics of the memory further still through its addition of the visual gerund, *watching*. None of these texts allow for the interpretation that Emma and Léon are walking over a moss-covered path.

But rather than undo the polyvocality of the ST, such shifts alter its inflection. The insertion of perceptual verbs grounds the phraseology to a greater, and to a more banal extent, in the reality of the narrative world; in so doing, it is the facile expression of the protagonist which is privileged. Disengaged from narratorial tinkering, the limitations of Emma's vocalization all but drown out the unhinged, illusory qualities of her inner cognition, qualities which could only have been formulated by the narrator. Therefore, the ambiguous balance of FIS is disrupted by the overemphasis placed in the retranslations on the additional prosaic verbal groups, and thus on the voice of the CV. On the other hand, however, the external vocalization is also modulated through the insertion of these verbs; if a narratorial voice is to be identified in these retranslations, it is one which, in opposition to the ST, overtly signposts the mental processes of the protagonist. As such, the move towards explicitly reporting Emma's aural world further distorts the balance of FIS by infusing a more diegetic, descriptive tone into the narrative. Contrary to the incertitude which underpins vocalization in ST passages of FIS, the role of the EV in the above versions can now be attributed to a recognizable and reliable omniscient narrator, more akin to the voice in indirectly reported discourse. In sum, the shortcomings of the voice of the CV can no longer be heard once divested of the narratorial tinkering of the EV which is necessary for the ironic juxtaposition to take place, and the voice of this latter confines itself to a more conventional, less ambiguous narratorial role of telling as opposed to showing. In this instance, the repeated insertion of these verbs of perception demonstrates the extent to which similar strategies are used across a broad stretch of retranslations, a scenario that significantly undercuts the argument that retranslation correlates with differentiation and challenge. For these overlaps come more forcefully to the fore in those instances where the (re)translations move further away from the interpretations suggested by the discursive choices of the ST.

It is TT1 Marx-Aveling, TT6 Wall and TT8 Thorpe which retain the singular ST fusion of vocalization in the earlier example of FIS: TT1 Marx-Aveling remarks that 'They had often walked there to the murmur of the waves over the moss-covered pebbles' (135), TT6 Wall states that 'They had walked along there many many times, by the same murmuring waves, over the moss-covered stones' (98–9) and TT8 Thorpe declares that 'They had walked there many times, to this same murmur of the waves, on pebbles coated in moss' (117). In none of these cases is the sensory experience explicitly tied to a reported mental process, allowing the EV the indeterminate space in which to fuse his speech with that of Emma and to enable the subtle contrast between the lyrical phrasing of the narrator and the implied dearth of the protagonist's own formulations. Yet another pattern emerges from this particular example which demonstrates that the initial translation and most recent retranslation adopt analogous approaches and, along with TT6 Wall, serve as examples which are attuned to the particular polyvocality of the original. The interim retranslations, however, represent something of a backwards trend given their augmentation of the narrator's reporting voice and their anchoring of Emma's voice in the world of the concrete. Again, several points of comparison between versions, and not points of discrepancy, emerge from this particular example.

Summary

Although this exploration of Flaubert's use of voice in FIS has been rather brief, it is nevertheless clear that no distinguishable pattern of improvement can be discerned from the various ways in which the (re)translations have interpreted and recast this fundamental vehicle for irony and impersonality. Granted, the initial translation does show some signs of Berman's supposed blindness in its treatment of the imperfect tense and ellipsis, while this latter category also attests to chronological improvement in the three most recent retranslations. However, the initial translation is by no means alone in its occasional splintering of FIS, given those intermittent versions where the addition of reporting verbs reinforces the voice of the narrator above and beyond that of the protagonist, and undermines his impersonality. Similarly, the resources of the target language grammar are such that no translation can hope to recreate the ambiguous use of ST aspect (which could be simultaneously pseudo-iterative, iterative and continuous), with the result that the uncertainty of the narrative is downplayed. If any signs of consistency are to be identified, then it is perhaps TT6 Wall which has remained most harmonized with the polyvocal specificities of the original across these examples. Subsequently, the following two retranslations, that is the most recent versions, go against the grain of the Retranslation Hypothesis.

Focalization

In the case of Flaubert's FIS, the fusion of speaking is also accompanied by the fusion of seeing. Focalization occurs on two different levels, as defined by Bal (1985): on an extradiegetic level, through the external narrator-focalizer (EF), and on an intradiegetic level, through the Character Focalizer (CF). In certain cases, the focalization of the latter is embedded seamlessly into that of the former, so that the intradiegetic perspective prevails: this has been termed 'double focalization'. In other instances, it becomes impossible to determine which perspective has been adopted: this is known as 'ambiguous focalization'. Moreover, various different facets of focalization can also be taken into consideration, in particular those which Rimmon-Kenan has defined as facets of perception and psychology, relating to 'the focalizer's sensory range', and 'mind and emotions' (2002: 80), respectively. This approach thus allows a distinction to be drawn between sensory perceptions and the cognitive or emotive workings of the consciousness.

It is also necessary to incorporate an examination of the focalized, namely that which is seen, whether animate or inanimate, perceptible or non-perceptible. The focalized elements of a given clause can be categorized in parallel with the SFG system of Transitivity, in particular with the categories of participant and circumstance. These are integral to the examination of who is experiencing what, or more precisely, who is seeing and what is being seen. Firstly, the participants, that is those involved in the verbal process of the clause, can function as both focalizers or focalized. But, it is crucial to bear in mind the clandestine EF who will essentially be hidden from view. Secondly, the circumstantial elements of the clause, that is the 'when, where, how and why' (Rimmon-Kenan 2002: 260), serve to qualify 'the unfolding of the process in space-time' (2002: 265), and can therefore function as focalized elements.

The picture becomes more complicated in situations of ambiguous focalization, since the source of the visual, sensorial, cognitive or emotional observations is questionable. In turn, the uncertainty, or the duality of the identity of the focalizer is brought to bear on the identity of the focalized; the specific qualities of the focalized participant or circumstance will necessarily change according to whose eyes are responsible for the depiction. Thus, the participants in and circumstances of focalization mediate the portrayal of a dislocated world within the ST, and construe two disparate levels of experience: the experience of the EF, and the experience of the CF. Any changes in these elements through translation will then distort that particular, yet often imprecise, picture, painted in ironic and scathing hues.

Focalized participants

Generalized participants

As was the case in the issue of who speaks, the presence of generalizations lends an even greater degree of ambiguity to the narrative: it becomes impossible to determine whether the focalized participants are viewed through the eyes of the CF, and are thus tinged with the clichés of her romantic education, or through the eyes of the EF, and are thus observed from an ironic distance.

We return here to the proposed axiom that

> C'était **cette** rêverie que l'**on** a sur ce qui ne reviendra plus, la lassitude qui **vous** prend après chaque fait accompli, **cette** douleur enfin que **vous** apportent l'interruption de tout mouvement accoutumé, la cessation brusque d'une vibration prolongée (MB 126),
>
> [*It was **that reverie one** has about what will return no more, the listlessness that comes over **you** after each fait accompli, in a word, **this** pain that the interruption of all routine movement, the brusque cessation of a lingering vibration, brings to **you***]

It is the use of the personal pronouns *on* and *vous*, along with the demonstrative pronoun *cette* which opens the narrative up to different layers of interpretation. Firstly, the pronoun *on* blurs the focal orientation of the narrative since, 'in all its uses, "on" confines the identity of its subjects to the shadows, merging them thus into an indeterminate collective' (Herschberg-Pierrot 1993: 34). From such shadows may emerge the focalization of a protagonist who sees the *on* as representative of a timeless body of people, a body into which she can fuse herself, if only through her reverie. From the ironic and distant stance of the narrator, the focalization changes, and the shadows may give rise to 'the eternal imbecile named *On*' (Flaubert 1930b: 337) and to the representation of Flaubert's detested received ideas. Secondly, the direct object *vous* also poses problems of identification: is the narrator pinpointing the reader, closing the distance between himself and the narratee in order to render the generalization more pertinent?; or, does the narrator focus on a *vous* which corresponds to the subject *on*, in the sense that it is global in its reach?; or is it a sweeping focalization that can be traced back to the protagonist, desperately trying to inscribe her personal experiences into a universal (romantic) dimension? As far as the ST register is concerned, the informality of the focalized pronoun may suggest that it is allied to Emma as opposed to the conventional omniscient narrator; however, in the same way as the narrator can yield voice to the character in moments of FIS, perspective can also be relinquished. Finally, the use of the deictic marker *cette* can be linked to one of the generalizing strategies as noted by Williams, namely the evocation of 'a fictional particular' which can be discerned through 'the use of the demonstrative adjective (either "ce" or "un de ces") coupled with a noun (usually abstract) and a defining relative clause' (1978: 492). Although Williams attributes the generalizing representation of 'particulars' solely to the EF, it may further be attributed to the viewpoint of a CF who sees the world through the filter of ingrained truisms.

As far as the translation of *on* is concerned, it is certainly the case that the TL system has a corresponding third person indefinite pronoun, *one*, which can also be 'used for general, indefinite, human reference and frequently includes the listener implicitly' (Gramley and Pätzold 2004: 100). But, whereas *on* occurs frequently in SL discourse, the extent to which one is employed in the TL is substantially lower; here, the preference would tend towards avoidance, in particular through the use of the passive or the insertion of a more definite pronoun. Indeed, this TL inclination is reflected in the (re)translations, where only two versions incorporate the impersonal pronoun: TT3 May pinpoints 'the dreams that come to one when one has bade farewell' (128), while TT4 Hopkins focuses on 'the mood which afflicts one when one dreams' (147). In so doing, these versions retain the incertitude as to the identity of the focalized participant and a relationship of closeness can thus be postulated with the ST. But at the same time, the infrequency with which the impersonal pronoun generally appears in TL discourse renders its usage in these versions somewhat conspicuous, calling a degree of attention to itself which is not inherent in its deliberately and ironically prosaic usage in the original.

Another strategy which preserves the indefiniteness of the ST focalized participant emerges in the two most recent retranslations, where the personal pronoun is conveyed in the second person singular: 'brooding which comes when you lose something forever' (TT7 Mauldon 110) and 'that type of waking dream you experience' (TT8 Thorpe 117). In this instance, the referent can indeed encompass the same generic scope as its SL counterpart, but yet again, in contrast to the unmarked form of *on*, the TL use of *you* may also be more conspicuous in light of the 'historical situating of second-person discourse as a typically postmodernist kind of *écriture*' (Fludernik 1994: 445, original emphasis). On the one hand, the focalized participant of the TT remains elusive in terms of classification, while on the other, the TL signifier gives way to historical connotations which do not exist for the SL form.

A further manipulation of the personal pronoun appears in the initial translation and first retranslation where the vagueness of *on* is attenuated by the more inclusive *we*: 'that reverie which we give to things' (TT1 Marx-Aveling 135); 'dreaming as we so often do' (TT2 Blanchamp 103). While the TL pronoun still retains the universality of the ST observation, the *we* referring to humanity at large, it does however imply that the EF places himself directly within the reach of its collectiveness. Of course, narratorial inclusion is made evident in other ST generalizations such as the oft-cited maxim that 'la parole humaine est comme un chaudron fêlé où nous battons des mélodies à faire danser les ours' [*human language is like a cracked cauldron on which we beat out melodies to make the bears dance*] (MB 196). But where this particular instance differs is that the pronoun occurs within a passage of FIS. Rather than preserve the ambiguous focalization of the ST, the use of *we* renders the EF 'complicit in the things about which he speaks' (Defaye 1998: 58, my translation), or more precisely in this instance, complicit in the things he sees. The shift in pronoun thus forces a definite and untenable collusion between the narrator and the object of his contempt, while presenting an identifiable source of focalization where none is evident in the ST. As a result, the extradiegetic perspective of the EF dominates the intradiegetic perspective of the CF, thereby cancelling the equifocalness of FIS and with it, the opportunity for the ironic clash between these two divergent viewpoints.

Likewise, disambiguation occurs in TT5 Russell and TT6 Wall, where the indefinite pronoun of the ST is simply omitted: 'It was the spell cast by the departed' (TT5 Russell 136); 'It was the kind of reverie that comes when something vanishes' (TT6 Wall 98). Here, the focalization becomes more explicit in its precision; the generality of the SL pronoun is supplanted by the sense of definitiveness which emerges from the contracted clause of TT5 Russell and from the revised subject in TT6 Wall. In turn, this explicitation undercuts the ambiguous focalization of the ST: the line of vision of the CF is obscured since no evidence remains of the protagonist's attempts to perceptualize her situation within the context of the global *on*. This leaves only the perspective of an EF who, in terms of the psychological facet of focalization, 'knows everything about the represented world' (Rimmon-Kenan 2002: 80), given the certitude of the observations. Once again, the equifocalness of FIS collapses into the single perspective of an external narrator-focalizer, while the generalizing dimension is also diminished, leaving little room for irony.

As far as the treatment of the second personal plural pronoun is concerned, the (re)translations bring a variety of strategies to light. The first point to note is that the use of *vous* in the ST as an indirect object is somewhat marked in terms of its informal register and it is indeed this familiar slant which intimates the presence of the CF. By translating the pronoun as *you*, both TT1 Marx-Aveling and TT7 Mauldon retain the uncertain universality of the ST observation: 'the lassitude that seizes you' (TT1 Marx-Aveling 135); 'that lassitude you feel […], that pain you suffer' (TT7 Mauldon 110). Moreover, the markedness of the TL pronoun within the context of nineteenth-century literature (in this sense, it is comparable to the SL pronoun) alters the texture of the narrative sufficiently so as to suggest that the gaze is not the gaze of the traditional omniscient narrator. This universality and markedness is perpetuated in TT8 Thorpe, but to a lesser extent given the omission of the second pronoun in: 'the lassitude that grips you […] the suffering that the interruption of any habitual motion […] brings' (TT8 Thorpe 117). The removal of this latter focalized participant deemphasizes the familiarity of the observation, and thus risks overshadowing the presence of the CF.

An amalgamation of omission and the use of *one* comes to the fore in TT3 May and TT4 Hopkins, while TT5 Russell remains consistent with the whole scale removal of all personal pronouns: 'the lassitude that comes over one […] the pain, in a word, which accompanies the interruption of habit' (TT3 May 148); 'the sort of lassitude which deadens the heart […] the pain that strikes at one' (TT4 Hopkins 147); 'the lassitude that follows the event, the pain caused by any accustomed motion breaking off' (TT5 Russell 136). In those instances where *one* is the focalized participant, the ambiguity remains alongside the potential for universality, while its markedness also points to the singularity of the narrative context; however, where the pronoun has been omitted, the observation becomes more definite in its focus, and as was the case earlier, the perspective of the CF is submerged.

The issue of complicity returns once again in TT2 Blanchamp, but also in TT6 Wall: 'the exhaustion which overtakes us […] that pain which the interruption […] produces in us' (TT2 Blanchamp 103); 'the lassitude we feel' (TT6 Wall 98). As was the case earlier, the use of the first person plural, whether as direct object, indirect object or subject, draws attention to the parameters of the focalized participant as a universal entity which necessarily encompasses the EF, but which is unlikely to have stemmed from the perspective of the CF. And so the hazy focalization of FIS has once again been subjected to a process of clarification from which emerges a determined focalized participant and a one-dimensional perspective.

The greatest bifurcation of FIS occurs in conjunction with the translation of the cleft construction and the deictic marker which characterize the phrase: 'C'était cette rêverie […], cette douleur' [*It was that reverie […], this pain*] (MB 126). This example revolves around what Williams defines as 'a fictional particular' (1978: 492), in other words, a definite constituent of the narrative world which serves as a basis for the ensuing generalization. Central to such definitiveness is the precision of the deictic marker which 'positions the receiver in a context where representation becomes *presentation*' (Laurent 2001: 96, original emphasis, my translation). However, in the context of ambiguous focalization, this act of presentation may be attributed intradiegetically to the CF, or extradiegetically to the EF. Moreover, the use of the cleft construction to set up the generalization is significant since, as Culler has highlighted, the 'introduction of *c'était* is generally a way of introducing a fact, presenting it shorn of its potential links with thought and activity' (Culler 1974: 205). Thus, the cleft construction cleaves the narrative, suspending the observation beyond what is concrete in mental or physical terms, and in so doing, demonstrates the extent to which the perspective of the CF is contorted, not least through cliché and over-idealization.

The generalization revolves around the dual axes of the demonstrative article and the cleft construction; in order to mirror the dynamics of the original focalization, a (re)translation must preserve the precision of the first and the singular prosaism of the latter. However, the only version to retain both elements of focalization is TT1 Marx-Aveling, which mirrors the ST in its observation: 'It was that reverie […], that pain' (TT1 Marx-Aveling 135). Therefore, the banality and orchestrated romanticism of the focalized constituent is preserved, facilitating both the perspective of the CF and the ironic distance of the EF. Elsewhere, the focalized generalization is somewhat diluted. While TT8 Thorpe retains the cleft construction and demonstrative as signposts for the hackneyed in 'It was that type of waking dream', the use of the definite article in 'the suffering' (TT8 Thorpe 117) detracts from the overall exactitude of the observation, and therefore attenuates the force of the ironic marker. In TT6 Wall comes the contracted observation that 'It was the kind of reverie' (TT6 Wall 98), which retains some degree of precision through the use of the nominal phrase, 'the kind of', but which omits the second demonstrative phrase 'cette douleur' [*that pain*], thereby limiting the frame of vision. Similarly, TT5 Russell preserves the cleft construction in 'It was the spell […], the pain' (TT5 Russell 136), but the omission of the deictic marker limits the sense of both intra- and extradiegetic proximity which emerges in the ST.

Nevertheless, the most evident and destructive manipulation of focalization comes to light in the remaining retranslations, in specific, through the treatment of the cleft construction. In TT2 Blanchamp, TT3 May, TT4 Hopkins and TT7 Mauldon, the focalized participant becomes the protagonist: '**She** was dreaming' (TT2 Blanchamp 103; TT3 May 148); '**She** was in the mood' (TT4 Hopkins 147); '**She** sank into that kind of brooding' (TT7 Mauldon 110). Consequently, the presence of dual focalization is all but eradicated – the viewpoint which emerges is one of an omniscient EF with a bird's-eye view on the happenings of the narrative world, thereby shattering both the indecidability of the ST focalization and the opportunity for the reader to glimpse the irony created when the critical gaze of the EF is superimposed on to the rose-tinted gaze of the CF.

Notwithstanding, some compensatory strategies appear in these versions which serve, if not to restore, at least to intimate the presence of an intradiegetic focalizer. Take for example TT3 May, which actually reinstates the ST cleft construction and deixis later on in the observation: 'It was, in a word, that pain' (TT3 May 148). Thus, the signalling of cliché is suspended in the clause complex, but not altogether omitted, while the incorporation of the demonstrative retains the allusion to an entity that may be considered as both intra- and extradiegetically located, thereby preserving the ambiguous balance of focalization. With regard to TT7 Mauldon, the demonstrative prevails in the clause complex 'that kind of brooding […], that lassitude […], that pain' (TT7 Mauldon 110), and reinforces such 'fictional particulars' as the converging point for internal and external focalization.

Conversely, TT3 May omits all deictic markers, thereby diluting the emphasis on the crux of the generalization, and by extension, diminishing the basis for irony. TT4 Hopkins follows suit in its exclusion of the demonstrative pronoun, albeit with an intimation of universality by means of the approximating phrase, 'the sort of lassitude' (TT4 Hopkins 147); but here the initial manipulation of the cleft construction is compounded further still with the inclusion of the subsequent observations that 'She felt in her bones […]. She felt the pain' (TT4 Hopkins 147). Thus, it is this repeated insistence on the protagonist as focalized participant which destroys the effect of FIS to the greatest extent: the equifocality of the ST is forced into a unified perspective which conceals the vision of the CF, undermining both the universal span of the ST observations and its exposure of cliché.

Animate participants

In addition to generalizations, the key passage further encompasses focalizations which centre on the human characters themselves. The following observation is a prime illustration of the ambiguous focalization that not so much underpins, as destabilizes the ST:

> quoiqu'**il** fût séparé d'**elle**, **il** ne l'avait pas quittée, **il** était là (MB 126)
> [*although* ***he*** *was separated from* ***her, he*** *had not left* ***her, he*** *was there*]

Viewed through the eyes of Emma, the CF, this statement builds into a crescendo as she convinces herself that Léon may have left, but that his essence somehow remains with her. The threefold repetition of the pronoun *il* places Léon in the role of the primary focalized participant and demonstrates the extent of Emma's fixation thereon. She herself appears as a secondary focalized participant whereby the use of the direct and then indirect objects show her to be the fixed point around which the action rotates. However, it is important to distinguish between the different ontological statuses accorded to the primary focalized participant within this ST observation: the first clause recognizes the real Léon, the one from which the CF is physically removed, while the remaining clauses insist on a Léon whose presence is ethereal. Thus, in terms of intradiegetic focalization, the CF concentrates initially on the concrete, and moves towards an illusion which will ultimately replace reality. When focalized through the eyes of the EF the experience becomes more complex: the self-delusion of the protagonist is exposed through the clear and ironic gaze of an EF who occupies a privileged position of unrestricted knowledge.

The strained polyfocality of the ST is subject to several manipulations in the (re)translations. Firstly, TT2 Blanchamp demonstrates a reversal of the focalized Participants in the phrase 'although she was separated from him' (104); whereas both the CF and the external focalizer EF in the ST have fixed their attention on Léon as the primary focalized, this retranslation skews the original dynamics by reassigning the prominence of each participant. Although the reversal does not impact on the potential inherent in the narrative for dual focalizers, Léon no longer occupies the key position as the primary focalized subject, which in turn undermines Emma's fixation, but also dulls the contrast between the real and the imaginary Léon. Consequently, it is the distance between the CF and the EF, between what is real and what is illusory, that is distorted, and with it the scope for irony is diminished. Similarly, TT4 Hopkins merges the two participants in its snapshot, 'Though **they** were separated' (147); here, the shift does not allow the CF to bring the conditions of their separation into as sharp a focus:

the fusion of Emma and Léon obscures the former as the immobile pivot of focalization and the latter as the focalized entity which has been removed from her. Also, the merger is perhaps more suggestive of an EF who has a panoramic overview of the represented narrative world; by encompassing both participants in one single observation, the orientation of the original CF is lost and the latent polyfocality of the ST disrupted.

Several minor alterations appear in TT1 Marx-Aveling and TT6 Wall where there is a reliance on cataphoric reference; the phrases 'Though separated from her, he had not left her' (TT1 Marx-Aveling 135) and 'though far away from her, he had not left her' (TT6 Wall 98) omit the initial focalized participant, and in so doing, underplay his predominance in the clause. As was the case earlier, the obsession of the CF is clouded and the discontinuity between the various representations of Léon is downplayed. TT5 Russell preserves the threefold emphasis on the protagonist in 'He was far away, and yet he had not left her, he was here still' (136). The concessive now qualifies the second clause, and although it does not disrupt the ontological move from the real Léon to the illusory one, it does misleadingly suggest that Emma is more accepting of that reality. It falls to TT7 Mauldon and TT8 Thorpe to restore the focalization of the ST in their observations that 'although he was separated from her, he had not left her, he was there' (TT7 Mauldon 110; TT8 Thorpe 117). The two most recent versions thus appear to corroborate the thinking that the passage of time engenders improvement, but it is also important to bear in mind that this improvement is more marked in reference to midpoint retranslations than it is in reference to Marx-Aveling's initial attempt.

In addition, ST focalization extends into the past; Emma and Léon are reunited as focalized participants in the recollection:

> Quels bons soleils ils avaient eus! (MB 126).
> [*What good days they had had!*]

However, only three retranslations look back with the same focalization: TT5 Russell evokes 'The fine sunny days they had had' (136), TT6 Wall opts for 'What sunny days they had had' (99), a togetherness which is also echoed in the TT8 Thorpe construction 'What lovely sunny days they had had' (117). In TT3 May and TT7 Mauldon, the pair remains focalized, albeit with lesser precision given their transitive shift from the subject position: 'what beautiful sunny days had been theirs' (TT3 May 149) and 'How brightly the sun had shone on them' (TT7 Mauldon 110). But it is in TT1 Marx-Aveling, TT2 Blanchamp and TT4 Hopkins that the greatest re-focalization occurs given the removal of the original subjects: in the observations 'How bright the sun had been' (TT1 Marx-Aveling 135; TT2 Blanchamp 104) and 'How brightly the sun had shone' (TT4 Hopkins 147), the escapist illusion of the CF and the mocking gaze of the EF lose their anchoring point, namely the ironic togetherness of Emma and the object of her fantasy. The elimination of the human focalized participants weakens the link to the subjective, internal focalization of the protagonist, pointing instead to a descriptive slant more redolent of a Balzacian narrator. Thus, effacing the identity of the focalized upsets the subtle balance that is fundamental to the functioning of FIS. If the behaviour of the (re)translations in this particular instance were to be represented through a line of best fit, then it may be possible to argue for an increased duality of focalization over time. However, there are still notable anomalies in TT4 Hopkins and TT7 Mauldon which frustrate this upward progression.

Circumstantial elements

Focalization extends beyond participants to encompass perceptions of what SFG terms circumstantial elements, namely prepositional phrases or adverbial groups which 'refer to examples such as the location of an event in time or space, its manner, or its cause' (Halliday and Matthiessen 2004: 260). Circumstantial elements in passages of FIS thus simultaneously construe (a) the narrative world as observed by the CF, and (b) the narrative world as created by the EF. Where the picture becomes complicated is with the issue of deictic markers in FIS: whereas in indirect discourse, spatio-temporal markers tend to be transposed and reported from the perspective of the EF, there are no hard and fast rules in either the SL or the TL for retaining or reorienting the original character focalization in instances of FIS. Accordingly, the circumstantial elements found in the ST may be attributed to the focalization of either or both the EF and the CF; once again, the source is uncertain and the narrative boasts a greater sense of ambiguity.

The perception of location within the narrative world can be examined in relation to the SFG category of 'the location of the unfolding of the process in space-time' (Halliday and Matthiessen 2004: 265). The seemingly straightforward focalization of space in the statement that 'il était **là**' [*He was **there***] (MB 127) nevertheless raises the issue of undecidability: in this instance of FIS, it is impossible to determine whether this distal deictic marker has been transposed or not from a proximal one. In the vast majority of the (re)translations, this ambiguity remains intact with the unspecified location 'there'; as is the case in the ST, this marker can be traced back in both directions, and may or may not have been transposed. However, a shift occurs in TT5 Russell, where the distal marker of the ST is rendered in proximal terms: 'he was here' (136). In other words, the degree of remoteness is refocused to become a degree of nearness, a transposition which suggests the restoration of direct discourse and which then points to the CF as its original source. Consequently, the polyfocality of the situation is downplayed since the intradiegetic focalization dominates; the immediacy of the deixis suggests that the EF has relegated his own gaze to that of the protagonist, that is double focalization (EF1+CF2), thereby limiting the ambiguity of the narrative, whilst foregrounding the subjective perspective of the CV.

Similarly, a further marker of location appears in the observation that 'Ils s'**y** étaient promenés' [They had walked **there**] (MB 126), where the SL pronoun implies an indistinct position relative to the focalizer(s), which may also have been proximal (ici/here) or distal (là/there) in origin. As far as the majority of the (re)translations are concerned, five – TT1 Marx-Aveling, TT3 May, TT6 Wall, TT7 Mauldon and TT8 Thorpe – opt for the more remote pointer, 'there'; TT2 Blanchamp renders the location more explicit in the statement that 'they had strolled beside the river' (101); TT4 Hopkins and TT5 Russell both employ anaphoric reference which situates Emma and Léon 'beside it' (TT4 Hopkins 147; TT5 Russell 136). The lack of precision and subsequent ambiguity which characterizes the ST focalization is preserved in those versions which construe location through the distal deictic marker; it remains uncertain as to where the original focalized location was, that is near or far, since the pronoun may have been transposed or retained, and thus, the source of the focalization is also undecided. However, the retranslations which define the spatial parameters more overtly risk overemphasizing the EF whose panoramic overview lends itself to a more involved descriptive act, while attenuating the spontaneity and incertitude of the focalized point of the CF.

Addition

As was the case with voice, the addition of any element into the clause risks undermining the subtle balance of Flaubert's ironic narrative. In the source text, the following example draws the attention of the reader to Emma's frustration and regret at not having taken Léon for a lover:

> Comment n'avait-elle pas saisi ce bonheur-là, quand il se présentait! (MB 126)
> [How had she not seized that same happiness, when it was presenting itself!]

However, the clause has been manipulated in TT2 Blanchamp, TT4 Hopkins and TT5 Russell with the introduction of a supplementary focalized location, to now ask why she had not seized such happiness 'when it might have been within her grasp' (TT2 Blanchamp 104); 'while she had had it within her reach' (TT4 Hopkins 147); or 'when it lay within her reach' (TT7 Mauldon 110). Here, the addition of focalized locations underpins the narrative with a stabilizing effect that runs counter to the original, in that they modify the transience of the situation by implying a greater degree of contact (although the modality of TT2 Blanchamp does go some way to reducing its certitude). It is this contact which then solidifies the memory, turning a perception into a conviction; in turn, the delusion of the CF is downplayed, and the irony as exposed by the EF, that is that happiness will forever elude Emma, is attenuated. Once again, it becomes impossible to align this attenuating behaviour with the bias of improvement over time, while this example further brings to light how retranslations, rather than distance themselves from their predecessors, can in fact mirror existing strategies.

The tendency of the median retranslations, TT4 Hopkins and TT5 Russell, to insert additional elements is also evident in their treatment of the observation that 'il était là' (MB 127), which is expanded to become 'He was there still' (TT4 Hopkins 147) and 'he was here still' (TT5 Russell 136). The addition of the adverb *still* in both instances effectively distorts the perceptions of time as encoded in the ST. This temporal reframing detracts from the immediacy of the perception of the CF, undermining Emma's confused, reactive state of mind through its contrastive, and therefore, logical presence. This disparity between the now and then implies the sweeping, panchronic focalization of an EF, whose single gaze frames all time relative to the protagonist.

Likewise, the reminiscence 'Quels bons soleils ils avaient eus' [*What good times they had had*] (MB 126) is qualified in TT2 Blanchamp by the inclusion of the temporal adverb 'then' (104). Where the ST achieves retrospective perception through the use of tense alone, the CF of TT2 Blanchamp is constrained in her escapist focalization; her incursion into the past is now tempered by an implicit and bitter contrast with the current abandoned state of her present. As with the above, additional circumstantial elements have the capacity to fracture the characteristic focal ambiguity of the ST.

Summary

In the same way as the study of vocalization brings to light irregularities in the behaviour of (re)translation, so too does the study of focalization expose significant deviations from Berman's teleological vector. Again, this is merely a snapshot of the (re)translations, but it does expose significant peaks and troughs in how the specificities of the source text are reconstructed in the respective target language narratives. In this instance, the initial translation proves to be much less blind to the ambiguous use of focalization in the ST than its immediate successor, TT2 Blanchamp, and the two intermediate versions, TT4 Hopkins and TT5 Russell. For these three retranslations stand out as particularly susceptible to modifying the panorama of the original narrative world by recasting or adding circumstantial elements which then emphasize the presence of an external focalizer – to the detriment of that of the Character Focalizer and thus to the fundamental inconclusiveness of Flaubert's narrative texture. Indeed, there is certainly evidence of parallel translation strategies across these three versions which also detracts from the argument that retranslation is differentiation. Furthermore, the behaviour of the three most recent retranslations appears to be characterized by inconsistency, a trait which in turn frustrates any forward, progressive movement. Both TT6 Wall and TT8 Thorpe focus with less precision on certain facets of the generalization, thereby obscuring in part the vapid truisms which frame the perspective of the CF, but both also preserve the ironic dynamics of separation and togetherness, which characterize Emma's reverie. Similarly, TT7 Mauldon goes some way to maintaining the double-edged ambiguity inherent in the use of universal pronouns, before discontinuing the uncertain focalization in its treatment of the cleft construction. Consequently, no single (re)translation re-construes a comparably complex and equifocal window on to Flaubert's narrative world, and no single (re)translation then creates an analogous space for impersonality and irony.

Organizing the narrative world: Temporality

In addition to passages of FIS, the particularities of Flaubert's writing also extend to the way in which the internal narrative world has been organized, that is to the narrative feature of temporality, which understands sequencing as 'an organizing principle in interpreting experience' (Baker 2006: 51). But any comparative analysis of sequencing must first recognize that Flaubert's work has been 'carefully structured by a systematic *perversion* of plot as a central system of narrative organization and meaning' (Brooks 1992: 171, my emphasis). For *Madame Bovary* is a 'book about nothing', and the key passage itself creates meaning through the suspension of narrative events which, in turn, underscore the stifling inertia of Emma's existence. However, the static nature of the plot is offset by the author's mania for unifying (non-)content with form. Only this flawless coalescence will allow prose to 'stand erect from one end to the other [...] forming a long, solid line' (Flaubert 1927a: 264, my translation). The various and idiosyncratic ways in which Flaubert has created this unifying line throughout the key passage will form the basis of the comparative analysis in the following section.

Relationships between clauses will first be investigated in order to determine how taxis and logico-semantics shape intradiegetic organization. This approach must be framed within the context of what Proust has termed Flaubert's 'grammatical singularities' (1971: 592, my translation), as a result of which the SL and the narrative world are marked by an anomalous use, or rejection of, conjunction. The issue of cohesion, that is how a text 'hangs together' (Halliday and Matthiessen 2004: 87) will then be addressed, bearing in mind Culler classification of Flaubert's writing as 'elegant prose straining to hold itself together' (1974: 60).

Taxis and logico-semantics

The investigative thrust of this section will hinge on how the narrative world is organized in the original tale and then reorganized in the (re)translations. From a systemic functional perspective, clause complexes 'serve to construe [...] local sequences in the flow of events that together make up [an] episode' (Halliday and Matthiessen 2004: 364), and these temporal or causal sequences are realized through the grammatical resources of taxis and logico-semantics: the first category is concerned with how independent and dependent clauses are presented, and the second with how clause nexuses are tied together on a logical and semantic level.

The first point to examine is the logico-semantic role of the conjunction *et*, the most renowned analysis of which appears in Proust:

> In Flaubert, the conjunction 'et' ['and'] serves no purpose assigned to it by grammar. It marks a pause in rhythmical measure and divides a tableau. Indeed, where anyone else would place an 'et', Flaubert removes it. [...] Conversely, where no one else would think of using it, Flaubert does. It is like a sign that another part of the tableau is beginning, that the ebbing wave is about to reform once again. [...] In short, with Flaubert, 'et' always begins a secondary phrase and almost never concludes a list. (1971: 591, my translation)

Furthermore, Le Hir notes that the conjunction 'also serves to launch a new movement' and classifies it as an *et* 'of contrast' (1965: 251, my translation).

Thus, the role of *et* in the ST is not one of addition; on the contrary, the additive conjunction dissects and contrasts narrative sequences, and introduces subordinate phrases, all the while contributing to the poeticism of the prose. A stipulation for closeness in (re)translation must then be the retention of this distinctive linking – or more precisely rupturing – device.

The first example to explore is the use of *et* in what Flaubert termed his 'prolonged comparison' (1927a: 398) between Emma's memory of Léon and a dying fire on a Russian steppe:

> Elle se précipitait vers lui, elle se blottissait contre, elle remuait délicatement ce foyer près de s'éteindre, elle allait cherchant tout autour d'elle ce qui pouvait l'aviver davantage; **et** les réminiscences les plus lointaines comme les plus immédiates occasions, ce qu'elle éprouvait avec ce qu'elle imaginait, ses envies de volupté qui se dispersaient, ses projets de bonheur qui craquaient au vent comme des branchages morts, sa vertu stérile, ses espérances tombées, la litière domestique, elle ramassait tout, prenait tout, et faisait servir tout à réchauffer sa tristesse. (MB 127)
>
> *[She was hastening towards it, she was huddling herself against, she was stirring delicately that hearth on the verge of burning itself out, she was going searching all around her for anything that might kindle it more;* ***and*** *the reminiscences the furthest away just like the most immediate occasions, what she experienced with what she imagined, her desires for sensual pleasure that were drifting away, her plans for happiness that were breaking off in the wind like dead branches, her sterile virtue, her fallen hopes, the domestic bedding, she was gathering it all, taking it all, and using it all to warm her sadness]*

Two distinct issues arise here with regard to taxis and logico-semantics, respectively: the absence of coordination between the first four independent clauses, and the segmenting use of *et*, a division rendered all the more acute given its position after a semicolon and which demarcates a move from a fourfold paratactic organization of Emma's actions towards a tableau which comprises seven subordinated categories of the protagonist's metaphoric fuel. In terms of rhythm, the unimpeded movement from one independent clause to the next represents Emma's frenetic, disordered search for happiness, while the conjunction introduces a comparatively more laboured and oppressive complex of subordinated clauses (the wave is reforming) before arriving at the main clause itself, 'elle ramassait tout' [*she was gathering it all*] (MB 127), creating a new tableau. As Schor puts it, this 'awkward piling up of syntagms adequates Emma's vain efforts to defer the death of desire' (1980: 31), thereby demonstrating how conjunction and syntax serve a larger sequential and thematic purpose.

But to what extent are these relations preserved in the (re)translations? To begin with the uncoordinated clauses in the first half of the example, only TT3 May and TT8 Thorpe uphold the exact dynamics of the ST construction; each nexus is characterized by parataxis, each individual clause retains its independent status. All other (re)translations avoid the fourfold repetition of the subject at the head of each clause. In TT1 Marx-Aveling, the final clause reads 'sought all around her anything that could revive it' (136), thereby rendering it dependent on the preceding clauses in order to provide the missing subject. Likewise, TT6 Wall retains three independent clauses, but modifies the third in the series into the embedded, and fundamentally hypotactic, minor clause, 'delicately rousing the greying embers' (99). The remaining retranslations, TT2 Blanchamp, TT4 Hopkins, TT5 Russell and TT7 Mauldon, all rely on zeugma, whereby the subject of the initial clause governs the whole complex, and a relationship of inequality is instigated. The hypotaxis of TT7 Mauldon is most substantial given the presence of two minor clauses, 'delicately stirring [. . .] and searching' (TT7 Mauldon 111), which are subordinate to the preceding verbal group as well. TT2 Blanchamp, TT5 Russell and TT7 Mauldon further manipulate the uncoordinated relations of the ST by inserting the conjunction and: '**and** sought' (TT2 Blanchamp 105); '**and** cast about' (TT5 Russell 137); '**and** searching' (TT7 Mauldon 111). Consequently, the distressed disjunction which prevails in the ST between the actions of the protagonist is, to varying degrees, reframed in a more hypotactic manner, that is a more logically dependent manner, in many of the TL versions. The grammatical logic which overarches these complexes then dissembles the irrational impetuosity of the protagonist, as well as this particularity of Flaubert's style. In this instance, the initial translation does loosen the cement which holds together form and content in the original, and this union is restored in the most recent retranslation. But, as has previously been the case, these start and end points mask the variable bearings of the interim retranslations; the reunification of form and content in TT3 May is short-lived and is followed by a move away from the specificities of the source text in the four subsequent versions. Likewise, the insertion of an additional 'and' in numerous versions once again points to a relationship between retranslations that can be characterized by coincidence, not difference.

The second section of this complex is introduced by the 'et' construction, which rhythmically gives way to a detailed tableau of the fuel which Emma collects in order to sustain the fire; in this particular tableau, each component, or group of components, is isolated between commas and serves as a direct object of the governing, yet suspended, main verb. Furthermore, the coordination within the tableau itself is conspicuous by its very absence. The semicolon plus additive conjunction is preserved in TT1 Marx-Aveling, TT5 Russell, TT7 Mauldon and TT8 Thorpe, thereby introducing a measure of deferral into the narrative before embarking on what Huss terms 'descriptive amplification' (1977: 142). However, the rhythmic pause is lessened in TT3 May, where the conjunction remains but is preceded by a comma: here, the narrative continues unhindered by a punctuation mark which dissolves the clear ST division between tableaux. TT4 Hopkins and TT6 Wall interrupt the flow of the narrative by inserting a dash in the first case and preserving the semicolon in the second; however, neither version incorporates the additive conjunction, with its suppression masking one of Flaubert's idiosyncrasies of style. But it is in TT2 Blanchamp that the greatest obstacle to Flaubert's style occurs: in this retranslation, the coordination and the syntax of the ST are reworked as 'She made use of everything, of the most remote memories' (TT2 Blanchamp 105). The sentence boundaries have been manipulated: the semicolon and conjunction are omitted, to be replaced by a new sentence wherein the suspension of the matrix clause is undone. In other words, the pace of the narrative is reworked; the build-up to the primary action is reversed, while the momentary pause between the two tableaux becomes more permanent. As a consequence, the disjunction evinced in the ST is tempered by the insistence on the conventional SVO patterning of the TL. In contrast to the example just mentioned, the initial translation is now on an equal footing with the two most recent retranslations, thereby creating another erratic pattern with sporadic peaks and troughs which cannot be contained by Berman's straight-line thinking.

The next issue to examine is the lack of conjunction in the ST list of fuels for the metaphorical fire; indeed, such absence lends weight to Proust's observation that Flaubert reverses expectations with regard to the usage of *et*. Here, it is TT2 Blanchamp once again which stands out as susceptible to concealing Flaubertian singularities. The uncoordinated enumeration of the ST becomes coordinated as the list progresses: 'She made use of everything, [...] of her desire for voluptuous pleasures which was increasing, **and** of her plans of happiness, [...] of her disappointed hopes **and** of the conjugal bed' (TT2 Blanchamp 105, my emphasis). When considered alongside the restructuring of the discourse flow, it is possible to surmise that these strategies were motivated by a desire to render the narrative easier to follow, but in so doing, the grammatical deviations of the ST are forced into an undisruptive, uniform target language sequence which moves forward at a faster pace than the original and subsequently belies Emma's overwrought and discordant movements.

Although TT2 Blanchamp is the only (re)translation which modifies the logico-semantics of the ST in this example, it is also of note that a prominent punctuation trait arises in the majority of the other versions: five of the (re) translations all replace the comma before the matrix clause with a dash: '– she gathered' (TT1 Marx-Aveling 136; TT3 May 149); '– all these she gathered' (TT4 Hopkins 148); '– anything and everything she gathered' (TT5 Russell 137); '– all this she gathered' (TT Mauldon 111). Despite retaining an analogous position to that of the ST, the list of fuel is now presented in a less disruptive manner given the overt typographical signal of digression; the single dash before the matrix clause alerts the reader to a pause which is greater than the one imposed by the comma of the ST. As such, the paratactic relationship between the main subject and predicate of the complex and its apposed objects is rendered in a more emphatic manner. In turn, the detachment is clearly highlighted, while the punctuation of the ST is harnessed into a less demanding configuration. Only TT6 Wall and TT8 Thorpe preserve the sweep of apposed objects linked by commas alone, and therefore do not seek to contain what Culler deems to be the 'awkwardness and clumsiness of Flaubert's sentences' (1974: 204). In all other versions, this 'deliberate distancing device' (1974: 204) is abandoned and the irony of futility is deferred. Thus, on a superficial level there is some evidence of a correlation with the Retranslation Hypothesis in the sense the shortcomings of an earlier version (TT2 Blanchamp) are rectified by later retranslations (TT6 Wall and TT8 Thorpe). On a more detailed level, though, the vista is more complex and thus exceeds the explanatory force of this assumption, while a certain critical mass of retranslations emerge, which all share the same coordinating strategy.

To return to Le Hir's concept, the *et* 'of contrast' (1965: 251), its juxtaposing role comes to light in the following clause complex:

> Pourquoi ne l'avoir pas retenu à deux mains, à deux genoux, quand il voulait s'enfuir? **Et** elle se maudit de n'avoir pas aimé Léon (MB 127)
>
> [*Why not have held on to it/him with both hands, on both knees, when it/he wanted to run away?* ***And*** *she cursed herself for not having loved Léon*]

Here, the additive conjunction serves as a marker of a certain narrative shift from the ambiguity of FIS to discourse reported by an omniscient, external narrator. But only half the TL versions retain the conjunction: '**And** she cursed herself for not having loved Léon' (TT1 Marx-Aveling 136; TT6 Wall 99; TT7 Mauldon 110; TT8 Thorpe 117). The remaining retranslations omit this significant juncture in the narrative, an omission which can perhaps be attributed to the erroneous, but 'persistent belief that it is improper to begin a sentence with *And*' (Burchfield

2004: 52, original emphasis). Regardless of motivation, the fact remains that the majority of the TL versions diverge from the original logico-semantic pattern. The paratactic relation between the two clauses of the ST is coordinated by what is known in SFG as an enhancing conjunction, that is one which expands on the former clause (cause) by introducing consequences (effect) in the latter. But where such coordination is absent in translation, the link between the two independent clauses is diluted, with the result that neither the relationship between Emma's mental workings and actions nor the shift in narrative voice is emphasized. The pattern of (re)translation behaviour here reveals that the three later retranslations actually evince the same paratactic strategies as the initial translation, leaving all other interim retranslations to obscure the specificities of the source text in this case.

The conjunction *mais* [*but*] appears in the following example where it is preceded by a semicolon and, like *et*, it marks a new, contrastive tableau which is characterized by a complex series of hypotactic and paratactic clauses:

> ; **mais**, comme l'ouragan soufflait toujours, et que la passion se consuma jusqu'aux cendres, et qu'aucun secours ne vint, qu'aucun soleil ne parut, il fut de tous côtés nuit complète, et elle demeura perdue dans un froid horrible qui la traversait. (MB 127–8)
>
> [*; **but**, as the storm was still blowing, and since the passion consumed itself to cinders, and since no help came, since no sun appeared, it was on all sides total night, and she remained lost in a horrible cold that cut through her*]

More specifically, the clause complex can be deconstructed as follows: the initial contrastive conjunction is a detached fragment of the first independent clause, that is 'mais […] il fut de tous côtés nuit complète' [*but […] it was on all sides total night*], which is then extended by the subsequent paratactic clause that provides additional information, that is 'et elle demeura perdue' [*and she remained lost*]. However, these independent clauses are preceded by a series of four subordinated, or hypotactic clauses, which both enhance the main clause (they qualify it by reference to cause) and, in two of the cases, explicitly extend each other (they coordinate certain causes).

The fragmentary texture of this passage attests to the obstacles in the life of the protagonist. As Huss notes, 'the meaning of the narrative is […] in its very reluctance to move forward' (1977: 144); or, the flow of the narrative is hindered by the elaborate convolutions of the logico-semantic markers employed by Flaubert, just as Emma's path to happiness is obstructed. The frustrated development of the clause complex, and of Emma's existence, therefore places grammar in a pertinent position with regard to the portrayal of narrative meaning(s). And yet this particular passage comes under considerable revision in the (re)translations; firstly, in terms of the segmenting use of the semicolon, and secondly, in terms of how the clauses relate to each other.

The dividing role of the semicolon functions on a rhythmic and a semantic level in this instance: the pause it commands in the progression of the narrative serves as a cadenced dislocation between a portrayal of Emma's desperate attempts to secure happiness and her subsequent failure, a failure which is further reinforced by the contrastive conjunction *mais* at the head of the ensuing clause complex. The majority of the (re)translations preserve the series as 'but' (TT1 Marx-Aveling 136; TT3 May 150; TT6 Wall 99; TT7 Mauldon 111; TT8 Thorpe 118), and therefore maintain the accentuated segmentation of the ST. However, the move towards futility becomes less fluid in TT2 Blanchamp, TT4 Hopkins and TT5 Russell where the semicolon is replaced with a full stop. The initiating clause complex is now cut off from the secondary complex, with the hesitant pause of the ST being reformed as definite break in the narrative; consequently, the link between the actions of the protagonist and their (non-)effect is lessened as the relation between the two complexes becomes more disconnected. Once more, the initial translation and the three later retranslations are on par in terms of closeness, this time joined by TT3 May, which demonstrates a good degree of consistency across the TL versions, except for a few isolated dips.

The logico-semantic chain of the secondary clause complex in the earlier example is also affected by disconnection, or at the very least by diversion, through translation. The clause complex is distinguished by a plethora of causative conjunctions ('comme' [*as*], 'que' [*since*]), which finally culminate in isolation and inertia; as such, progression is realized through grammar alone, namely through the climactic and frenzied succession of logico-semantic markers, which then give way to a dramatic chute towards emptiness. However, the singular ST progression is revised in many of the (re)translations, particularly in TT4 Hopkins where the complex is remoulded as: 'But still the tempest raged, and passion died down to a powdery ash. Help came not, nor did the sun shine. All around was deepest night. She lived on like a lost soul racked by an icy cold' (148). In short, all the logico-semantic markers of cause have been omitted, while the involved hypotactic gradation of the ST dissolves into a simplified and relatively uncoordinated succession of paratactic clauses. To reprise Culler's phrase, the narrative is no longer 'straining to hold itself together' (1974: 60); rather, the TL sequence hastens forwards, unhindered by an awkward patterning of subordinated conjunctions. Consequently, this TL version removes the grammatical obstacles to fluency, and by extension to Emma's advancement, thereby camouflaging the sudden fall and the subsequent stasis of the ST.

However, the earlier mentioned version by Gerard Hopkins was reissued in a revised form by OUP in 1981 where several differences emerge: 'But **as** the tempest raged on, and passion **burnt itself to ashes, no help came**, nor did the sun shine; ***all*** around was deepest night. She lived on like a lost soul racked by an icy cold' (1981: 111). In addition to the verbal modifications, the main revisions hinge around logico-semantics and taxis: the introduction of the causal conjunction *as* allows the first two clauses to relate hypotactically to the initial independent clause, while the shift from full stop to semicolon increases the degree of interrelatedness between segments. Nevertheless, it is still parataxis which dominates the construction of the complex, with the result that the frustrated movement of the ST remains flattened out in the TL version.

Likewise, TT1 Marx-Aveling, TT6 Wall and TT7 Mauldon all evince this inclination towards unobstruction, particularly through the rejection of the hypotactic 'et que' [*and since*] and 'que' [*since*] conjunctions in the third and fourth clauses. In all these versions, the dependent, causative clauses of the ST become independent resultant clauses in the TL: 'no help came, no sun rose' (TT1 Marx-Aveling 136); 'no help came, no sun appeared' (TT6 Wall 99); 'no help came and no sun rose' (TT7 Mauldon 111). As far as TT2 Blanchamp and TT5 Russell are concerned, it is the use of zeugma which serves to intimate the hypotactic progression of the ST; in other words, the initial causative conjunction governs the series of dependent clauses in 'as the storm was still raging, and passion was consuming itself […], and no help came and no gleam of sunlight appeared' (TT2 Blanchamp 105), and 'since the storm still blew, and passion burned to ashes, and no help came nor sun shone out' (TT5 Russell 137). However, the reliance on a single conjunction along with the repetition of the additive conjunction facilitates the flow of discourse, once again obscuring the faltering movement of the ST. It is TT3 May and TT8 Thorpe which incorporate the greatest frequency of causative markers: 'since the storm ceased not […], since no succour came' (TT3 May 150); 'as the storm was still blowing, […] and since no help came' (TT8 Thorpe 118). However, neither retranslation preserves the taut and intricate dynamics of the ST sequence, meaning that there is scant evidence here for improvement over time.

Cohesion

Halliday and Matthiessen note that 'it is important to be able to think of text dynamically, as an ongoing process of meaning' (2004: 254) and it is the lexicogrammatic and semantic resource of cohesion which allows patterns of meanings to be created across the text as it evolves. Cohesion comprises four elements: '(i) conjunction, (ii) reference, (iii) ellipsis and (iv) lexical organization' (2004: 533). The primary focus of this analysis will centre on the cohesive links created by reference and by lexis; the relations enabled by conjunction have already been addressed in the logico-semantic analysis mentioned earlier, while ellipsis tends to be a predominant feature of dialogue and, as such, is of less relevance to the present study. By examining referential and lexical cohesion, it will be possible to determine the extent to which the (re)translations reconstruct or destabilize one of the stylistic mainstays of this masterpiece which unifies form and content.

Reference

The first subcategory of reference to examine is that of demonstrative reference, which 'creates cohesion by creating links between elements' (Halliday and Matthiessen 2004: 534). Such referential cohesion appears between the nominal phrases in the following clause complex:

> Dès lors, **ce souvenir** de Léon fut comme le centre de son ennui; […] Elle se précipitait vers lui, elle se blottissait contre, elle remuait délicatement **ce foyer** près de s'éteindre (MB 127)
>
> [*Henceforth, that memory of Léon was as the centre of her ennui; […] She was hastening towards it, she was huddling herself against, she was stirring delicately that hearth on the verge of burning itself out*]

The demonstrative deictic markers are employed by the omniscient narrator who locates the particular referents in a relationship of endophoric and anaphoric nearness. In other words, the points of reference are found within the text, have antecedents within that same text and are in immediate proximity to the protagonist. The two examples above form part of Flaubert's extended fire metaphor, but serve different functions of textual cohesion: the first deictic marker initiates the comparison, creating a tie between the preceding cogitations of the protagonist and their figurative consequences; the second deictic marker follows on closely from the first and reinforces the metaphorical fusion of the tenor with its vehicle, that is *ce souvenir* [*that memory*] with *ce foyer* [*that hearth*], by mirroring its grammatical construction. Consequently, these demonstratives are charged with binding together the narrative, the former initiating and the latter continuing, whilst both pointing towards the immediacy of the situation.

And yet the first demonstrative is nowhere to be found in any of the (re)translations. The pointing action is neutralized in TT1 Marx-Aveling, in TT3 May, in the revised version of TT4 Hopkins and in TT8 Thorpe to become '**the** memory' (TT1 Marx-Aveling 136; TT3 May 149; TT4 Hopkins 110; TT8 Thorpe 117) or '**the** recollection' (TT2 Blanchamp 104). The fundamental difference is that '*the* merely announces that the identity is specific; it does not specify it' (Halliday and Matthiessen 2004: 558), so the link which is established between the specific, and preceding, reminiscences of the protagonist in the ST is diminished, along with the precision of its location as emphasized by the narrator. The majority of the retranslations, that is TT4 Hopkins (148), TT6 Wall (99) and TT7 Mauldon (110) reinstate a degree of specificity by portraying '**her** memory' or '**her** remembrance' (TT5 Russell 136); while the use of possessive reference establishes an endophoric link, it does so with anaphoric reference to the protagonist and is therefore unmarked since most narratives comprise a consistent chain of reference to key characters. Consequently, the markedness of the ST demonstrative is also diminished in these versions, and with it, the transition between the two stages of the text.

Similar strategies arise with regard to the translation of *ce foyer* [*that hearth*]; the demonstrative is replaced in four versions by the specific, but non-specifying determiner: 'the dying embers' (TT1 Marx-Aveling 136; TT4 Hopkins 148; TT7 Mauldon 111); 'the greying embers' (TT6 Wall 99). The possessive also comes to light in TT3 May with 'its dying embers' (TT3 May 149), whose antecedent is the fire. Closely linked to this is the strategy which appears in TT2 Blanchamp and TT5 Russell where the noun group is replaced by anaphoric pronominal reference, so that Emma 'fanned it' (TT2 Blanchamp 105) and 'stirred it' (TT5 Russell 137). Again, the demonstrative reference of the ST has been stripped of its markedness, and the immediacy of the protagonist's turmoil is arrested. While TT1 Marx-Aveling remains consistent in its pointing technique towards the two metaphoric components (employing *the* on both occasions), the lack of explicitness mutes the cohesive echo of the ST. Only TT8 Thorpe instigates the use of the demonstrative here, pointing towards 'this hearth' (118), but the cohesive link with the actual tenor of the metaphor is diminished since this has been signalled merely as 'the memory' (117). Consequently, the connectedness between form and content, between the use of the proximal demonstrative and the immediacy of Emma's distress, becomes disconnected in all of the TL interpretations.

In a further example of reference, the non-selective determiners of the following observation cohere to a larger sense of ironic detachment within the text, whereby the protagonist finds herself one step removed from reality as the tragic heroine of her own fiction:

> elle prit même **les** répugnances **du** mari pour **des** aspirations vers **l'**amant, **les** brûlures de la haine pour **des** réchauffements de la tendresse. (MB 127)
>
> [*she took even* ***the*** *repugnance to* ***the*** *husband for* ***some*** *aspirations towards* ***the*** *lover,* ***the*** *burns of hate for* ***some*** *warmings of tenderness*]

Firstly, the reference evinced in *le* mari [the *husband*] and *l'*amant [the *lover*] 'signal[s] that the identity is known, or knowable' (Halliday and Matthiessen 2004: 558), but without any great degree of explicitness. In other words, the identity of the referent may be recoverable from either the immediate endophoric context, identifying Charles and Léon in particular, or from a wider exophoric context, simply identify the broader categories of 'husband' and 'lover'. Given that 'Emma's reading impinges on the narrative texture of the novel' (Lloyd 1990: 82), it may well be the case that the neutral determiner acts cohesively as a reflection of the protagonist's inability to distinguish between the reality of her situation and the fictional tropes of romantic literature.

However, the detachment achieved in the ST by means of the non-selective determiners undergoes a process of re-attachment in all the (re)translations save TT5 Russell and TT8 Thorpe, where the designation of 'the husband' and 'the lover' (TT5 Russell 137) and the general categories of 'husband-hating' and 'lover-longing' (TT8 Thorpe 118) facilitate both an endo- and an exophoric identification of the referents, thereby preserving the influence of fiction on the protagonist and intertwining with an essential thematic thread that runs through the ST narrative. In all remaining versions, the referents are bound endophorically through the use of personal reference as 'her husband' and 'her lover' (TT1 Marx-Aveling 136; TT2 Blanchamp 105; TT3 May 150; TT4 Hopkins 148; TT6 Wall 99; TT7 Mauldon 111). In other words, the nouns are identified expressly with possessive determiners, and since these are 'used primarily in anaphoric reference' (Halliday and Matthiessen 2004: 554), their function can only be textual, forming part of the chain of reference items tied to Emma. In turn, the potential for situational reference, that is for cohesion with the tropes of romantic literature, is impeded. Therefore, the potential for an ironic reading is restricted across a substantial number of (re)translations, having been enabled at only two points. Although one of those points happens to be the most recent version, a restorative move had also been instigated in TT3 May, before disappearing over the subsequent four retranslations and simultaneously frustrating the path of progress.

The second issue which arises from this example is the referential juxtaposition between the definite determination of *les répugnances* [*the repugnance*] and the indefinite determination of *des aspirations* [*some aspirations*], and again between *les brûlures de la haine* [*the burns of hate*] and *des réchauffements de la tendresse* [*some warmings of tenderness*]. While all are non-selective in nature, that is there is no explicit establishment of identity, it is of note that the definite articles qualify the unequivocal emotions and the indefinite articles point to the protagonist's misconceptions. Reference thus serves as a grammatical border between the real and the imaginary, and continues to weave the disjunction inherent in the mind of Emma into the text.

As there is notable inconsistency between the ways in which each TL version deals with the two contrastive sets, the strategies evident in the treatment of the first pair will be examined before progressing to the second pair. To begin, TT1 Marx-Aveling, TT2 Blanchamp and TT3 May demonstrate a strategy whereby the definite article of the initial noun group is replaced by the less marked possessive pronoun, while, in line with normal TL practice, reference is simply omitted for the abstract noun: 'her repugnance' is contrasted with 'aspirations' (TT1 Marx-Aveling 136); 'her loathing' with 'yearning' (TT2 Blanchamp 105); and, 'her detestation' with 'longing' (TT3 May 150). Thus, the opposition persists between the definite and the dubious sentiments; nevertheless, the use of the possessive binds the emotion firmly to Emma, obscuring any cohesive ties to concepts gleaned from reading material, and therefore the sense of detachment is lost since the protagonist can no longer be contextualized as the tortured heroine of her own melodrama. A further juxtaposition is retained in TT4 Hopkins and TT6 Wall which opt for omission in conjunction with the use of indefinite reference: 'dislike' precedes 'a craving' (TT4 Hopkins 48), and 'disgust' is opposed to 'an aspiration' (TT6 Wall 99). But here, the lack of reference impacts negatively on the specificity of the concrete emotion, and renders the abstract sentiment in more precise terms, thereby reversing the contrastive strategies of the ST. Furthermore, the division is dissolved in TT5 Russell and TT7 Mauldon given the use of the same reference in 'an aversion' and 'an aspiration' (TT5 Russell 137) in the former, and the omission of any cohesive reference in 'aversion' and 'desire' (TT7 Mauldon 111) in the latter.

The contraction of the sentiments in TT8 Thorpe as 'husband-hating' and 'lover-longing' (118) may have preserved the endo- and exophoric scope of the nominal references, but the shift which reworks the emotions as gerunds also disallows the juxtaposition inherent in the original. Therefore, the discordant inner life of the protagonist remains unmarked through the system of reference; cracks appear in the cohesive cement of the ST as one of the straight lines of the narrative, that is Emma's inability to distinguish between the real and the imagined, is interrupted in all (re)translations.

Most (re)translations then perpetuate these cohesive cracks by discarding the referential differences in the second pair of contrastive emotions. Both noun groups are identified by the definite article in TT1 Marx-Aveling, TT3 May, TT5 Russell, TT6 Wall, TT7 Mauldon and TT8 Thorpe by conflating, for example, 'the searing touch of hatred' with 'the rekindling of love' (TT7 Mauldon 111), or 'the scorch of spite' with 'the rekindling of tender love' (TT8 Thorpe 118). In this case, the prevalence of the definite article may have been instigated by the more physical bent of the noun groups in comparison to the first pair, but the lack of referential discontinuity both dislodges the cohesive theme of Emma's lack of judgement and attributes the fictional component with a greater degree of determination. Of the remaining versions, TT2 Blanchamp inserts a contrast between 'her burning hatred' and 'the warmth of tenderness' (105), but this now ties the first noun group exclusively to the protagonist, implying a greater degree of awareness, whilst overstating the definitiveness of the second. Finally, though, TT4 Hopkins also changes tack to oppose 'the burning touch' and 'tenderness rekindled' (148); whereas the initial strategy saw omission and the use of the indefinite article, that is a reversal of the ST determination, here the distinction between the real and the imaginary is intimated given the exactitude of the first reference and the imprecision of the latter. Subsequently, it is the only retranslation to ensure the same degree of unity between form and content which underpins the original.

Lexical cohesion

One of the most overt signs of cohesion within a text is the pattern created by words through reiteration or collocation. In the key passage is evidence of one of Flaubert's particular stylistic predilections; as Le Hir remarks, 'the ternary construction is doubtless a constant feature of Flaubert's style' (1965: 253, my translation), and this comes to the fore in the next example where the clausal triptych is reinforced by the threefold lexical repetition of tout: 'elle ramassait **tout**, prenait **tout**, et faisait servir **tout** à réchauffer sa tristesse' [*she was* *gathering it* ***all****, taking it* ***all****, and using it* ***all*** *to warm her sadness*] (MB 127). In this instance, the lexical reiteration of the direct object functions cohesively by embedding a sense of Emma's turmoil into the text. Nevertheless, the exact dynamics of this repetition are absent in nearly all of the TL versions. It is TT8 Thorpe alone which retains all three instantiations: 'she gathered **all**, seized **all** and let it **all** serve to rekindle her sadness' (118). There is also a fair degree of repetition in TT1 Marx-Aveling which mirrors the ternary construction of the ST, but insists less on the lexical presence of *tout* [*all*] given the use of synonymy: 'she gathered it **all** up, took **everything**, and made it **all** serve as fuel' (TT1 Marx-Aveling 136). Certainly, the repeated emphasis on Emma's mania persists, although the cohesive parallelism of the ST is unravelled to a certain degree by the use of an alternative lexical item. Henceforth, the rate of repetition decreases in the retranslations: two adverbial instantiations appear in TT7 Mauldon, that is '**all** this she gathered up, **all** this she took, and used to feed her unhappiness' (TT7 Mauldon 111), while two synonyms are employed in TT5 Russell, that is '**anything** and **everything** she gathered up and used to feed her grief' (TT5 Russell 137). Only one reference comes to light in TT2 Blanchamp, TT3 May and TT4 Hopkins: 'She concentrated it **all**, and made it help' (TT2 Blanchamp 105); 'she gathered them **all** together and made of them the wherewithal' (TT3 May 149); '**all** these she gathered, taking what came to her hand' (TT4 Hopkins 148). At this point, the cohesion of the ST has all but collapsed since only the very first link of the lexical chain remains, but it is in TT6 Wall that the chain dematerializes completely: 'these she collected up and used' (TT6 Wall 99). Thus, the lexical strand which binds together the ongoing narrative and the theme of Emma's desperation has been torn from this TL version, misshaping one of the author's predominant stylistic features. It also follows that there is a notable move away from the specificities of the original at a moment which both comes later than the more restorative attempts of the initial translation and immediately before the fully corrective interpretation of the most recent retranslation. This serves as yet another example which distorts the undeviating path of the Retranslation Hypothesis.

Perhaps the most striking use of lexical cohesion in the key passage is the one used to underpin Flaubert's famous extended fire metaphor which Bopp describes as 'a tour de force, […] the longest metaphor in French literature, a prolonged, coherent metaphor' (1951: 199, my translation). Moreover, Flaubert himself claims that 'My comparison […] is a thread, I use it to make a transition' (1927a: 233, my translation). As such, lexical cohesion plays a decisive role both in the internal coherence of the metaphor itself, and in the progression of the narrative from one moment in the protagonist's life to another, namely from Emma's inner turmoil following the departure of Léon to her return to daily monotony and ennui. In the ST, the fire metaphor is instigated by the verbal phrase 'il y pétillait' [*it was crackling there*] and concludes with its extinction when 'la passion se consuma jusqu'aux cendres' [*the passion consumed itself to cinders*]. Between these two points is a succession of verbal or nominal phrases, all of which are tied together in a chain of lexical collocation and reiteration; dispersed throughout the text are lexical items which frequently co-occur with regard to fire, and stand in a synonymic or antonymic relation to each other. These items are 'ce foyer près de s'éteindre' [*that hearth on the verge of burning itself out*], 'aviver' [*kindle*], 'réchauffer' [*warm*], 'les flammes s'apaisèrent' [*the flames subsided*], 'la provision [...] s'épuisât' [*the supplies were exhausted*], 'l'entassement' [*the piling up*], 's'étouffa' [*was stifled*], 's'effaça' [*faded*], 'brûlures' [*burns*] and 'réchauffements' [*warmings*] (MB 127).

On the whole, the (re)translations take up and maintain the reiterative cohesion of the ST, thereby reinforcing the exposition of what Schor terms 'Emma's pathetic struggle to keep a memory alive' (1980: 31) and facilitating the narrative flow towards her subsequent failure and chagrin. However, the very initiating verb of the extended comparison, *pétiller* [*to crackle/sparkle*], is problematic given both the aural and visual breadth of its meaning: the SL concept encapsulates both the dry and repeated crackling sound and the brightness of the fire, a semantic range which is mirrored in the TL verbal phrase to sparkle. Indeed, this is incorporated into TT3 May where the fire 'glowed and sparkled' (149), and again into TT4 Hopkins with 'sparkled' (148). Nevertheless, TT2 Blanchamp retains only the visual implications with 'shone' (105), as is also the case in TT7 Mauldon with 'glittered' (110). Conversely, TT5 Russell (136), TT6 Wall (99) and TT8 Thorpe (117) all opt for the onomatopoeia of 'crackled', while TT1 Marx-Aveling flattens the action with the non-sensory verb, 'burnt' (136). Evidently, all TL lexical choices collocate with the superordinate category of fire, but in all versions save TT3 May and TT4 Hopkins, the collocation is restricted to one angle – either sound, or vision, or general word – as opposed to the dual approach of the SL item. Consequently, limitation of the scope of the verbal phrase also equates to limitation of the bridging and internal cohesion of the metaphor: the move from the psychological to the allegorical is effected on the single basis of what Emma sees or what Emma hears, while the ensuing lexical chain is bound only to the initiating verbal phrase by one sensory link. The behaviour of the (re) translations can then be conveyed as reaching a pinnacle in TT3 May and TT4 Hopkins, as opposed to in the later versions.

Finally, the issue of collocation comes to the fore in certain retranslations. Given that cohesion is reinforced through collocation, that is the tendency of words to co-occur, any weakening of this tendency will necessarily undermine its cohesive effect. A case in point is the following clause complex where there is a strong collocation, not only between the nominal and verbal phrases in 'cette lueur d'incendie [...] s'effaça par degrés' [*that glimmer of fire faded gradually*] (MB 127), but also between the verbal phrase and the metaphorical tenor, namely the memory of Léon. This two-way collocation is preserved in TT1 Marx-Aveling, TT6 Wall and TT7 Mauldon, which employ the verb *to fade* – lights fade, as do memories – and to a lesser extent in TT2 Blanchamp and TT4 Hopkins where the action is one of dying. However, TT3 May opts for the co-occurrence of 'glare' and 'disappeared' (150), TT5 Russell for 'glow' and 'obliterated' (137) and TT8 Thorpe for 'fiery glimmer' and 'blotted out' (118). None of these pairs occur together with any notable frequency in the TL, nor do they collocate specifically with memory. The result is a weakening of the cohesive chain within the extended comparison and beyond, from which a pattern of variance in retranslation behaviour emerges.

Summary

Of all the analytical sections thus far, the organization of the narrative world appears to be the most resistant to relationships of closeness between a given TT and the ST, with the subcategories of taxis (non-coordination; causative conjunctions), and cohesion (demonstratives; contrasting articles; lexis) proving to be persistently unwieldy as far as the preservation of Flaubert's idiosyncratic style is concerned. Furthermore, there is no identifiable template against which the teleological assumptions regarding retranslation might hold true. Instead, a plethora of configurations come to light, even within the pages of a single (re) translated work. Accordingly, the most recent retranslation by Thorpe (2011) may exhibit strategies which sustain, for example, Flaubert's use of parataxis, his singular application of *et* and cohesive lexical repetition, but the same version also betrays moments of abandon which fragment the original chains of cause and effect, blur the juxtaposition between lexical items and break down collocational patterns. Looking back towards the initial translation, it is clear that it too shares the inconsistent approach of the latest version, preserving some of Flaubert's stylistic particularities, such as the foregrounding of conjunctions, and lexical repetition or collocation, and obscuring others, such as the logico-semantic relationship between clauses, as well as lexical juxtaposition and polysemy. Of the points in between, these retranslations provide further evidence in support of the argument that degrees of closeness to the source text fluctuate over time and inside a given work, since no linear invariance towards improvement can be detected. The only common denominator between the individual retranslations here is their fundamental irregularity in the interpretation and treatment of the original narrative organization.

Conclusion

This chapter set out ascertain whether or not the assumed progressive movement of retranslation could be identified in the British versions of Flaubert's *Madame Bovary*, while simultaneously exploring how the very act of translation can affect the particularities of Flaubert's style, with specific reference to the questions of who speaks and who sees in FIS, and to narrative organization.

In the first instance, the narratological approach was supplemented by a systemic functional approach, in that explorations of focalization were aligned with explorations of the clause as representation, while investigations into voice were carried out alongside scrutiny of the clause as exchange. By establishing a checklist of features under each category, it was possible to undertake a consistent and repeatable comparison between each TT and the ST, and also between the (re)translations themselves, paying close attention to how each one conveyed the polyfocality and polyvocality of the original, and the ensuing undecidability of the narrative device. In order to be deemed 'close' to the original *Madame Bovary*, that is to have effected a return to the source text and its specificities, a given (re)translation must have preserved the narrative features of causal emplotment and relationality whereby the impersonality of the author leaves the reader bereft of any explicit guiding markers, and the banality of bourgeois society is implicitly exposed to scorn.

However, these narrative features were subject to dissipation or disappearance in numerous reworkings of FIS. The question of who speaks was liable to oversimplification as a result of the universal and ironic scope of the gnomic present being collapsed into more restricted, less ironic configurations; of the grammatical asymmetry between the SL and TL imperfect aspects which, in most cases, imposes a greater degree of certainty; of the removal of ellipsis which obscures both the inner workings of the protagonist and the underlying criticism of her inadequacy; and finally, of translatorial tinkerings which privilege the material over the abstract, thereby stabilizing the fundamentally unstable voice(s) of the ST.

Similarly, the question of who sees also found itself refracted in a more limited sphere in translation. Again, grammatical asymmetry exposes the translation of the indefinite pronoun as problematic given its unmarkedness in the SL and markedness in the TL; subsequent compensatory strategies in the (re)translations can impose a reduction in the uncertain universality of pronouns and imply the complicity of narrator, undermining the impersonality of the narrative. In the most extreme cases, a clear-cut focus on the protagonist shatters FIS. Where the precision of the demonstrative is curtailed, the clichéd nature of the observation is underplayed, along with irony of the ST, not least as a consequence of shifts to the possessive article which negate ambiguous focalization. As regards focalized participants, a certain blurring of focus downplays Emma's psychological fixation, suggesting instead the panoramic viewpoint of an EF. The indefinite balance shifts to favour the EF once again in those cases where deictic markers are interpreted as proximal or are overspecified, while the addition of temporal markers may emphasize either the panchronic logic of an EF, or the immediacy of time relative to the CF, thereby constricting the undecidability of ST focalization. Where circumstantial elements are added to retranslations, the move from metaphysical to physical endows Emma with a clarity of vision that runs contrary to her crippling ST disconnection from what is real. In many of the examples mentioned earlier, a certain overlap of strategies between (re) translations comes to the fore which goes some way to repudiating any claim that each new retranslation has differentiation as its goal. This is particularly apparent in those examples where the (re)translations correlate by diverging significantly from the features of the ST.

The second part of this chapter then turned its attention to the organization of the narrative world, and again drew on SFG in order to establish consistent points of comparison between the specific way in which the ST clause complexes are held together by taxis and logico-semantics and Flaubert's particular use of cohesion across clauses. In turn, this approach facilitated a study of how the narrative feature of temporality is impacted by (re)translation, that is how the narrative flow of the original is impeded, rerouted or promoted. Various translation strategies came to light here which exerted a negative impact on the distinctive way in which Flaubert constructs and holds together his narrative. By reversing the ST absence of coordination and conjunction, the actions of the protagonist can erroneously be attributed with a sense of logic or made to flow in a less fragmented manner which opposes her confusion and desperation. By suppressing or modifying the famous 'et' construction, the specific flow of the ST is redirected with greater or lesser pauses which fail to introduce the subsequent tableau in a comparably idiosyncratic manner. Also, elaborate, hypotactic ST complexes tend to be oversimplified, thereby disguising the strained narrative texture of the original and the afflictions of the protagonist which are mirrored in its tautness and final chute. Finally, the cohesive threads which run through the ST find themselves unravelled in those instances where the ironic precision of the demonstrative is rendered imprecise, weakening the ties to Emma's misguided romantic conceptions, and, similarly, where the non-specific definite article is replaced with the possessive, thereby obstructing the exophoric reach of the marker towards the tropes of fiction. Lexical repetition can also be diminished in translation, which in turn attenuates the emphasis accorded to the given item in the ST, and the dislocation evidenced with regard to lexical chains and collocation further destabilizes the particular Flaubertian texture of the narrative.

The above overview of the attendant risks of translation on Flaubert's impersonality, irony and narrative flow is also significant in the sense that these risks are not confined to the earliest, initial translation, or even to the earlier (re)translations. Instead, the manifold shifts which came to light in all TL versions and under each analytical rubric (FIS and narrative sequencing) attest to the inconsistencies which pervade the (re)translations and which ultimately destabilize the premises of Berman's progressive model and therefore the Retranslation Hypothesis. According to the logic of the latter, closeness is a unified concept and gains in magnitude as time advances: however, this particular case study demonstrates that when examined on a more intricate level, certain facets of a given TT may prove to restore the specificities of the original, while other facets instigate a move away from its narrative features. Thus, the conflicting relationship to closeness within individual TL versions jars against the uninterrupted trajectory of both the Retranslation Hypothesis and Berman's move towards perfection, exposing instead a tangle of similarities and incongruities which defy containment within a one-way path. Admittedly, there are moments where the assumptions on retranslation appear to hold – the preservation of ellipsis in TT6 Wall, TT7 Mauldon and TT8 Thorpe, the move of focalized participant from real to illusory in TT7 Mauldon and TT8 Thorpe, the absence of conjunction in TT6 Wall and TT8 Thorpe. Nevertheless, these validations are relatively isolated when contrasted with the frequency of other instances where the only pattern to emerge is one of oscillation over time. Another shade of subtlety emerges from those examples which show a high degree of correlation between the strategies employed in the initial translation and the later retranslations. In these cases, the polarized positioning of the

TL texts has no bearing on whether the specificities of the original have been revealed or concealed, but instead affirms that the passage of time and experience has been accompanied only by inertia. Furthermore, when the behaviour of the retranslations that fall in between the start and end points is taken into consideration, there is very little evidence in recurrent patterns beyond the apparent propensity of TT2 Blanchamp, the first retranslation, to be particularly blind to Flaubert's style. Instead, if each example could be plotted graphically, the prevailing trend would be one of oscillation and the linear representation would be characterized by peaks and troughs, not by the smooth line of upward progression. In short, the empirically identified twists and turns of the *Madame Bovary* (re)translations betoken a fundamentally capricious pattern of behaviour which is at variance with and far exceeds any teleological move from inchoate deficiency to later accomplishment. Viewed in this light, logic such as Berman's is reductive, and the shortcut which it imposes bypasses all the intricacies which constitute the interpretative potential of (re)translation.

6

Tales from Le Berry

Introduction

The primary goal of this chapter is to bring another corpus of (re)translations into direct dialogue with thinking that posits retranslation as a corrective, restorative and enhancing phenomenon. To this end, the following comparative analyses will examine the various ways in which the uniqueness of Berrichon cultural identity has been remediated by those TL versions of *La Mare au diable* which actually preserve the ethnographic Appendix to the pastoral tale. In this case study, the overarching benchmarks for comparison will be the narrative features of temporality, relationality and selective appropriation. Temporality and relationality will allow an examination, respectively, of how the (re)translations have dealt with the physical sequencing of the Appendix, and how they have framed the narrative in temporal and spatial terms. Selective appropriation is of pertinence since certain vernacular, acoustic and material elements of the Berry are privileged by Sand over others to give an idealized as opposed to realistic portrait of the region. Since Sand ultimately set out to imbue her narrative with a social message of understanding between the town and country, causal emplotment is inextricably linked to all the narrative features. The comparative focus in what follows will essentially be on individual matricial, lexical and typographical choices; it is therefore not necessary to reinforce the analysis with the metafunctional components of SFG, as was the case in the previous chapter, since these choices are located either far above or below the level of the clause and, in contrast to the translation of Flaubert, are not frustrated by questions of undecidability. The (re)translation strategies will also be evaluated according to whether and how they re-encode Sand's specific portrayal of Berrichon traditions and patois, and facilitate cultural understanding between peoples, no longer on an intranational level, but on an international one.

Temporality

According to Baker, the 'set of events, relationships and protagonists that constitute any narrative […] ha[ve] to be embedded in a sequential context and in a specific temporal and spatial configuration that renders them intelligible' (2006: 51). This is certainly true of the ST Appendix which follows chronologically and structurally after the events of the main narrative tale. The preceding love story becomes a premise for the Appendix to engage in its ethnographic study of a country wedding, and the same narrator requests a digression to:

> raconte[r] en détail une noce de campagne, celle de Germain, par exemple, à laquelle j'eus le plaisir d'assister il y a quelques années. (MD 154)
>
> [*recount in detail a country wedding, that of Germain, for example, which I had the pleasure of attending a few years ago*]

Although the Appendix may initially have been devised as a means of adding more material to the short tale, there is nevertheless an integral link between the two sections of the ST which serves to retain the curiosity of the reader as a continuation of the main events, whilst providing Sand with the opportunity to chart the particular cultural identity of the Berry region and accentuate its richness for the reader.

However, of the seven TL versions of *La Mare au diable* to be published in Britain, the initial translation along with the following two retranslations omit the Appendix altogether. The initial translation (TT1 Anon) and first retranslation (TT2 Anon) of the pastoral tale were both published in 1847, while the second retranslation (TT3 Shaw) was made available in 1848. The eight chapter divisions in these three TL texts would suggest that they are all based on the serialized version of the ST, published in February 1846: 'the novel comprised eight chapters in *Le Courrier français*', whereas the book version, published in May of the same year, 'comprised seventeen chapters' (Cellier 1999: 216, my translation). This fact may go some way to explaining why the Appendix is not included in these (re)translations as the main body of the ST was published by *Le Courrier* independently of the Appendix, which appeared later in March and April 1846. Despite the possibility of gaining access to this additional source material, it would appear that TT1 Anon, TT2 Anon and TT3 Shaw treat the main narrative events in isolation. Consequently, the spatial ordering of the original work is discontinued, in that the sequential move from the tale of Germain and Marie to an ethnographic study of their wedding rites is interrupted.

Since temporality allows narratives to 'project a chronological end that is also a moral end, a purpose, a forecast, an aspiration' (Baker 2006: 54), the suspension of temporality in the (re)translations further brings about a fragmentation of the work's idealism. As Hamilton remarks, the Appendix with its 'final portrait of Germain, newly married to Marie, fuses the novel's ideas into a unified whole. It acts as a concluding statement on life which contradicts the pessimism of Holbein's "Laboureur" criticized in the first pages' (1978: 181). The omission of the Appendix thus disrupts the original dialectal schema; the joy and love finally discovered by the protagonist is not brought to its full conclusion in these (re) translations, and the potential for Sand's humanitarian message of progress and understanding is severely attenuated.

As an addendum to the RH, Susam-Sarajeva notes that 'the *non-existence* of retranslations under particular circumstances should be given the importance it merits in translation research' (2003: 5, original emphasis). In this case, the non-existence of any translation, let alone retranslation, of the Appendix before TT4 Sedgwick is certainly significant. On a superficial level, the non-existence of the Appendix that spans from the initial translation to the second retranslation, followed by its recovery in TT4 Sedgwick and all subsequent versions appears to support the notion that retranslations fulfil a restorative function, to the extent that both the regional identity of the Berry and the moral unity of the original work are re-established in the later versions.

But it is also important to note that the dynamics of retranslation are, in this instance, more complex than the simple binary of absence/presence. Rather, the very boundaries between initial translation and retranslation become blurred when we consider that TT4 Sedgwick is at once a retranslation of the main body of the ST and an initial translation of the Appendix. It is essentially a hybrid text, an amalgam of antecedents and precedents, which defies uniformity of classification. Paloposki and Koskinen have also uncovered evidence of hybridity in the Finnish (re)translations of Hugo's *Les Misérables*, prompting them to conclude that 'the actual categorizing of translations into first and subsequent translations, which has formed the basis for almost all theorizing about retranslations, is ultimately misleading' (2010: 37). For this theorizing has made the assumption that (re)translations are unified entities, which are invariable in their macro- and micro-level approaches to the original. Rather, it is impossible to contend that later translations are closer to the source text when those later translations comprise discontinuous, fractal relationships with the original in the first instance. The fundamental hybridity of TT4 Sedgwick thus skews the Retranslation Hypothesis, since its dual points of reference to the original – as both an initial translation and a retranslation – create an anomaly which cannot be assimilated into any linear idea of progress.

Relationality

Relationality is the narrative feature which renders events intelligible by linking them to their wider contexts of space and time. The ethnographic study of the Appendix depends very much on markers of physicality (in particular, the positioning of the narrator) and temporality (tradition) as a means of conveying its message of fraternity and humanistic progress. However, Baker points out that translation necessarily entails a reconfiguration of contextual markers and that 'translating a narrative into another language and culture inevitably results in a form of "contamination", whereby the original narrative itself may be threatened with dilution or change' (2006: 62). In this case, any dilution of or change to the original orientations will have a negative impact on how the TL reader is brought to an understanding of the Other, while diminishing the reach of Sand's idealism.

The narrator of the Appendix plays a fundamental role in the original as a mediator between the ways of the Berry and the Parisian audience, allowing the latter access to those traditions through his own personal experience thereof. A key linguistic feature of this mediation is the use of deixis, namely those 'features which relate utterances to the spatiotemporal co-ordinates of the act of utterance' (Lyons 1977: 636), and which therefore draw the reader into the narrative world that they are invited to appreciate. The following analyses will focus on the specific categories of social, place and time deixis. Social deixis, that is 'those aspects of language structure that encode the social identity of participants' (Levinson 1983: 89), will be examined in the context of the complex relationship between narrator and reader. Place deixis will be investigated as a means of discerning how the narrator negotiates his position of dual-belonging, while time deixis will highlight the specificities of the Berrichon calendar as well as the ravages of progress on tradition.

Social deixis

The relationship between narrator and reader is already established in the opening chapter of the pastoral tale itself ('L'auteur au lecteur' [*The writer to the reader*]), where the reader learns that 'C'est l'histoire d'un laboureur précisément que j'avais l'intention de vous dire et que je vous dirai tout à l'heure' [*It is the story of a labourer precisely that I had the intention of telling you and that I will tell you later*] (MD 37). In this sense, the transmission of Berrichon identity and culture is based on a dialogic mode between narrator and narratee, which is all the more fitting given the oral tradition of the peasants. However, it is of note that there are amendments to the tone of this relationship by the time the Appendix is reached; here, the deictic 'referent honorific system' (Levinson 1983: 91) turns from vouvoiement towards tutoiement when the narrator states in his opening gambit that 'Je te demande pardon, **lecteur ami**' [*I ask your pardon, **reader friend***] (MD 153) and 'j'espère t'amuser encore un instant, **cher lecteur**' [*I hope to amuse you for another moment, **dear reader***] (MD 154). It may well be that this increase in familiarity is a direct consequence of the narrator and the reader having experienced together the trials of the preceding tale, or the result of the two sections having been written separately. In any case, the TL does not have the grammatical means to convey this distinction, and evidence of the proximity between the two parties must necessarily be restricted to the epithets of 'ami' [*friend*] and 'cher' [*dear*] when examining the (re)translations.

Firstly, the label of 'lecteur ami' [*reader friend*] (MD 154) reinforces the sense of camaraderie between the addresser and the addressee, instilling an easiness which will facilitate understanding. This dynamic is preserved in TT4 Sedgwick as '**kind reader**' (95), in TT5 Miles as '**good reader**' (133) and in TT6 Cowan as '**dear reader**' (99). However, in TT7 Brown the address comes abruptly as '**Reader**' (89), where the omission of the apposed noun is compounded by the presence of capitalization, all of which lends a greater degree of formality or austerity to the happy companionship evinced in the ST. In turn, the basis of familiarity on which the narrator functions as a mediator is undermined. Furthermore, this typographical device draws even more attention to the fact that the narrative is in written form and as such it distances the translation from the oral tradition of the peasants, as opposed to attempting to bridge the gap. Contrary to the progress anticipated by Berman, it is in fact the most recent retranslation which points further away than the original narrator, weakening the association between this mediating figure and his addressees.

Secondly, the phrase 'cher lecteur' [*dear reader*] (MD 154) further bolsters the amity inherent in the ST by incorporating a different epithet to denote proximity. Here, TT7 Brown persists with its capitalization but does include the adjectival marker in '**dear Reader**' (154), thereby lessening the degree of formality, but still emphasizing the written medium. Both TT4 Sedgwick and TT6 Cowan duplicate their previous phrasing of '**kind reader**' (95) and '**dear**

reader' (100), respectively, and although this strengthens the relationship through accumulative effect, it is TT5 Miles alone which mirrors the precise synonymic devices of the ST since it diverges from its previous adjectival choice to invoke, in its turn, the '**dear reader**' (134). It follows that there is no evidence here in support of retranslation as a corrective measure.

The narrator is also aligned to the Berry region, and this relationship of dual-belonging is perhaps most keenly felt in the ST through the use of the social deictic *nous* [*we*] which serves to demarcate his allegiance to both the rural and the urban. To begin, the relationship with the reader can be characterized in terms of proximity; the ST narrator, wishing to close the gap between the two worlds, incorporates certain narratorial strategies which engage the reader in the communicative situation, fostering a sense of inclusivity. Thus, when the narrator muses, 'Pourquoi ne dirions-**nous** pas son costume?' [*Why don't* ***we*** *describe his suit?*] (MD 184) and coyly quips that '**Nous** ne parlerons pas de la rôtie [***We*** *won't mention the roast*]' (MD 188), the *nous* of the narrator can be described as a *nous de modestie*, in that the use of the plural pronoun avoids an overstated use of the first person singular. In this sense, the narrator positions himself as a mediator in the service of his target audience, and the rejection of the outright authoritativeness of *je* [*I*] is also in keeping with the deferential stance, feigned or otherwise, evinced in the opening lines of the Appendix: the story will be told on the condition that 'tu me permets que je te [la] raconte' [*you permit that I tell it*] (MD 154). As such, the pronoun *nous* becomes an important signpost in the communicative situation, signalling both inclusivity and an implied willingness to serve the needs of the reader.

In the first example, the majority of the TL versions retain the allusion to the reader in 'Why should **we** not' (TT4 Sedgwick 115; TT5 Miles 160) and 'Why shouldn't **we**' (TT7 Brown 106). But in TT6 Cowan, there is a significant omission of the personal pronoun: '**Why not** describe her costume?' (121). The infinite construction erases all specific participants in the act of narration; while the generality of the question could be regarded as all-encompassing, and the lack of pronoun certainly goes some way to conveying the narrator as unassuming, the absence of explicit interaction between narrator and reader nevertheless weakens the basis on which the ST depiction of the Berry rests. The overall pattern of retranslation behaviour in this case is one of consistency, but with a notable move away from the source text in the penultimate retranslation.

In the second example, several more manipulations of the inclusive use of *nous* [*we*] come to light. It is TT4 Sedgwick and TT5 Miles which remain consistent in their preservation of the pronoun in the statements that '**We** shall not speak of' (TT4 Sedgwick 118) and '**We** shall not deal here with' (TT5 Miles 164), thereby safeguarding against an overbearing or individualistic use of the first person singular pronoun. Conversely, TT6 Cowan and TT7 Brown place all emphasis on the narrator alone who claims that '**I** will not mention' (125) and '**I** will pass over' (108), respectively. As such, the reader is disengaged from the storytelling dynamic, and the sense of exclusivity inherent in the first person pronoun enlarges the distance between town and country. The chronological ordering of these (re)translations thus demonstrates a definite disengagement from the social configuration of the source text, and runs counter to the notion of increased proximity with time.

Turning to the other side of the narrator's loyalty, tonic pronouns are employed as a means of framing his own roots in the Berry region, not least through the clear spatial marker of belonging, *chez nous* [*where we live*]. This stamp of identity appears early on in the Appendix when the narrator notes that winter is an appropriate time '**chez nous** de faire les noces' [***where we live*** *to have weddings*] (MD 154). Three versions maintain the possessive element of the SL to delineate '**our** country' (TT4 Sedgwick 96), '**our** parts' (TT5 Miles 134) and '**our** part of the world' (TT7 Brown 89). While TT6 Cowan does convey geographical precision with the phrase 'in these parts' (100), the emphasis on the narrator's physical location in the Berry does not, however, have the same function as the ST emphasis on belonging. In other words, the ST narrator strives to establish his Berrichon origins from the outset, and in so doing, his voice adopts a more emotive and authoritative tone as mediator for the urban reader; this tone is then modulated in TT6 Cowan, where the native associations of the narrator are underplayed. In this case, there is a repeat of an earlier pattern, whereby it is also TT6 Cowan which disrupts the accurate pointing of the other versions.

Social and spatial deictics overlap when the narrator maps out certain physical dimensions of the Berry, noting that 'c'est à **une demi-lieue de chez nous** qu'il fallait aller chercher la bénédiction nuptiale' [*It is* ***half a league from where we live*** *that must be travelled in search of the nuptial blessing*] (MD 181). In this case, only TT4 Sedgwick retains the exact bearings of the ST, incorporating the precise distance, the point of departure and the collective sense of belonging: '**we** had to go **half a league from home**' (113). The journey outlined in TT7 Brown, namely that '**we** had to go **half a league away**' (104), incorporates the collective pronoun, but is somewhat vague on the point of departure, thereby weakening the indigenous ties between the narrator and the region. This is also true of TT5 Miles, where not only does the orientation become vaguer, but the distance is converted into quintessentially British terms, fundamentally appropriating the way in which the Berrichon inhabitants quantify the world around them: '**we** had to go **a good mile and a half**' (157). Finally, all communal sense of identity disappears in TT6 Cowan where the focus shifts to the protagonists alone: '**they** had to travel **half a league**' (119). According to Laurent, 'the third person pronoun is normally not deictic' (2001: 96, my translation) since it refers to an element in the utterance, as opposed to the situation of that utterance. By narrowing the reference to Germain and Marie, elements in the utterance, the narrator effectively removes himself from his privileged communicative position, that is from inside the narrative situation; his authoritative footing as insider is destabilized, which in turn undermines his role as mediator. The initial translation of Appendix is thus the only TL version to preserve this particular socio-spatial deictic, demonstrating a high degree of precision which disaffirms the supposed blindness of initial translation attempts.

The mediation of Berrichon identity is further ensured in the ST by the use of the social deictic *on* [*one*] which serves as a means of accentuating the collective nature of Berrichon activities. In addition, its indefiniteness attenuates the sense that the Berrichon peasants are expressly the 'Other'; as Jaubert notes, the 'primary effect of this deictic reference is the creation of a common world' (1990: 107, my translation). In the Appendix, the use of the indefinite pronoun goes some way to establishing a sense of inclusivity, or, at the very least, to curtailing exclusivity. In the same way as the *nous de modestie* harbours the urban reader from the disruptive feeling that the narrator is too firmly planted in the foreign, so too does the ambiguity of the indefinite pronoun allow the narrator to adopt a stance as an outside observer, but without overtly denying his potential place as a participant. Take for example the prevalence of the indefinite pronoun in the following description of the wedding rituals:

> **On** se réunit peu à peu, et l'**on** dansa sur la pelouse [...]. Quand la nuit fut venue, **on** commença d'étranges préparatifs, **on** se sépara en deux bandes, et quand la nuit fut close, **on** procéda à la cérémonie des *livrées*. (MD 157–8, original italicized emphasis)
>
> [***One*** *got together little by little, and* ***one*** *danced on the grass [...]. When the night had drawn in,* ***one*** *started some strange preparations,* ***one*** *separated into two bands, and when the night had fallen,* ***one*** *proceeded to the ceremony of the* livrées]

On the one hand, the repeated use of the pronoun points to a sense of Berrichon village spirit, with an undefined number of peasants taking part in the celebrations. On the other, the polysemousness of the pronoun serves to moderate the foreignness of the situation, creating a shared world which escapes an 'us and them' dynamic, whilst allowing the narrator to play down, but not erase, his own involvement in the interests of retaining his position as an intermediate.

Of course, a wide-scale use of the indefinite pronoun in the TL would be much more marked than is the case in the SL, and is therefore likely to meet with more resistance. As far as the example just mentioned is concerned, the (re)translations demonstrate three main approaches to the translation of *on*: the use of a nominal group, the third person plural pronoun or a passive construction. The first, introductory instance of *on* is rendered with much greater specificity in TT4 Sedgwick as '**the guests**' (98), which then reinforces the division between those who have been invited and those who have not, isolating the reader, excluding the narrator and collapsing the sense of a shared world. The remaining versions opt for the slightly vaguer category of '**people**' (TT5 Miles 137; TT6 Cowan102; TT7 Brown 91), a choice which is not so blatant in its exclusivity. The subsequent observation that 'l'on dansa' [*one danced*] (MD 157) brings further strategies to light: TT4 Sedgwick uses the initial subject to govern the second verbal group, that is '**the guests** assembled and danced' (98), and therefore corrodes the ST emphasis on collectiveness through pronominal repetition; in turn, the third personal plural is incorporated in '**they** began dancing' (TT6 Cowan 102) and '**they** danced' (TT7 Brown 91), a strategy which at once categorically distances the narrator from the event and heightens the sense of separation for the reader. TT5 Miles relies on a passive construction in order to preserve the ambiguousness of the ST, in that the phrase '**there was** dancing' (137) does not alienate the reader, nor does it preclude the involvement of the narrator. But it does obscure the human element and, therefore, understates the importance of village involvement. Indeed, all these strategies are repeated in various configurations for the translation of the remaining uses of the indefinite pronoun: TT4 Sedgwick and TT7 Brown go on to solely employ *they*, and in that way, widen the divide between narrator and peasant, between narrator and reader; TT5 Miles persists in the use of passive constructions, again dissimulating the communal presence of the village folk, but fostering a general arena into which the narrator or the reader may project themselves; finally, TT6 Cowan wavers between the third person plural and the passive so that '**strange preparations** began; **they** divided into two parties and [...] **the ceremony of the "liveries"** started' (102). It seems as if the asymmetry in normal patterns of language has prevented the inclusiveness of the SL pronoun being transferred into the TL versions, with the result that no (re)translation exhibits a return to the original.

A further example of sustained emphasis on the impersonal pronoun appears in the narrator's description of the wedding ritual which involves the planting of a cabbage:

> **on** apporte la corbeille, et le couple païen y plante le chou [...]. **On** l'entoure de terre fraîche, **on** le soutient avec des baguettes [...]; **on** pique des pommes rouges au bout des baguettes [...]; **on** chamarre le tout de rubans et de banderoles; **on** recharge le trophée sur la civière [...], et enfin **on** sort du jardin (MD 195–6)
>
> [***One** brings the basket, and the pagan couple plant the cabbage there [...] **One** surrounds it with fresh soil, **one** props it up with sticks [...]; **one** spikes red apples on the end of the sticks; **one** adorns the whole thing with ribbons and streamers; **one** loads the trophy up again on to the stretcher [...], and lastly **one** leaves the garden*]

Once more, this is a collective activity for the peasants, but the use of the pronoun in conjunction with the gnomic present extends its reach to incorporate not just those who are in attendance specifically for the wedding of Germain and Marie, but all those who have taken part in the custom since its inception. As was the case in the example just mentioned, the (re)translations employ both the third person plural pronoun and passive constructions as alternatives to the impersonal pronoun of the ST, although there are no instances of the incorporation of more precise nominal groups. Consistent with the aforementioned strategies, TT5 Miles is dominated by passive phrases whereby '**the basket** is brought [...]. **It** is surrounded [...], propped up [...]; rosy apples are stuck on the ends [...], and springs [sic] [...] are set all around; **the whole** is titivated [...] the trophy is loaded' (171–2), although the final instantiation is rendered as '**they** come forth' (172). The remaining versions demonstrate a greater degree of alternation between the two options. However, this oscillation leads to a significant misrepresentation of the ceremony in two of the TL versions: by opting for *they* in the translation of 'on l'entoure' [*one surrounds it*] (MD 195), TT4 Sedgwick (123) and TT6 Cowan (130) introduce an anaphoric reference back to the preceding nominal group of 'le couple païen' [*the pagan couple*] (MD 195). Thus, the observations that 'the "infidel" pair plant the cabbage [...]. **They** surround it' (TT4 Sedgwick 123) and that 'the two "heathens" plant the cabbage [...]. **They** pack fresh earth round it' (TT6 Cowan 130) restrict the actions to the two peasants who have assumed the ceremonial role of 'les païens' [*the pagans*]; however, in the traditional Berrichon order of things, as charted in the ST, the planting formalities are less inhibited, extending to the community at large. Ultimately, an asymmetry between language preferences has resulted in the distortion of a particular ritualistic facet of Berrichon cultural identity across all the (re)translations.

Spatial deixis

In terms of spatial deixis, the ST narrator frequently mediates cultural identity through the demonstrative. The Appendix is replete with these deictic markers that point from the position of the narrator directly into the region, and, as Massardier-Kenney notes in reference to her translation of *Valvèdre*, but of no less relevance here: 'the very frequency of these demonstratives is significant and they should not be removed in English since they attest to the desire expressed throughout the text to bring the reader closer to the narrative world' (2004: 74, my translation). The demonstrative affords readers a sense of immediacy, of direct access to the otherness of the context, but they are simultaneously shielded from the full disruptive force of such a relocation by the guiding presence of the narrator. In the Appendix, there is a particular concentration of demonstratives in the description of the ritual mock siege of the bride's home by the groom and his party. This episode is characterized by a series of verbal and physical mêlées between the two sides, and assumes an almost frenzied tone; the use of deictic markers then keeps readers anchored amidst the ensuing chaos, providing them with specific points of reference which in turn underscore the cultural importance of these symbolic acts.

Table 6.1 gives an overview of how each demonstrative marker of the ST is treated in the (re)translations. It is evident that the strategies for dealing with the translation of the demonstrative are diverse and that no one (re)translation demonstrates a consistent use of the TL equivalent marker. The version which demonstrates the least degree of manipulation is TT4 Sedgwick, shifting to the definite article in only two of the eleven examples. However, this quantitative measurement does not allow for the significance of some shifts over others: while TT5 Miles shows the greatest degree of modifications, altering the demonstrative to the definite article on five instances, the three shifts discernible in TT7 Brown are in point of fact more disruptive to the spatial framing of the ST. On one hand, the frequent use of the definite article in TT5 Miles leaves the reader without specific compass points in unfamiliar and disordered territory. On the other, TT7 Brown transforms the demonstrative into the possessive pronoun, observing that this is specifically '**their** struggle' (102); rather than facilitate access to the peasants, this deictic marker calls attention to the otherness of the country folk, but erects a barrier in the path of the reader. In addition, the second instantiation of '**cette** lutte' [***this** fight*] (MD 178) is replaced by anaphoric reference with the pronoun '**it**' (TT7 Brown 102), and as a result, both the overall presence and the pointing power of the ST marker are diminished. Likewise, the shift from demonstrative to paraphrase, that is from '**ce** germe d'incendie' [***this** germ of fire*] (MD 178) to '**what** might have turned into a real fire' (TT7 Brown 102), reverses the immediacy afforded by the framing device. In other words, the ST deictic shortcut which submerges the reader into the Berry takes a more circumlocutious route in TT7 Brown.

Table 6.1 Demonstrative markers

MD	Literal translation	TT4 Sedgwick	TT5 Miles	TT6 Cowan	TT7 Brown
cet intérieur (164)	this interior	these (102)	this (143)	the (107)	this (95)
ce siège (165)	this siege	this (102)	this (144)	this (107)	this (95)
cette scène (165)	this scene	The (102)	The (144)	The (108)	This (95)
cette attaque (172)	this attack	this (106)	the (148)	this (112)	this (98)
cette époque (177)	this time	this (110)	those (153)	those (116)	that (102)
cette lutte (177)	this fight	this (110)	the (153)	It (116)	their (102)
Ces jeux (178)	These games	these (110)	these (153)	these (116)	these (102)
Cette lutte (178)	This fight	this (110)	the (153)	it (117)	It (102)
Cet incident (178)	This incident	This (111)	The (154)	This (117)	This (102)
Ce germe (178)	This germ	the (111)	this (154)	the (117)	what (102)
Ces fantômes (180)	These ghosts	these (112)	these (156)	these (118)	these (103)

Certain demonstratives are preserved in all the (re)translations, namely '**ce** siège' [***this** siege*] (MD 165), '**Ces** jeux' [***These** games*] (MD 178) and '**ces** fantômes' [***these** ghosts*] (MD 180), but there is no obvious logic which might explain why these nominal groups are more susceptible to this treatment than the others: they are no more or less concrete in terms of their physical presence, nor are they alone in having textual antecedents. A further nominal group to maintain its specific marker in translation is '**cette** époque' [***this** time*] (MD 177), although the TL variations in proximal and distal demonstratives temporally frame the ST setting in diverse ways. A sense of immediacy emanates from TT4 Sedgwick with '**this** time' (110), bringing the reader as chronologically close to the narrative events as possible; but the other versions locate the events in a more distant past through the use of the distal phrases '**those** days' (TT5 Miles 153; TT6 Cowan 116) and '**that** time' (TT7 Brown 102), and in so doing, allows a sense of temporal removal to pervade the narrative. In this particular example, what we have is a reversal of the logic of improvement over time, in that the later versions increase the distance between reader and ST. But an examination of the treatment of the demonstrative as a whole reveals an apparently unsystematic strategy of choice; certainly, the balance is weighted in favour of the demonstrative in all the TL versions, but without a full-scale retention of the markers, no TT pinpoints the nominal groups with as much precision and transparency as the ST.

Temporal deixis

Berrichon cultural identity is further negotiated by the narrator through the use of temporal deixis. In this rural environment, life is governed by the natural laws of time; everything has its season or its time of day which is reflected in the ST by the repeated foregrounding, or thematizing, of temporal adjuncts. According to Baker, 'Thematizing temporal adjuncts is […] common in any type of narrative text, that is, any text which recounts a series of events' (1992: 132), and in this instance, the position of the temporal adjunct reinforces the inextricable link between events and their natural timeframe in the Berry region. This strategy can be seen at numerous points in the ST: the observation that '**C'était en hiver**, […] époque de l'année où il est séant et convenable chez nous de faire les noces. Dans l'été on n'a guère le temps' [***It was in winter,** […] a time of the year when it is fitting and seemly where we live to hold weddings. In summer one scarcely has the time*] (MD 154) highlights how the agricultural calendar presides over all other occasions. As far as other rural occupations (and supernatural activity) are concerned, '**C'est particulièrement la nuit** que tous, fossoyeurs, chanvreurs et revenants exercent leur industrie' [***It is particularly at night** that all, grave diggers, hemp beaters and ghosts ply their trade*] (MD 159). Specifically, '**C'est à la fin de septembre**' [***It is at the end of September***] (MD: 132) that the hemp crushing begins, as a result of which '**C'est alors** qu'on entend la nuit, dans les campagnes, ce bruit sec et saccadé' [***It is then*** *that one hears at night, in the countryside, this sharp and fitful noise*] (MD: 132), generated by the crushing process. These nocturnal goings-on then foster a sense of mystery and foreboding in the autumnal region since '**C'est le temps** des bruits insolites et mystérieux' [***It is the time*** *of strange and mysterious noises*] (MD 160), and '**C'est durant** ces nuits-là, nuits voilées et grisâtres, que le chanvreur raconte ses étranges aventures' [***It is during*** *these same nights, bleak, misty nights, that the hemp beater tells of his strange adventures*] (MD 161). The use of the cleft construction evidently becomes an important framing device for the narrator as it allows him to convey the crucial interaction between the natural calendar and particularities of the region.

Only a few modifications come to light in the (re)translations, with the majority mirroring the cleft constructions. Take for example the following: each TL version records that '**It is** especially at night' (TT4 Sedgwick 99), '**It is** by night particularly' (TT5 Miles: 138), 'It is chiefly at night' (TT6 Cowan 103) and '**It is** particularly at night' (TT7 Brown 92) when the aforementioned work takes place. However, TT6 Cowan reworks the ST report '**C'était** en hiver' [***It was*** *in winter*] (MD 154), opting to foreground the event itself instead, whose prominence is further increased by the use of the demonstrative: '**This wedding** took place in winter' (TT6 Cowan 100). Consequently, the syntactic emphasis is on the event, while the seasonal frame is consigned to the Rheme element, to reprise the language of SFG, that is the remainder of the clause. Also, TT5 Miles removes the cleft construction, '**C'est** à la fin de septembre' [***It is*** *at the end of September*] (MD 159), and although the temporal setting remains foregrounded in the phrase which commences '**Late** in September' (TT5 Miles 139), the specific stress of the ST begins to ebb. Similarly, TT6 Cowan compresses the ST timeline, '**C'est** alors qu'on entend la nuit' [***It is*** *then when one hears at night*] (MD 159), where both adjunct and noun underscore the night-time backdrop, into '**At night**, the countryside resounds' (104). Again, the temporal aspect comes first, but the emphatic structures of the ST are denied. Given the loss of emphasis on seasonality in TT5 Miles and TT6 Cowan, it is the initial translation of the Appendix and the most recent retranslation which emerge as closest to the temporal configurations of the original.

Finally, temporal deixis is significant with regard to Berrichon traditions. As Didier notes, Sand 'is writing at a time when the situation is evolving very quickly' (1994: 78); in other words, this is a time when the sweep of progress and industrialization threatens the very existence of Berrichon language and customs. Sand's narrator also proves to be acutely aware of this conflict, and on the whole, the majority of the (re)translations mirror those deictics which underscore the juxtaposition between the narrative past and present. The narrator observes that '**Déjà** la moitié des cérémonies celtiques, païennes, ou moyen âge [...] **se sont éffacées**' [***Already** half of the celtic, pagan or medieval ceremonies [...] **have faded***] (MD 154), where the temporal adjunct in conjunction with the perfective tense mark the irreversibility of the situation. These temporal deictic markers are well preserved in the (re)translations: '**Already** half the ceremonies, Celtic, Pagan or of the Middle Ages [...] **have disappeared**' (TT4 Sedgwick 96); '**Already** there **has vanished** a good half of those Celtic, pagan or medieval ceremonies' (TT5 Miles 134); 'Half the Celtic, pagan and medieval ceremonies [...] **have already vanished**' (TT6 Cowan 100). However, in TT7 Brown there is the observation that: '**Already**, half the Celtic, pagan or medieval ceremonies [...] have **become obsolete**' (89). Consequently, while most TL versions point to the cultural vulnerability of the region, and in so doing, underpin the author's attempt to stem the threat, the most recent retranslation seems to claim that the traditions of the region have simply been discarded due to their age. Here is an example which reveals the most recent retranslation to obstruct the pertinent temporality of the original and to prevent readers from feeling the full force of the threat faced by the rural traditions.

In comparison to the progress of other provinces, the narrator remarks that 'Le Berry **est resté** stationnaire' [*The Berry **has remained** stationary*] (MD 153) with the result that 'c'est le pays le plus conservé qui se puisse trouver à l'heure qu'il est' [*it is the most preserved countryside that can be found at the present hour*] (MD 154). In this instance, the use of the perfect tense draws attention to an action whose effects can still be felt at that present narrative moment. The temporal deictic marker is maintained in TT5 Miles, where 'Berry, in contrast, **has remained stationary**' (134), and in TT7 Brown, where 'The Berry area **has stood still**' (89); both TL versions then identify the narrative situation of the narrator as a contemporary observer of the state of the region. However, TT4 Sedgwick and TT6 Cowan opt for the simple past in, respectively, 'Berry **remained** as she was' (95) and 'Berry, on the other hand, **remained** static' (99), thereby inscribing a sense of temporal distance into the narrative which dissociates the narrator from his privileged ST position, that is in the moment, and which, in turn, reduces the sense of immediacy for the reader. In this instance, the distribution of proximity to the source text across the (re)translations is rather uneven, alternating between strategies which distance the narrator from and then realign him to his original temporal point of reference.

Summary

The deictic markers of the ST all point to the way in which the narrator negotiates the distance between the reader and the Berry, and are thus fundamental to the configuration of relationality in the narrative; social deixis shapes the relationship between the interlocutors, while the spatial and temporal orientations of the narrative highlight the narrator's dual-belonging and raise awareness of the importance of the seasons and of the survival of Berrichon traditions. Together, these deictic markers assist in bringing narrative events into a coherent, intelligible whole. When the relational composition of the ST is transposed into the TL versions, several issues emerge. Firstly, the grammatical asymmetry between SL and TL in terms of the indefinite pronoun *on* gives way to an inconsistency in strategy across all the (re)translations, regardless of whether they appear later or not, and ultimately conceals the sense of social collectiveness. Similarly, the irregularity with which the demonstrative pronoun *ce* is translated prevents a relationship of closeness from being posited between the ST and any of the (re)translations. Secondly, the above examples appear to indicate that TT6 Cowan and TT7 Brown are both susceptible to skewing the relational points of reference established in the original, undermining the narrator's attempt to include the reader, obscuring his allegiance to the region and removing him from the immediacy of his narrative position. Indeed, TT7 Brown reconfigures the original reference points further still by attenuating the demonstrative links into the narrative world, as well as the external threat to traditions. Baker's warning that the original narrative may be diluted or changed through translation (2006: 62) is therefore most pertinent to the two most recent retranslations. The resultant downward trend in how the relationality of the original is treated provides further counter-evidence to claims that retranslation advances towards a richer, closer interpretation of the source text. Instead, the hermeneutic potential of the original is here shown to be restricted in the very versions which Berman, and Goethe before him, might have assumed to approach a pinnacle of greatness.

Selective appropriation

The Berrichon cultural identity constructed in the ST Appendix rests on the narrative process of selective appropriation, whereby certain aspects of reality are incorporated into the narrative and others omitted. The reader is subsequently exposed, not to a minute study of the region and all its singular facets, but to those specificities of the region that have been privileged by Sand, and subsequently, by the narrator. In this instance, the choices made by Sand as to which cultural qualities to highlight, and to what extent, can all be related to the author's overarching concern with how to make the urban reader comprehend the 'paysan' in such a way as to enable a more concordant society. The rationale which underpins the author's strategy is certainly one of 'instruire en amusant', that is select those features of le Berry which will entertain and charm the Parisian reader but simultaneously foster a progressive understanding of the richness and value of the rural way of life.

The close alliance between selective appropriation and causal emplotment, the injection of moral meaning into the narrative, is readily observable in Sand's use of Berrichon patois. As Didier notes, Sand's work 'is essentially made up of a process of *selection* rather than of creation with its overabundant richness of language' (1994: 79, my emphasis and translation); this selection is necessarily perturbed by the simultaneous need to instil a sense of otherness in the narrative (without which there would be no gap to breach and no bridge to social progress) and to, in Schleiermacherian terms, leave the reader in peace as much as possible as a prerequisite to entertainment on the first level, and understanding on the second. The following comparative analysis will examine evidence of specific selection criteria within the ST, and will then chart whether or not these criteria are modified in the TL versions, alongside the effects that any alterations might have on the desired rapprochement between town and country.

Likewise, Sandian selective appropriation is motivated by a desire to 'create this indispensable impression of the real' (Didier 1994: 79, my translation) which is needed to promote otherness. In addition to the richness of the Berrichon patois itself, Sand foregrounds the poetic merits of the 'paysan' as expressed in the oral tradition of the region. But rather than focus solely on the lexis used, the Appendix also emphasizes the fundamental link between Berrichon patois and personality, and between traditional music and the land itself, whilst also providing auditory descriptions of voice and typical country sounds. Consequently, the reader is protected from a potentially overwhelming exposition of unfamiliar signifiers, and is instead given access to the reality of the auditory characteristics of the region through the labelling of sounds. In this sense, timbre is at once universal and specific, a common aural language through which to express the intonations of the Berrichon people and countryside.

Furthermore, the material reality of the region is expressed by Sand's descriptions of local costumes, produce, wildlife, and even the soil of the

Berry. Their physical presence and labelling serve as touchstones of Berrichon identity; as well as adding local colour to the narrative, the tangible objects adopt a greater significance as concrete markers of native customs and ways of life. In essence, they are a meronymic representation of Berrichon alterity. So, the comparative analysis must take into account how the sonic and the material reality of the Berry region is conveyed in the (re)translations; closeness will be measured against the prevalence of these reference points in the TL narratives, and the extent to which the reader can thus experience the otherness of the region, an experience which should ultimately promote cultural comprehension.

Berrichon patois

The task which Sand sets herself in the translation of the Berrichon patois is a frustrated one, especially given its anti-Babelian aspirations: undo the linguistic and cultural confusion between a major and a minor tongue, but by striking a balance that will ensure comprehension in the former and the preservation of linguistic identity in the latter. As Vincent remarks, Sand:

> discovered a simple, innocent poetry in the life of the man of the fields that she sought to carry over into her novels. But this poetry could scarcely be expressed in the language of the cultivated, refined man. She was forced to seek out a new form. And that is what troubled the author of the *Mare au Diable*. (1916: 36, my translation)

Both the author and the Appendix narrator appear to be acutely aware of the limitations of this intranational transfer, and the latter regrets 'de n'avoir pas su te la [l'histoire] traduire mieux; car c'est une véritable traduction qu'il faut au langage antique et naïf des paysans que *je chante*' [*not having known how to translate it [the story] better; because it is a veritable translation that is necessary for the ancient and native language of the peasants that* I sing] (MD 153, original emphasis). Thus, cultural mediation is frustrated by the challenge of rendering the patois to a Parisian readership. Unimpeded access to the source language, that is to the dialect, would be to the detriment of linguistic comprehension, and consequently to understanding on a fraternal level. On the other hand, uprooting the patois by translating it into standard French would be to destroy its significance as a source of alterity, not least since 'a vernacular clings tightly to its own soil and completely resists any direct translating into another vernacular' (Berman 2000: 294).

How then does Sand resolve this double bind? Various translation strategies may be discerned, the most overt of which is Sand's attempts to let the linguistic specificity of the region shine through by code-switching and typography, that is by introducing into the text Berrichon lexical items, 'almost always appearing in italics in order to signal their inevitable alterity' (Bordas 2006: 72, my translation). This strategy is tempered by the addition of synonyms or explicatory paraphrases in standard French, with the result that the reader stumbles only momentarily over the linguistic presence of the other. Furthermore, Louise Vincent's comprehensive survey of *La langue et style rustiques de George Sand dans les romans champêtres* reveals that a number of lexical items 'are, by no means, to be found in the language of the peasants' (1916: 22, my translation), and thus only masquerade as part of the Berrichon dialect. Similarly, 'amongst the words classed as Berrichon patois, those which belong to Old French are much greater in number' (1916: 31, my translation). Consequently, Sand appears to have supplemented the regional idiom with what Venuti would classify as 'discursive peculiarities designed to *imitate* a foreign text' (1995: 101, my emphasis); in other words, the reader is shielded from the full force of Berrichon alterity through lexical choices (selective appropriation) which signal difference, whilst simultaneously and conversely signalling something more familiar – a common linguistic heritage. In this sense, Sand's inclusion of antiquated terms goes hand in hand with her presentation of the Berrichon dialect as 'trop français pour nous' (MD 153). The peasant way of speaking is also approximated through the inclusion of certain antiquated and sociolectic expressions which, being removed from standard patterns of French, further emphasize otherness.

Moreover, Sand's medial position permits a manipulation of language that establishes what can be termed a 'third code which arises out of the bilateral considerations of the matrix and target codes; it is, in a sense, a subcode of each of the codes involved' (Frawley 1984: 168). Indeed, it is this third code that Naginski alludes to when she defines Sand's pastoral novels as 'a series of attempts to provide […] a synthetic language' (1991: 237), and that Didier identifies as 'a certain language forged by [Sand], midway between the language of the towns and that of the countryside' (1998: 645, my translation), an amalgamation designed to narrow the divide between the two. But the technical difficulties of translating a dialect aside, Sand's primary concern was perhaps to create a simulacrum of alterity onto which she could project her idealistic aims. Cronin argues that in order for minority languages to survive, they must 'champion difference' (1998: 156). While Sand's inclusion of Berrichon lexical items certainly facilitates their preservation, the accompanying admixture of old French terms and sociolect champions difference on a much wider scale, allowing the author a more diverse backdrop against which to inspire and encourage fraternal harmony across all divides. In order for a (re)translation to realize the full differentiating potential of the original, the alterity of Sand's linguistic construct – her act of choosing – must remain intact.

Italics and synonymy

The first issue to be investigated is the typographical use of italics to emphasize difference, in particular, those words which are accompanied by a synonym, in the sense of a standard French equivalent, as a means of softening the blow for the urban reader. Given the specificity of the Appendix, it is not surprising that there is a strong italic presence within this section, not least in the presentation of the wedding customs. This is evidenced in the narrator's exposition of 'les cadeaux de noce, appelés ***livrées***' [*the wedding presents, called* **livrées**] (MD 155), where the Berrichon word follows after the standard French phrase. The strategies evinced in the (re)translations are diverse. TT4 Sedgwick incorporates a synonym in the phrase 'her wedding gifts – **favours**, as they call them' (96); but this alternative merely intimates the presence of the Other as there is no real linguistic clash between the minor and the major, with both words stemming from the same standardized source. Also, the narrator distances himself somewhat from his own native tongue through the deictic marker 'they'. As far as TT5 Miles is concerned, the tactic is one of omission as it simply alludes to 'the wedding gifts' (135); by erasing the foreign element from the narrative, the Parisian reader is left entirely unalerted to the linguistic richness of the region. With TT6 Cowan comes the restoration of linguistic alterity in the description of 'the wedding presents known as the **"liveries"**' (100). According to Vincent, the lexical item *livrées* is to be classified under the rubric of words 'which do not have the same meaning in modern French' (1916: 190, my translation), that is it is a loan word from standard French, but does not have the same semantic equivalence. As such, TT6 Cowan adopts precisely the same approach: the transliteration of the Berrichon term allows for a standard TL term, that is 'liveries', to be employed in a wholly different semantic context. A further sense of distance is registered into the narrative given its somewhat old-fashioned connotations, and the use of typographic markers to signal its particularity. Likewise, TT7 Brown preserves both the italics and the synonymic construction in 'the wedding presents, called the ***livrées***' (90). Here the presence of the foreign is at its most prevalent: on the one hand, the retranslation mimics the ST strategy of non-translation, thereby clearly underscoring the incongruity of the dialect; on the other, however, it could be argued that the distance inscribed is greater than that of the ST where the lexical item is at least recognizable to the reader. But TT7 Brown is not without its compensatory measures, namely the use of a note: 'The word *livrée* (livery) often also referred to the ribbon given to the bride' (117). Consequently, TT7 Brown mediates the foreignness of the Berrichon noun through explicitation and transliteration, allowing the reader an easier passage through linguistic uncertainty whilst highlighting a thought-provoking discontinuity between minor and major languages. It follows that, in keeping with the Retranslation Hypothesis, the two most recent versions, TT6 Cowan and TT7 Brown, are closest to the ST in terms of both preserving the specificity of the dialect item and attenuating the disruption to the reader.

Nevertheless, the subsequent use of italics plus synonym reveals certain inconsistencies in the approach of the (re)translations: 'un tablier d'***incarnat***, indienne rouge' [an *apron in* **incarnadine**, *a red indienne*] (MD 155) becomes 'an apron of carnation, – an Indian red' (TT4 Sedgwick 96), 'an apron of ***incarnate*** (a red print […])' (TT5 Miles 135), 'a pinafore of **pinkish** printed calico' (TT6 Cowan 100) and 'an apron of ***incarnadine***, a red calico' (TT7 Brown 90). In this case, Vincent classifies the italicized item as belonging to words 'which are only found in dictionaries of Old French' (1916: 181, my translation), and as such, otherness is reinforced through its antiquated tone. Once again, TT7 Brown creates a sense of alterity along similar lines: incarnadine is an archaism, and the version persists in its use of the typographic marker. The same holds for TT5 Miles which also incorporates the use of italics (contrary to its treatment of the *livrées* in the earlier example), and which opts for the obsolete adjective incarnate. With TT6 Cowan comes a reversal of strategy, where, rather than maintain lexical otherness, the signifier is omitted. As regards TT4 Sedgwick, its approach is consistent with its strategy for the *livrées* in that two lexical items are employed, but both are subsumed into the major language; in addition to the fact that there is a mistranslation (discussed later in reference to the material world), the heteroglossia of the ST is drowned out. In this case, the initial translation of the Appendix is admittedly deaf (rather than 'blind') to the Berrichon patois, but this shortcoming is not corrected in all subsequent (re)translations, with the result that no unbroken line can be drawn towards the alterity of TT7 Brown.

Conversely, one of Marie's wedding gifts is described as 'un beau ***devanteau*** (tablier)' [*a beautiful* **devanteau** *(pinafore)*] (MD 176), where the standard term in parenthesis decodes the vernacular term which, in Vincent's taxonomy, belongs both 'to the patois of Central France and to Old French' (1916: 136, my translation). This act of code-switching is suppressed in TT4, TT5 and TT6 where only standard TL terminology prevails in their respective depictions of 'a handsome apron' (TT4 Sedgwick 108), 'a fine apron' (TT5 Miles 152) and 'a fine pinafore' (TT6 Cowan 115). It therefore falls to the most recent version to re-establish a degree of distance from contemporary language by presenting 'a ***fine front*** (apron)' (TT7 Brown 101); beyond the obvious dialectal quality of the word, the typographic accentuation and the archaic tone reinforce its specificity, allowing linguistic dissonance to be felt. Precisely the same dynamics are to be found in the treatment of the lexical item, 'mes pauvres ***mondes*** (mes pauvres gens)' [*my poor* **mondes** *(my poor people)*] which comes under the category of words which have a different sense in the Berrichon patois (Vincent 1916: 215). The particularity disappears in three of the retranslations where the ST description is collapsed into familiar TL lexis: 'my poor people' (TT4 Sedgwick 119); 'good people' (TT5 Miles 166); 'Poor folks' (TT6 Cowan 126). In this instance, TT7 Brown forces distance into the narrative by means of an obsolete and italicized TL item in 'my poor ***worldlings*** (my poor people)', whilst also approximating the SL semantic context, that is 'monde' is transposed to 'world'. It could therefore be argued that the restorative capacity of retranslation is at play in this particular context, although a number of retranslations do appear before the recovery of ST alterity is attained.

The final example of synonymy is the ST allusion to 'le dernier charroi, appelé la ***gerbaude***' [*the last cart, called the* **gerbaude**] (MD 196), which is adorned with a decorative sheaf. The word itself is classified by Vincent as appearing 'either in the glossary of Central France or in the lexicons of Berrichon patois' (1916: 128, my translation), and as such, is one of the more inherently local terms. A range of subtly different strategies appears in the (re)translations. TT4 Sedgwick opts for 'the last load, called **"the cart of sheaves"**' (124), and TT6 Cowan for 'the last wagon (known as the **"sheaf-wagon"**)' (131). Both employ the alternative emphatic device of quotation marks, but fail to incorporate a sense of otherness, disentangling the patois item into its general component parts, and thereby flattening its specificity. On the contrary, TT7 Brown intensifies the level of alterity evinced in the ST by a process of non-translation alongside the emphasized use of a synonym: 'the ***gerbaude***, or "sheafage"' (114). Here, the TL item is not to be understood in its standard context, that is as an aggregate of sheaves, but assumes a different meaning, thereby mirroring one of Sand's own strategies. Non-translation comes to the fore again in TT5 Miles and its depiction of 'the last cart especially, the ***gerbaude*** as it is called' (173). On the one hand, the preservation of the Berrichon word underscores the gap between the linguistic and cultural contexts, but is tempered by the TL synonymic phrase. On the other hand, however, the TL reader is left with a comparatively greater sense of cultural disorientation given that their SL counterpart would have recognized the 'gerbe' root of the patois item. It follows that none of the TL versions manage to retain the original, and exacting, balance between foreignness and familiarity.

Italics and explanation

Moving on to the use of patois, which is bolstered by paraphrases or explanations, the narrator makes frequent use of the phrase *c'est-à-dire* [*that is to say*] as a means of introducing reformulations or extended definitions. Take for example the ST description of a laurel branch decorated with ribbons and placed on the fireplace, known as 'l'***exploit***, c'est-à-dire la lettre de faire part' [*the* **exploit**, *that is to say, the letter of announcement*] (MD 156). In TT4 Sedgwick this is depicted as 'the ***writ*** – that is to say, the letter of announcement' (97); in TT5 Miles, we find 'the ***exploit***, **or writ**, as it is called, the announcement of the wedding' (136); in TT6 Cowan, the reader is presented with 'the **"summons"** [which] serves as the notice announcing the wedding' (101); finally, TT7 Brown describes 'the ***exploit***, in other words the letter of invitation' (90), but adds the additional note that 'the *exploit* was also often a branch decorated with a ribbon fixed to the bed of those invited to the wedding' (117n14). On one level, it is true that all versions draw attention to the lexical item, using quotation marks in the case of TT6 Cowan and italics elsewhere. Indeed, TT5 Miles and TT7 Brown both employ non-translation, and in so doing, they mirror the ST use of *exploit* as a familiar word which assumes a different meaning, while TT4 Sedgwick, TT5 Miles and TT6 Cowan all hint at the origins of the SL word in their legal-sounding terminology (an exploit being a summons left by the bailiffs).

However, the ST instigates a subtle juxtaposition in its reformulation between the non-written and the written, that is between the non-written medium of the peasant (*exploit*) and the written medium of the reader (*lettre*). But this juxtaposition is broken down in TT4 Sedgwick and TT5 Miles, where mention of a 'writ', that is a record that appears specifically in writing, substantially undermines the latent presence of the oral and symbolic traditions of the Berry region. Thus, TT6 Cowan proves itself to be close to the ST in terms of emphasizing orality with 'summons', not to mention alluding to the judicial roots of the word; TT7 Brown also perpetuates the alterity of the lexical item, whilst providing the reader with a crutch of familiarity. A dynamic of closeness in the two most recent versions then provides further micro-level corroboration of thinking which aligns retranslation with improvement.

The wedding invitation is extended to a given guest's '***compagnie***, c'est-à-dire, tous ses enfants, tous ses parents, tous ses amis et tous ses serviteurs' [**compagnie**, *that is to say, all his children, all his relatives, all his friends and all his servants*] (MD 156). In this regard, the italics point to the atypical use of the term (it too belongs to that category of words whose meaning is not the same as in modern French), while the ensuing definition serves to clarify its semantic scope for the uninitiated. As far as the (re)translations are concerned, all mark out the specificity of the term either through italics in TT4 Sedgwick (97) and TT7 Brown (91), that is 'his ***company***', or through quotation marks in TT5 Miles (136) and TT6 Cowan (101), as 'his **"company"**', and consequently, the same relationship of unfamiliarity holds. However, there is one instance of mistranslation where TT4 Sedgwick restricts the explanation to 'all his children, all his friends, and all his servants' (97), thereby omitting the category of 'tous ses parents' [*all his relatives*] (MD 156) and essentially distorting the specific Berrichon usage of the term. Conversely, a compensatory tactic comes to the fore in TT6 Cowan, which translates 'serviteurs' [*servants*] (MD: 156) as 'retainers' (101), and in so doing, sustains the archaic qualities inherent in the ST. In light of the shortcomings of TT4 Sedgwick, the remaining versions necessarily behave in accordance with the trajectory outlined in the Retranslation Hypothesis, preserving the otherness of the region which is to be celebrated and worked through to arrive at an enlightened understanding of the country and its people.

Another ST strategy for highlighting alterity is to be found in the narrator's explanation of hemp production:

> Quand le chanvre est ***arrivé*** à point, c'est-à-dire suffisamment trempé dans les eaux courantes et à demi séché à la ***rive***, on le rapporte dans la cour. (MD 159)
>
> [*When the hemp is suitably* **arrivé/*embanked*, that is to say sufficiently soaked in the running waters and half dried on the rive/*bank***]

Here, the italicized verb is deceptive in its familiarity: a SL reader would initially interpret the action in its standardized sense of 'arrived', but the subsequent typographical emphasis on the physical location of the action, that is *la rive*, points to the specificity of the Berrichon usage whereby the peasants experience the world in such a way as to derive the process from its concrete position. Although TT7 Brown retains the italicization in 'the hemp is finally ***done***, in other words […] half dried on the ***river bank***' (92), its standardized interpretation of the Berrichon verb renders the TL link between action and location futile, and denies the reader a dialectal source of otherness. Elsewhere, no TL version retains the typographical echo between the two elements, and all opt for the common, that is non-Berrichon, sense of the verb, where the hemp has simply '**reached**' (TT4 Sedgwick; TT5 Miles 138) a certain point, or is '**ready**' (TT6 Cowan 103) or '**done**' (TT7 92). In this case, none of the TL versions truly retain the specificity of a verb which encapsulates the environmental conditions of hemp production, and the restorative potential of retranslation is notable here only by its absence.

Similarly, Berman argues that 'vernacular language is by its very nature more physical, more iconic than "cultivated" language. The Picard "bibloteux" is more expressive than the French "livresque" (bookish). The Old French "sorcellage" is richer than "sorcellerie" (sorcery)' (2000: 294). Such expressiveness is evident in the ST portrayal of 'le ***treizan***, c'est-à-dire treize pièces d'argent' [*the* **treizan**, *that is to say thirteen pieces of silver*] (MD 116), given to the bride by the groom on their wedding day, but there is a substantial flattening of the lexis in TT6 Cowan where only the explanation remains, that is 'thirteen pieces of silver' (122), while TT4 Sedgwick relies on metonymy and punctuation, merely repeating the quantity in its depiction of 'the **"thirteen"** – that is to say, thirteen pieces of silver' (116). Nevertheless, two versions preserve the iconic foreignness of the item, plus its explanation, as 'the ***trezain***, or the thirteen coins' (TT5 Miles 162) and 'the ***treizan***, in other words thirteen coins' (TT7 Brown 107), although it is not clear whether the spelling in TT5 is a result of a typographical error or an attempt at transliteration. But, as was the case with *gerbaude*, the familiarizing link with the lexical item's standard SL root, that is *treize*, is absent, and the resonance between the patois and the explanation is diminished. So, although TT5 Miles and TT7 Brown may be more expressive in their alterity, the TL reader is cut off from the anchoring point present in the original. As the risk of both non-mediation and over-standardization is the lack of comprehension, none of the (re)translations have fully returned to the carefully selected third code of the original.

Freestanding italics

The Appendix further comprises italicized patois items which are unsupported by synonyms or by paraphrases, but these items tend to appear in instances where the meaning is immediately recoverable from the context, or where the deviation from the standard French equivalent is so low as to not impede comprehension. This latter category is evident in the narrator's report of the wedding invitation '***à la divertissance, à la dansière***' (MD 156), items which Vincent places under the classification of 'words which are in the glossary of

Central France, or in the lexicons of Berrichon patois' and which stand for 'divertissement, plaisir' [*entertainment, pleasure*] and 'bal, danse' [*ball, dance*] (1916: 123–4, my translation), respectively. However, the slight orthographical transpositions of the ST do not transpire in the (re)translations: TT4 Sedgwick formulates '***sports***' and '***dance***' (97) which rely on typography alone to intimate otherness; TT5 Miles alludes to '**merry-making**' and '**dancing**' (136), with no linguistic or paralinguistic markers of alterity; in the same way, TT6 Cowan refers simply to '**the entertainments and the dances**' (101). But there is some degree of compensation in TT7 Brown, where the juxtaposition between the modern '***party-night***' and the antiquated '***dancery***' (91) is suggestive of the ST modulation, while the italics also highlight the specificity of the lexical items. The evidential trail in this example can therefore be mapped on to a trajectory of improvement if the start and end points are isolated, although it is important to bear in mind that the diminished alterity of the initial translation does persist over the interim retranslations.

Additionally, Sand incorporates the Berrichon (or Old French) word '***pastoures***' (MD 158), a variant of 'bergère' [*shepherdess*], which is translated in the TL versions as '**shepherdesses**' (TT4 Sedgwick 98; TT6 Cowan 102), '**shepherd lasses**' (TT5 Miles 137) and '***shepherdlasses***' (TT7 Cowan 117). Thus, there is no typological or linguistic markedness inherent in TT4 Sedgwick and TT6 Cowan. However, the introduction of the noun '**lass**' in TT5 Miles adopts a decidedly dialectal tone, enough to make the distance between the rural and the town felt. Its foreignizing impact is taken even further in TT7 Brown, where the italicization again reinforces the particularity of the lexeme. The treatment of this lexical item thus alternates between the negation and the restoration of otherness, and the ensuing discontinuity of the closeness initiated in TT5 Miles breaks with the linear vector of the Retranslation Hypothesis.

The ST narrator also focuses on 'une petite provision de chanvre en ***poupées***' [*a small provision of hemp in* ***dolls***] (MD 178), where the italicized patois word alludes to the particular shape into which the hemp is worked. This form is decomposed in TT4 Sedgwick and TT6 Cowan, where the distinctive form shape is blurred into the more general configuration of '**sheaves**' (111) in the former and '**bunches**' (117) in the latter. But it is re-sculpted in TT5 Miles as '**"dolls"**' (154) and in TT7 Brown as '**dolls**' (102), the difference being that the former emphasizes the specific provenance of the word through quotation marks, while the latter, in contrast to previous approaches, does not opt for the use of italics. The alternating pattern thus mirrors the dynamics of the above example, where the progressive moves between the commonplace and the unfamiliar detract from the credibility of the Retranslation Hypothesis.

Speech

The final way in which the Berrichon peasant is given a voice in the ST is through the use of reported speech. The frequency of patois words used by the peasants is extremely low in comparison to those used by the narrator, a trait which is most likely due to a reticence on the part of the author to interrupt the flow of direct speech with the synonyms and explanations necessary for the Parisian readership as these interruptions would undermine the oral texture of the narrative. Instead, the reported speech of the Appendix is marked by the use of antiquated and idiomatic expressions which underscore the distance between the speaker and the reader, but also enhance the entertaining facet of the narrative.

The 'cérémonie des livrées' [*ceremony of the livrées*] in the second chapter of the Appendix comprises a verbal standoff between the hemp beater and the gravedigger, and the otherness of their badinage is first intonated through the inclusion of expressions such as '**oui-da!**' (MD 167), an archaic exclamation, which ordinarily would signal the agreement of the speaker, but which here sarcastically rejects the gravedigger's requests that the groom's party be allowed to enter the house of the bride. Furthermore, this expression is marked in terms of sociolect. As Riffaterre observes, language must be regarded 'not just as a lexicon and grammar, but as a repository of the myths and stereotypes with which a society organizes and allegorizes a consensus of its members about what they imagine reality to be' (1990: 930). In this case, the reality of the Berrichon members is refracted through the narrator, but the expressions he uses to tell the public story inscribes the peasants as distinctively belonging to the lower echelons of society. The mocking tone carries across in TT5 Miles as '**Oho!**' (145), in TT6 Cowan as '**Very likely!**' (109) and in TT7 Brown as '**Oh yes**' (96), but the TT4 Sedgwick interjection of '**I rather think not**' (103) is stilted, introducing an air of formality into an otherwise jocular communicative situation. Nevertheless, none of the (re)translations mirror the significance of the word choice as a marker of social status, with sociolect proving to be another obstacle in the supposed restorative path of retranslation.

Closely related to the earlier example is the interjection of '**Oh! que nenni! pas si sot**' [along the lines of: ***Oh! Nay! Have some wit***] (MD 169), which not only lends a dated timbre to the hemp beater's speech, but also reinforces the working class roots of the region. In this instance, TT4 Sedgwick further diminishes the droll eloquence of the hemp beater in the awkward construction '**Oh, no, not quite so foolish**' (104), and fails to incorporate the sociolectal impact of the ST. As was the case in the first example of 'oui-da', the remaining versions do restore the fluency and colloquialism of the hemp beater's articulation: TT5 Miles asserts '**Oh! Not at all, not at all!**' (146), TT6 Cowan claims '**Oh no no! We're not such fools!**' (111) and TT7 Brown interjects '**No, you don't! We are not so stupid**' (97). But again, none of these versions retain the archaic tone of the ST exclamation, nor do they reflect the social implications, and therefore drown out a crucial note of alterity.

The dialectal properties of peasant speech are further conveyed through grammar. This is illustrated in the 'chant des livrées' [*song of the livrées*] with the refrain, '**J'ons** *de beaux cadeaux à vous présenter*' [**I has** *beautiful presents to present to you*] (MD 175); here, typographical emphasis (in an otherwise italicized song) highlights specificity in the shape of the regional conjugation of 'avoir' [*to have*]. The disruptive impact of its presence in the ST is imitated in TT7 Brown, where the line '**I done got** fine presents for you with me here' (100) attempts to approximate regional dialect by unsettling the standard rules of grammar usage. Elsewhere, however, the specificity of the ST is flattened by the conforming tendencies of the (re)translations: '***I have*** *presents for you*' (TT4 Sedgwick 108); '*And show the gifts* ***we bear***!' (TT5 Miles 151); '*Here* ***we've*** *fine presents to give to you*' (TT6 Cowan 115). However, TT5 Miles does demonstrate a degree of compensation by incorporating obsolete language in the italicized verses '*My mother weeps, my father is* ***wroth***,/*And I am a maid who keeps good* ***troth***' (152), thereby retaining a sense of strangeness in the TL. Indeed, more compensatory tactics come to light in TT5 Miles in other instances of reported speech, namely syntactical inversion in the gravedigger's comment that 'at Sainte-Solange we've been for sure' (145), and grammatical manipulation in the hemp beater's question, 'Think you there is room **and** to spare in our house?' (147). Therefore, both TT5 Miles and TT7 Brown make concerted efforts to ensure that the atypical speech patterns of the Berrichon peasant are represented in the TL. This behaviour also reinforces the impression gained from the earlier examples that it is in fact TT5 Miles and TT7 Brown which best preserve the particular orality of the region, thereby confounding further still the notion that retranslation represents a sustained, even movement towards betterment.

The colloquial tone of the peasants' speech is also bolstered by the inclusion of idiomatic expressions, as illustrated by the hemp beater's taunt: 'Allez plus loin chanter vos sornettes' [*Go away to sing your bagatelles*] (MD 168). In this instance, all TL versions retain the vernacular inflection of the expression in 'Go away with your nonsense' (TT4 Sedgwick 104), 'Go somewhere else to spin your yarns' (TT5 Miles 146), 'Go off and tell your silly stories somewhere else' (TT6 Cowan 110) and 'Go and sing your silly songs elsewhere' (TT7 Brown 97). But two significant issues arise from these TL choices. First, the ST expression underpins the oral tradition of the region, and while TT5 Miles, TT6 Cowan and TT7 Brown all allude to the verbal categories of 'yarns', 'stories' and 'songs', TT4 Sedgwick conceals this important characteristic in its more ambiguous allusion to nonsense. Secondly, TT5 displays yet more compensatory strategies since the idiom '**spin your yarns**' reinforces both the prevalence of voice in the Berry and a local industry, that is hemp production and spinning. Similarly, TT5 Miles translates the question 'Quelle bêtise nous contez-vous?' [*What nonsense are you telling us?*] (MD 168) as 'What **cock-and-bull** tale is this?' (147), where the rural imagery is once more in harmony with the verbal context. In accordance with Berman's definition of initial translations as faltering, TT4 Sedgwick does indeed prove to defer the oral texture of the original. Nevertheless, it is the immediate successor, TT5 Miles, which is most attentive here to both the oral and physical landscape of the region, meaning that the repeated translation efforts of TT6 Cowan and TT7 Brown do not result in more accomplished renderings of the original.

Summary

A cursory glance at the examples discussed above might suggest that the logic of the Retranslation Hypothesis is at play as far as Sand's hybrid use of language is concerned. For it is TT4 Sedgwick, the initial translation of the Appendix, which is least sensitive to the cultural otherness of the ST, flattening the dialectal items and drowning out both idiomatic and antiquated tones. It is also TT7 Brown which demonstrates a relatively persistent tendency to underscore the alterity of the patois and to reinforce the orality of the ST. Consequently the most recent version mirrors the selective appropriation of the ST narrative and its subsequent underscoring of the richness of regional language, while at the same time preserving the sense of difference necessary for the engagement and understanding of the reader.

But beyond, or between, these two points, this path from faltering initial translation to restorative retranslation is not without its aberrations. The first retranslation, TT5 Miles, also shows itself to be as attuned to the alterity of Berrichon patois as TT7 Brown, if not more so given its frequent recourse to compensatory tactics. In contrast, TT6 Cowan wavers in its progress, at points preserving, and at others negating, the linguistic identity of the peasant. Consequently, there is no teleological progression towards closeness; rather, the divergence of the initial version and the proximity of the most recent frame a more fragmented, inconsistent trajectory.

Sounds of the Berry

It is not just the selected lexical items which signal alterity; the Appendix is also replete with the auditory qualities of the region, not least the vocal qualities of the peasants. Didier recognizes the powerful 'presence of voice in the text' (1998: 694, my translation) in terms of the emphasis on storytelling and the inclusion of songs, but the qualification of how the stories are told or the songs sung further discloses part of the oral identity of the region to the reader. The narrator of the Appendix outlines the inextricable links which exist between the country dwellers and their tonality, as well as the particular noises which pervade the Berrichon landscape. He does so by using the framing technique of labelling, which entails 'using a lexical item, term or phrase to identify a person, place, group, event or any other key element in a narrative' (Baker 2006: 122). The following comparative analysis will focus on those labelling devices which identify the idiosyncratic soundscape of the Berry in order to determine the extent to which it resounds or is dampened in the TL versions.

To begin with the sonant qualities of the peasants' speaking and singing voices, the ST Appendix abounds with epithets that give the reader access to the specific tones and pitches which are to be heard across the region, not least during the 'cérémonie des livrées' [*ceremony of the livrées*]. There are many instances where all the (re)translations record the audible features of Berrichon voice with precision: take for example the description that 'les matrones chantaient d'une **voix perçante**' [*the matrons sing in a* ***piercing voice***] (MD 171), which reverberates in the TL versions as 'the matrons sang in **piercing voices**' (TT4 Sedgwick 105), 'in **shrill tones**' (TT5 Miles 148), 'in their **shrill voices**' (TT6 Cowan 112) and 'in **piercing tones**' (TT7 Brown 98). Similarly, the hemp beater sings 'd'une voix un peu **enrouée mais terrible**' [*in a voice that is a little* ***hoarse but terrific***] (MD 173), and these vocal characteristics are echoed as 'slightly **hoarse but terrible**' (TT4 Sedgwick 107), 'a little **hoarse,**

but tremendous' (TT5 Miles 150), '**husky but dreadful**' (TT6 Cowan 113) and '**hoarse but still awe-inspiring**' (TT7 Brown 99) in all the (re)translations. It follows that this is an isolated example of accuracy across all TL translation attempts, including the initial translation, a trait which in turn confounds the assumed need for improvement over time.

However, another act of vocal labelling occurs in the ST when the narrator observes that 'on entendait la voix **rude et enrhumée** du vieux chanvreur beugler les derniers vers' [*one would hear the voice of the old hemp beater,* ***hoarse and husky,*** *bellow the last verses*] (MD 174). The two ST epithets which allow the reader to sense the sound of the hemp beater's voice linger on in TT4 Sedgwick as 'the **hoarse croaking**' (107), in TT5 Miles as 'the **hoarse rough** voice' (151) and in TT7 Brown as 'the **rough pinched** voice' (100). But, the omission of an epithet in TT6 Cowan, which simply expresses 'the old hackler's **hoarse** voice' (114), modifies the tone and denies the reader an additional aural label, thereby reframing the voice in a more restrictive manner.

Similarly, the ST presents the reader with an auditory experience of 'les bonnes commères' [*the good womenfolk*] who '**nasillaient**, d'une voix **aigre** comme celle de la mouette, le refrain victorieux' [***sing through their noses,*** *in a* ***shrill*** *voice like that of the gull, the victorious refrain*] (MD 175). Once more, the ST verbal choice labels both the action and its attributes, while the ornithological comparison underscores the natural affinity between the peasants and their rural environment. Both these facets are retained in TT4 Sedgwick as 'the good gossips chanted the victorious refrain **through their noses** with voices **shrill** as a sea-mew's' (108) (although the labelling of the women is perhaps somewhat unjust); in TT5 Miles as 'the worthy dames, in a **nasal tone** as **sharp** as a gull's, would sing out the victorious refrain' (151); and in TT7 Brown as 'the good women struck up, in their **nasal** voices, **mewing** like sea-gulls, the victorious refrain' (100). As was the case earlier, TT6 Cowan stifles one of the vocal qualities in its description that 'the goodwives would raise their **shrill** sea-mews' voices and intone the triumphant refrain' (114); in specific, the shift from 'nasiller' to 'intone' leaves the TL reader with the sense that the action is carried out in a particular tone, but is not made privy to its nasal articulation. These two examples illustrate the inability of the Retranslation Hypothesis to encompass all nuances of translation behaviour; rather than an incomplete initial translation, it is now a later retranslation which marks a significant decline in auditory specificity.

An innate nexus is also established by the narrator between the rhythmic qualities of a Berrichon wedding march and the geographical lie of the land:

> une marche de circonstance, sur un rythme un peu lent pour des pieds qui ne seraient pas indigènes, mais **parfaitement combiné** avec la nature du terrain gras et des chemins ondulés de la contrée' (MD 157)
>
> [*a march suited to the occasion, in a rhythm a little slow for any feet who may not be indigenous, but* ***in perfect harmony*** *with the nature of the soft ground and the winding paths of the countryside*]

Both TT5 Miles and TT7 Brown play on the musicality of the ST; the former observes that the rhythm '**accords perfectly**' (137), the latter that it is '**perfectly in harmony**' (91) with the land, while TT6 Cowan retains the connection between the two elements which are '**perfectly suited**' (102), albeit with a diminished use of musical terminology. In TT4 Sedgwick, however, the relationship is somewhat altered in that the rhythm is simply '**admirably adapted**' (98) to the terrain; this lexical choice fails to convey the absolute synchronism of the ST labelling, and therefore weakens the indissoluble link between the cadence of the march and the Berrichon landscape. This unhearing initial translation and subsequent span of restorative retranslations thus conform to the anticipated path of the Retranslation Hypothesis.

Finally, the ST Appendix records many of the noises which are to be heard in the Berry countryside at specific times of the year and in specific circumstances. However, not all of these sounds survive the transition from the Berry to the various TL versions. Certainly, the ST observation that autumn is 'le temps des bruits **insolites et mystérieux** dans la campagne' [*the time of* ***strange and mysterious*** *sounds in the countryside*] (MD 160) is maintained in all versions as '**unwonted and mysterious** sounds' (TT4 Sedgwick 99), '**unwonted and mysterious** noises' (TT5 Miles 139), '**strange and unfamiliar** sounds' (TT6 Cowan 104) and '**unusual and mysterious** noises' (TT7 Brown 93). But the same cannot be said of the more specific stirrings of 'mille **crépitations inusitées**' [*a thousand* ***unusual cracklings***] (MD 161) amongst the trees. Here, the majority of the retranslations all preserve the sonorous qualities of the ST expression with '**unaccustomed**', '**unwonted**' and '**unusual cracklings**', respectively (TT4 Sedgwick 100; TT5 Miles 141; TT7 Brown 93), where the onomatopoeia of the TL noun choice further enhances the aural dimension of the narrative. Conversely, TT6 Cowan draws the reader's attention towards 'a myriad **strange patternings**' (105), and in so doing, makes a transition from the aural to the visual which frustrates the ST creation of Berrichon identity through sound. As has previously been the case, TT6 Cowan both disallows the reader access to the aurality of the region and frustrates any attempt to regard retranslation as consistently restorative.

Given the local industry of hemp production, the region is also characterized by the auditory presence of the hemp beaters:

> on entend la nuit, dans les campagnes, ce bruit **sec et saccadé** de trois coups frappés rapidement (MD 159)
>
> [*one hears at night, in the countryside, this* ***sharp and fitful*** *noise of three rapidly hit blows*]

The alliterative adjectives of the ST announce the distinct and irregular sounds of the machine, and are conveyed in TT4 Sedgwick as 'that **sudden, sharp** noise of three blows in quick succession' (99) and in TT5 Miles as 'the sound of three **short sharp** blows, rapidly struck' (139). Although the sibilance of the ST is preserved, if not intensified, the two TL versions only retain the semantic scope of the first ST adjective, *sec*, which can mean both sharp and swift, thereby quietening the fragmented rhythmic qualities of the distinctive Berrichon sound. An even greater degree of dissimulation comes to the fore in TT6 Cowan where 'the noise of three **quick sharp** taps' (104) drowns out the [s] alliteration and the staccato breaks in the rhythmic movement of the machine. While the monosyllabic pace of the phrase in conjunction with the onomatopoeia of 'tap' goes some way to restoring the auditory facet of the narrative, this latter lexical choice nevertheless reduces the intensity of the ST sound. But both the tone and the rhythm of the hemp beater resonates in TT7 Brown with 'that **dry, staccato sound** of three **blows** being **rapidly struck**' (92), and being the only TL version to fully portray the aural dimensions of the ST, this example can be used in support of the notion that time will engender improvement. However, the muting of sound evinced in TT6 Cowan also means that, compared to this low point, the earlier (re)translations proved more alert to the sonorous choices of the author.

Summary

From this survey of the sounds of the Berry in (re)translation, TT6 Cowan stands out as a comparatively disparate version, muffling many of the typical Berrichon qualities. Conversely, it is the most recent version which consistently preserves the regional soundscape. Two conclusions are to be drawn from this overview: first, that it is the selective appropriation of the peasants' vocal tones and pitches which undergo the greatest degree of preservation, while the characteristic noise of hemp beating is rather diminished. In this sense, the oral tradition and its aesthetic merit are emphasized, but the sounds of the industrial tradition and its work ethic are down played. Secondly, that the Retranslation Hypothesis is but partially supported in this particular rubric of sound; despite the most recent version echoing the acoustic identity of the Berry more precisely than any of the preceding versions, these same do not vouch for a continual march towards closeness.

The material world

Cultural otherness is also discernible in the material objects which lend a more concrete identity to the Berry region. As Didier remarks, 'The presence of reality is also the presence of objects and clothes' (1998: 695, my translation), and it is certainly the case that the world of the Appendix is permeated with physical descriptions of traditional wedding attire, local produce and items that are essential to the observation of rituals. Indeed, much of the realism of the Appendix can be attributed to Sand's descriptions of those material objects which are particular or significant to the Berry region. However, it is also important to note, as Lane does, that 'the pastoral novel does not open out on to reality, but rather […] on to a utopia' (1988: 83, my translation), which privileges the world as it should be, as opposed to how it actually is. Thus, Sand's selective appropriation and labelling of specific physical items serves as a means of symbolizing cultural identity, and therefore, of instigating causal emplotment by presenting the reader with a window onto the Other which should encourage respect and bridge the distance between the urban and the bucolic. The benchmark for comparison in the following analysis will be the extent to which these totems of cultural identity survive when the narrative is replanted abroad, and subsequently, the extent to which the TL reader is given access to these carefully chosen emblems.

One of the most evident and concrete ways in which the ST establishes specificity is through the narrator's descriptions of the traditional Berrichon dress. In this instance, the oft-cited metaphor of translation as clothing can be taken in its literal sense, with the (re)translations dressing the ST characters with different degrees of precision. One detailed description of Marie appears in the first chapter of the Appendix, where she

> était vêtue de ce qu'elle avait de mieux dans **ses hardes modestes**: une robe de gros drap sombre, un fichu blanc à **grands ramages de couleurs voyantes**, un tablier d'incarnat, indienne rouge fort à la mode alors et dédaignée aujourd'hui,

une coiffe de mousseline très blanche, et dans cette forme heureusement conservée, qui rappelle la coiffure d'Anne Boleyn et d'Agnès Sorel. (MD 155)

[*was dressed in the best of her* ***modest old clothes***: a dress in ***thick, dark woollen material***, *a white scarf with* ***large foliage patterns in bright colours***, *an apron in* incarnadine, *a red indienne very much in fashion at the time but spurned today, a very white chiffon headscarf, and in this happily preserved form which brings to mind the headdresses of Anne Boleyn and Agnès Sorel*]

This catalogue of traditional dress undergoes some modification in the TL versions, and even the most general of terms, that is 'ses hardes modestes' [*her modest old clothes*] is open to alteration. On one hand, three versions conserve the ST portrayal of '**her simple clothes**' (TT4 Sedgwick 96), '**her own modest finery**' (TT5 Miles 135) and '**her own humble clothes**' (TT6 Sedgwick 100). On the other, the TT7 Brown representation of '**her modest and ragged wardrobe**' (90) incorporates both the standard and pejorative meanings of the SL epithet *modeste*, with the result that the raggedness of Marie's dress overemphasizes the poverty of the peasant. As Godwin-Jones emphasizes, 'Again and again in her rural novels Sand sets forth the beauty and poetry of rural existence. There is scarcely a hint of a possible darker side to the picture' (1979: 56); so, by underscoring the deprivation of the peasant, TT7 Brown turns more in the direction of realism, and away from Sand's utopian ideal of life in the country. As a result of this oppositional move, it is possible to determine a reversal of the Retranslation Hypothesis.

All the TL versions convey the fabric of Marie's dress – '**dark, heavy cloth**' (TT4 Sedgwick 96); '**dark heavy stuff**' (TT5 Miles 135); '**thick dark dress**' (TT6 Cowan 100); '**dark, coarse cloth**' (TT7 Brown 90) – as well as her donning of a white 'fichu', 'scarf', 'neckerchief' and 'shawl', respectively. However, this second item is decorated 'à grands ramages de couleurs voyantes' [*with large foliage patterns in bright colours*] (MD 155), a pattern which reinforces the link between the rural setting and its traditional dress; the natural motifs are repeated in the majority of the (re)translations as a '**flower pattern**' (TT5 Miles 135), a '**floral pattern**' (TT6 Cowan 100) and a '**foliage patterns**' (TT7 Brown 90), but disappear from view in TT4 Sedgwick where the embellishment survives only as '**great spots**' (96). Similarly, this initial version of the Appendix mistranslates the nominal group 'indienne', that is a type of fabric, as an adjective in 'Indian red' (1979: 56) and thereby distorts both the colour and the stuff of Marie's attire. Thus, the later retranslations are closer to the natural hues of the ST, thereby lending empirical support in this instance to the progressive dynamics of retranslation.

This relationship between nature and dress becomes apparent once more in the ST depiction of the wedding attire of other characters. According to Vincent, 'comparisons drawn from nature, animals or plants abound in the Berry region. G. Sand used a certain number of them' (1916: 74, my translation), and this is certainly evidenced in the epithet applied to Petit-Pierre's 'habit complet de drap **bleu barbeau**' [*full suit in **cornflower blue** material*] (MD 182–3). But this suit 'of **cornflower blue**' (TT6 Cowan 120; TT7 Brown 105) only appears in these two versions, since TT4 Sedgwick (114) and TT5 Miles (158) exchange the botanical reference for the more general adjectival construction of '**light blue**' and thus weaken the inherent connection with nature. It follows that the oversight of the initial translation and first retranslation is corrected in the two subsequent versions, thereby lending further credence to the restorative properties of the phenomenon.

Likewise, Marie's wedding dress itself is made 'de drap fin **vert myrte**' [*a fine **myrtle green** woollen cloth*], which is accompanied by 'un tablier de soie **violet pensée**' [*a pinafore in **pansy purple** silk*] (MD 185), a colourful ensemble which further represents the Berrichon way of viewing the world through the filter of nature. In this instance, all the (re)translations preserve the first instantiation of organic colour as Marie is dressed in a 'cloth gown of **myrtle-green**' (TT4 Sedgwick 116), 'her gown of fine **myrtle-green** stuff' (TT5 Miles 161), 'her fine cloth gown of **myrtle green**' (TT6 Cowan 122) and 'her negligee of fine cloth in **myrtle green**' (TT7 Brown 107). And yet the second allusion to the floral tone of her apron disappears in TT4 Sedgwick (116), TT5 Miles (161) and TT6 Cowan (122), where the latter has recourse to the generalized epithet of '**deep violet** silk', while the earlier versions restrict the description to '**violet** silk'. Therefore, in accordance once more with the idea that repetition leads to accomplishment, it is the most recent version, TT7 Brown, which restores the natural metaphor in its portrayal of 'a silk apron as **purple as a pansy**' (107).

Even the very texture of the Berry soil comes under the descriptive pen of the author who singularizes 'la nature du **terrain gras** […] de la contrée' [*the nature of the soft ground […] of the countryside*] (MD 157). Once uprooted into TT5 Miles, however, the identifying characteristics of the Berrichon earth are submerged in the antonymic depiction of 'the comfortable landscape' (137) which undermines the previously discussed relationship between the earth and the slow rhythm of the march. Also, TT7 Brown focuses on the positive image of '**fertile terrain**' (91), thereby attenuating the significance of the ST emphasis on viscosity. In this case, it is the initial translation, TT4 Sedgwick, which best conveys the qualities of the ST exposition of 'the **heavy ground**' (98), that is ground which 'clings or hangs heavily to the spade, feet, wheels, etc.' (OED), while the increased degree of specificity in the TT6 Cowan description of 'the **heavy clay soil**' (102) further reinforces the bond between land and feet. The versions which then retain this selected attribute of the region are not those anticipated by the Retranslation Hypothesis, and its unbroken line of progress is here severed by the behaviour of the first and most recent retranslations.

Closely associated to the Berrichon land is the production of hemp, and Sand ensures that its characteristic ubiquity is conveyed in the Appendix where the reader is exposed not only to the manufacturing process, but also to its presence in peasant homes and rituals. One significant modification occurs in TT5 Miles, where 'une petite provision de **chanvre**' [*a small provision of* ***hemp***] (MD 178) turns into 'a small store of **flax**' (154). Whereas all other versions retain the particularity of the ST fibre, TT5 Miles presents the TL reader with a plant that, arguably, is more familiar in light of the tradition of flax production in Britain. Ultimately, this act of appropriation dissembles the traditional Berrichon industry, masking a facet of its identity and disrupting the coherence of the narrative with inconsistent reference. TT5 Miles therefore introduces an irregularity in the otherwise consistently accurate depictions of the initial translation and remaining retranslations.

The rural setting of the ST is also underscored by descriptions of game, such as 'une **oie plumée**, **passée dans** une forte broche de fer' [*a* ***plucked goose, skewered*** *on a strong iron spit*] (MD 169) which will symbolically be placed on the bride's hearth during the ceremony of the *livrées*. In another example of misrepresentation, TT5 Miles portrays 'a **feathered goose**, **slipped into** a strong iron band' (147), where the adjectival labelling gives the bird its feathers back, while the prepositional phrase fails to precisely covey its pierced state. All remaining versions, however, depict the goose as '**plucked**' and '**spitted**' (TT4 Sedgwick 104), '**on a strong iron spit**' (TT6 Cowan 111), or as '**skewered**' (TT7 Brown 97), thereby preserving the ST traits of this marker of Berrichon cultural identity. Once again, the general proximity exhibited in the majority of (re)translations is undone in TT5 Miles, making the line that extends from the initial version remarkable not as a consequence of its steady upward rise, but as a result of this deviating milestone.

Summary

It is clear from the above that TT5 Miles repeatedly modifies the material objects selected by Sand, while, contrary to previous patterns, TT6 Cowan appears to sustain a high level of proximity to the original markers of Berrichon cultural identity. The natural palette of the wedding attire perhaps undergoes the greatest concentration of material modifications, which then skews the way in which the peasants relate the manmade to the natural and restricts the window of the reader on to the customs and celebrated alterity of the region. Overall, no clear and repeated evidence emerges in support of the restorative traits of retranslation; the initial translation may have altered the fabric of the source text in the literal sense, but the accumulation of undiscerning translation shifts and mistranslations in its successor, TT5 Miles, have a more significant impact on the idealized fabric of the original. The teleology of improvement over time is also curbed by the fact that the most recent retranslation is surpassed in accuracy by TT6 Cowan.

Conclusion

By undertaking a comparative study of the way in which Berrichon cultural identity is framed in the ST and in the four (re)translations through relationality, temporality and selective appropriation, alongside the latent feature of causal emplotment, it has been possible to identify a rather unsystematic array of translation behaviour across the corpus and within individual TTs.

On the first level of temporality, the absence of the Appendix in TT1 Anon, TT2 Anon and TT3 Shaw equates to the fundamental absence of narrative itself. Not only does this deprive the TL reading public of the entertaining tales told by the narrator, but it also conceals the underlying ethnographic, idealistic and instructive aims of the author. For much of the narrative meaning of the Appendix is derived from its positioning after the main tale; the wedding ceremony provides a coherent resolution to the love story between the two protagonists, which in turn allows the author to record the ways of the region and simultaneously to stress the culturally and morally edifying qualities of the peasants. The restoration of the Appendix and its causal emplotment in three following retranslations can thus be read as a sign of the corrective attributes which Berman distinguishes in retranslation. Nevertheless, the subsequent hybridity of TT4 Sedgwick, as both initial translation of the Appendix and retranslation of the main tale, confounds the definitional parameters of retranslation. Whereas previous thinking appears to rest on the assumption that one integral translation will be succeeded by one integral retranslation, and so forth, the fractional profile of this particular (re)translation signals a schism in linear rationalities of retranslation.

Secondly, the feature of relationality allowed for an investigation of how the narrator mediates his position of dual belonging through social and spatial deixis, while temporal markers delineate the natural tempo of the Berry region and underscore the latent threat of time to its age-old customs. In this case, the Retranslation Hypothesis undergoes something of a turnaround, with the two most recent retranslations evincing behaviour which distances them from the dynamics of the original. Specifically, both TT6 Cowan and TT7 Brown alter social deixis in such a way as to disrupt the relationship between the narrator and the reader, thereby hindering the necessary process of mediation. TT7 Brown also attenuates the use of the demonstrative, removing the reader further from the narrative world and undermining the potential for engagement, and then underplays the vulnerability of the Berrichon traditions when confronted with industrial progress, which fails to alert the reader to the ethnographic significance of the work. Nonetheless, all TL versions were challenged by the collectiveness of the SL indefinite pronoun; grammatical asymmetry meant that a certain divergence was imposed away from the portrayal of Berrichon commonality, with the result that the window on to the specificities of the rural setting is restricted.

Finally, Sand champions particular facets of Berrichon life through the process of selective appropriation, on the basis of which the narrative is instilled with an ennobling, fraternizing message of respect and understanding. In this sense, the regional dialect certainly comes under the spotlight, not so much as a concerted study in lexicology, but rather as the creation of a linguistic space into which cultural otherness can be projected and felt without overly disconcerting the reader. Likewise, the sounds and the concrete objects of the region are brought to the fore as vehicles of both entertainment and enlightenment. The unique personality of the Berrichon peasants and their surroundings are captured in the ST portrayal of voice and rural noises, of dress, flora and fauna; and all with a view to underscoring a cultural alterity which will charm and challenge the reader. It is under the category of patois that the Retranslation Hypothesis is tentatively corroborated: TT4 Sedgwick and TT7 Brown represent the furthest point away from and the closest point to the ST, respectively. However, as is frequently the case, the line from initial to most recent version shows no signs of straightforward, incremental progression. This fluctuation is evidenced again in the comparative analysis of sound; while TT7 Brown records a very accurate soundscape, its immediate precedent, TT6 Cowan, produces a high level of distortion and suppression. Conversely, the material world of TT6 Cowan reveals a careful reproduction of artefacts, suggesting that it sees better than it hears, while it is now TT5 Miles which most dissimulates the physical identity of the region. Overall, the wavering behaviour of the (re)translations creates peaks and nadirs in Sand's idealistic conception of the peasants and in the opportunity afforded to the TL reader to recognize the cultural merits of the Other. Such modulation fundamentally troubles the ordered, undeviating teleology of the Retranslation Hypothesis which is ineffectual in accounting for the sheer diversity of (re)translation practice over time.

It is also worth noting here that the examples discussed in this chapter attest to a reasonably consistent pattern of dissimilarity across the choices made by the individual (re)translators. In other words, there is little evidence that one (re)translation has informed another. However, it is unclear whether this is a consequence of a deliberate eschewal on the part of the (re)translator of versions that have come before, so as to avoid undue influence, or of a calculated attempt to consult those versions, proceeding then from a logic of differentiation. Or, in more practical terms, this difference may simply indicate that the (re)translators did not have access to the work of their precursors. In any respect, these possibilities show that the textual lines of influence that might hold between (re)translations are varied, if not wholly speculative; all of which suggests that retranslation may veer off its predicted course at any moment.

7

Conclusion: Retranslation, Doxa and Genetic Criticism

A synthesis of findings

This book has been concerned with uncovering the range of interpretative, mediative and interactive processes which have shaped the contours of the (re) translations of Flaubert's *Madame Bovary* and Sand's *La mare au diable*, and with bringing those contours into relief against existing thinking on the phenomenon of retranslation itself. The emergent landscape is a complex one, with each shift of perspective revealing a different configuration of contextual and discursive elements, some of which fit with rationales of progress and challenge, but many of which do not.

When confronted with the intricate knot of translation choices – considered, perfunctory, circumspect, constrained, idiosyncratic, changeable, innovative, hasty, ill-advised and so on – which are constitutive of a given translation and which are compounded over time in retranslation, it is scarcely surprising that Berman's abstracted, essentialist paradigm should be found wanting. The consistent inconsistency, or polymorphous behaviour, evinced in both the comparative textual analyses strongly suggests that the process of retranslation cannot readily be channelled into an unequivocal course which starts blindly and hesitantly at a low point of incompletion, far removed from the source text, and moves steadily upwards towards a pinnacle of achievement and restoration. Although retranslations are more or less temporally sequential, their interpretative motions are not, and the moments at which this straightforward design comes into view in the case studies are few and far between. Instead, the (re)translations appear to be best characterized by ebbs and flows of accomplishment, across individual narrative features and across time. Similarly, the extent to which retranslations show signs of differentiation from their predecessors fluctuates, with more notable parallels emerging from the *Madame Bovary* corpus than from the more variable *La Mare au diable* one. Indeed, the potential hybridity of a given (re)translation further complicates the lay of the land, making it difficult to discern the originary locus of translation against which improvement can be measured. Of course, the present study is unavoidably partial, restricted as it is in scope and by the subjective evaluations of the researcher. It may well be the case that alternative points of comparison in alternative sections of the texts would have yielded different results, as might similar investigations into retranslation corpora in other languages and genres. But the prevalent variability demonstrated in this particular corpus is compelling, and if any retranslation pattern is to be hypothesized, it is an intricate and intractable one.

How then have teleological narratives come to be so codified in respect of retranslation? One reason might be sought in Bourdieu's concept of *doxa*, the term he uses to denote commonly held beliefs which are 'taken for granted' and perceived as 'self-evident and undisputed' (1977: 166). It would seem as though the history-as-progress model of (re)translation, as proposed by Goethe and re-emphasized by Berman, has become one such doxa, having permeated the two (interconnected) fields of academia and literature where it remained for a long time uncontested. While the growing body of empirical scholarship in Translation Studies is certainly beginning to challenge the arbitrariness of this discourse, it is likely that the 'new equal improves' doxa of the literary field will endure. There, it has become integrated into hierarchical struggles, and is exploited frequently by publishers and translators as a self-legitimizing and self-aggrandizing strategy. As Bourdieu remarks, 'the dominant classes have an interest in defending the integrity of doxa' (1977: 169), and so, for as long as this assumption is widely held and effectively defended, it will continue to be harnessed in the interests of status and of sales.

It is thus clear that (re)translation is as much a socially and a culturally embedded phenomenon as it is a textualized one. Indeed, the rivalry promoted by doxa is indicative of the logic of challenge which shapes the literary field as a whole, and which determines when (re)translations are produced and by whom, as well as how they are promoted and received. However, not all challenges are played out along such overt lines. Instead, any survey of how (re) translations behave and interact within a given literary field should always be mindful of strategic attempts to remain disengaged from the fray, as a means of circumventing censure or of obscuring the very game itself, and therefore the other players. In other instances, the challenge may not be centred on the content of the (re)translations per se, but rather on their physical format or the symbolic capital of their producers (translator, preface-writer, etc.), while a (re)translation which occupies a position presumed to be secure may deem itself (erroneously) to be beyond challenge. Furthermore, struggles are not necessarily confined to interactions between versions of the same source text; (re)translations may vie for visibility against other (re)translations of any text from an author's body of works, or against other paratextual and textual material which is bound inside the same volume of work. Nor can temporal restrictions be placed on the capacity of retranslations to rival each other since position-taking in the literary field is contingent on the history of the same. In this sense, the past is present in the present, and any former (re)translation can theoretically exert an influence on the configuration of the field at any moment, rendering Pym's (1998) notion of the passive retranslation redundant.

Retranslation has thus far been conceptualized as a fragmented phenomenon, with each text acting independently from, or against, other texts. However, by enlarging the frame of reference to include the accumulated history of a given corpus of (re)translations, a new dimension is added to the conceptual map. This new, broader optic reveals differentiated patterns of behaviour which appear, in this particular instance, to be dependent on the canonical status of the source text. Where the original work has been legitimized as a classic, retranslation can assume a rejuvenating role which staves off banalization. Where the original work occupies a more uncertain canonical position, retranslation may have an adverse effect, compounding its outmodedness and eroding its symbolic capital.

Retranslation, interpretation and genetic criticism

In light of the findings that retranslation is protean, unbounded and inexplicable in teleological terms, a paradigm shift is needed to better conceptualize the manifold modulations that can occur within the textual and contextual complexities of the phenomenon. The first step towards this shift might be as follows. Rather than conceive of (re)translations in the restrictive terms of textual proximity, these multiples of one should be viewed as instantiations of the interpretive potential of the source text. For there can be no definitive reading of the original, no singular path to restoration if we understand all texts to be unfinished, as Charles does: 'the text is not totalizable, for the pure and simple reason that it never ceases to be modified through reading, and that this very instability is constitutive' (1995: 383, my translation). With each reading and each (re)translation, the source text is pluralized and one new and possible text comes to light. In this sense, it is the impermanence of the original, and not the deficiency of translation, which gives impulse to the reiterative act of retranslation.

Such emphasis on the unfinished leads us to the discipline of genetic criticism which has been described as 'contemporaneous with an aesthetic of the possible' (Contat et al. 1996: 2) and which focuses on the '*avant-texte*, everything – drafts, sketches, outlines etc. – that comes before the published text' (Contat et al. 1996: 2, original emphasis). Specifically, this avant-texte, as a privileged window onto the development of the writing process, 'allows us to be present at the birth of the motivations, strategies and metamorphoses of writing' (de Biasi 1996: 29). Of interest, therefore, are the transformations and mutations which precede the moment where a text becomes (more or less) fixed in its published form. If we then reverse or mirror this logic, posterior retranslations are comparable to avant-textes since they too are a series of re-workings and metamorphoses wherein various motivations and strategies can be pinpointed.

This critical analogy between the avant-texte and translation has already been drawn by Scott who observes that the 'translator transforms the text of the ST into an *avant-texte* (draft), transforms the text back into a process of writing [...]. [This transformation] "unfinishes" the ST, multiplies its possibilities of being' (2006: 107). However, while Scott acknowledges the value of the genetic model for Translation Studies which has 'invested heavily in a theory and analytic methodology based on the objective of a single-version translation', its applicability is rather restricted to accounting for a translator 'constrained to produce, say, six versions' (2006: 116). Heuristically, the scope of this multiple-component framework is broader still, presenting as it does the opportunity to incorporate any number of retranslations, not simply by the same person, but by different translators and across different periods of time, under the banner of the avant-texte.

The very lexicon of genetic criticism implies a parallel with the study of retranslations, with de Biasi pointing to the 'deletions, [...] additions, missing fragments, multiplicity of versions, contradictions between these versions' (1996: 100) as the material traces or clues in manuscripts that facilitate a new, more involved reading of the work as a whole. The fluid mutability of the rough draft allows for a comparative viewpoint on to the unfolding process of creation, rather than on the end result, in the same way as a comparative study of a corpus of (re)translations brings to light how the potentiality of the source text has been exploited in non-finalist terms. Furthermore, Ferrer states that textual material is 'altered or disrupted by the slightest addition to the represented universe. This is why it is undoubtedly necessary to consider that the different versions, even those which are very *close*, always reflect different worlds' (1998: 27, my translation and emphasis). Indeed, it is this notion of 'different worlds', or of different modalities or degrees of existence which can help inform our framing of retranslations; rather than entities which cooperate through time to restore the linguistic or the cultural closeness of the ST, they are individual and different worlds, albeit rotating around the same axis, but worlds which have wavering interpretations of the meanings, the style, the structure of the ST. However, the analysis is not confined to the text itself; genetic critics also attempt to discern 'the influence of external social, economic, and cultural circumstances on the text' (Deppman et al. 2004: 5), thereby recognizing that texts will often bear the mark of the conditions in which they were born.

Genetic criticism, with what de Biasi terms its 'multidimensional conception of textuality' (1996: 59), thus offers a new paradigm for the study of retranslation that is richer and less rigid than any history as progress model. The emphasis placed on metamorphoses and instability, on finding clues as to interpretative processes and external pressures, and on the world of possibilities that opens up in the avant-texte can surely serve as an antidote to universalist assumptions, revealing in turn the transformative potentiality inherent in retranslation. Consequently, the pattern that best fits retranslation is one of possible worlds radiating outwards from the source text, some reflected darkly and others with clarity, some replete and others lacking, but always with the process to be begun again.

Notes

Introduction

1 The term 'retranslation' has also been used in relation to acts of relay translation, that is translation which is effected through an intermediary language (e.g. from Sinhalese, via Portuguese, into English). In addition, 'retranslation' is sometimes used to designate retro-translation, that is the translation of a text into a given TL, and then back again into the SL (see Gambier 1994: 413). However, 'retranslation' in this book will be restricted to the concept of the repeated translation of a given work into a given language.

Chapter 1

1 Most of the following section originally appeared as part of an article in *Essays in French Literature and Culture* (Deane-Cox 2012) and is reproduced with the kind permission of the publishers.

Chapter 2

1 Parts of this chapter have already appeared in an article in *Essays in French Literature and Culture* (Deane-Cox 2012) and have been reproduced here with the kind permission of the publishers.

Chapter 4

1 Capitalization will be used throughout for those lexicogrammatical terms which are used in a specific context in SFG, in opposition to any general usage they may also have.
2 This argument against point of view is well rehearsed in narratology; see, for example, Bal 1985; Rimmon-Kenan 2002; Nelles 1990; Nünning 1990; O'Neill 1992.

References

Abrams, D. (2013), 'Do We Need So Many Re-translations of Classics?', *Publishing Perspectives* [online]. Available at: http://publishingperspectives.com/2013/11/do-we-need-so-many-re-translations-of-classics/ [Accessed 19 December 2013].

Adams, J.R.R. (1987), 'Irish Booklore: Simms and M'Intyre: Creators of the Parlour Library', *The Linen Hall Review*, 4(2): 12–14.

Anon. (1842), 'George Sand', *The Mirror of Literature, Amusement and Instruction*, 1(25), June: 395–8.

———. (1843), 'Œuvres Complètes de George Sand', *The Foreign and Colonial Quarterly Review*, 1(2), April: 478–508.

———. (1847a), 'Book Review', *Literary Gazette*, 1588, June: 468.

———. (1847b), 'Fiction', *The Critic*, 6(143), September: 197.

———. (1847c), 'George Sand', *Howitt's Journal of Literature and Popular Progress*, March: 128–30.

———. (1847d), 'Literary Notices', *Howitt's Journal of Literature and Popular Progress*, 2, July: 119.

———. (1847e), 'Marie', *The Examiner*, 2053, July: 432.

———. (1847f), 'New Novels', *The Athenaeum*, 762, July: 762–3.

———. (1847g), 'Second Notice', *Howitt's Journal of Literature and Popular Progress*, 3, July: 317–18.

———. (1847h), 'The Old Convents of Paris', *The Critic*, 6(145), October: 230.

———. (1847i), 'The Old Convents of Paris', *The Athenaeum*, 1051, December: 1295–7.

———. (1848a), 'Advertisement', *The Athenaeum*, 1088, September: 894.

———. (1848b), 'Fiction', *The Critic*, 7(179), September: 382.

———. (1848c), 'Memoir of George Sand', in G. Sand (ed.), *The Devil's Pool*, London: H.G. Clarke.

———. (1848d), 'The Literary Examiner', *The Examiner*, 2086, January: 51.

———. (1849), 'Advertisement', *The Examiner*, 2177, October: 672.

———. (1850), 'Advertisement', *The Critic*, 9(210), January: 2.

———. (1851), 'George Sand', *Reynold's Miscellany of Romance, General Literature, Science and Art*, 6(152), June: 317.

———. (1853), 'George Sand', *Reynold's Miscellany of Romance, General Literature, Science and Art*, 11(280), November: 261.

———. (1858), 'George Sand', *The National Review*, 11, January: 37–69.

———. (1862), 'Les Misérables', *The Quarterly Review*, 112(224), October: 271–306.

———. (1876), 'George Sand', *The Pall Mall Gazette*, 3530, June: 71–2.

——. (1877), 'George Sand', *Blackwood's Edinburgh Magazine*, 121(735), January: 70–93.

——. (1886), 'Novels of the Week', *The Athenaeum*, October: 428–30.

——. (1895), 'J.M. Dent & Co.'s New Books', *The Pall Mall Magazine*, 7(32), December: 14.

——. (1911), 'Biographical Note', in G. Sand (ed.), *The Devil's Pool and François the Waif*, London: Everyman's Library.

——. (1930), 'Black Magic', *The Bookman*, 78(463), April: 66–7.

——. (1959), 'World's Classics for Christmas', *The Guardian*, 27 November: 14.

——. (1966), 'Front Matter', in G. Sand (ed.), *The Devil's Pool*, London and Glasgow: Blackie.

——. (2005a), 'Andrew Brown Biographical Note', in G. Sand (ed.), *The Devil's Pool*, London: Hesperus Press.

——. (2005b), 'Back Cover', in G. Sand (ed.), *The Devil's Pool*, London: Hesperus Press.

——. (2005c), 'Victoria Glendinning Biographical Note', in G. Sand (ed.), *The Devil's Pool*, London: Hesperus Press.

Arnoux-Farnoux, L. (2010), 'Traduire et retraduire Cavafis, ou les métamorphoses de Protée', in R. Kahn and C. Seth (eds), *La Retraduction*, Rouen and Le Havre: Publications des Universités de Rouen et du Havre.

Auerbach, E. (1953), *Mimesis: The Representation of Reality in Western Literature*, tr. W. R. Trask, Princeton: Princeton University Press.

Baker, M. (1992), *In Other Words: A Coursebook on Translation*, London & New York: Routledge.

——. (2006), *Translation and Conflict: A Narrative Account*, London and New York: Routledge.

Bal, M. ([1985] 2009]), *Narratology: Introduction to the Theory of Narrative*, 3rd edition, Toronto: University of Toronto Press.

——. (2006), *A Mieke Bal Reader*, Chicago: University of Chicago Press.

Barnes, J. (2010), 'Writer's Writer and Writer's Writer's Writer', *London Review of Books*, 32(22), Available at:http://www.lrb.co.uk/v32/n22/julian-barnes/writers-writer-and-writers-writers-writer [Accessed 08 April 2014].

Béghain, V. (2011), '"A Dress of French Grey": Retraduire *Villette* de Charlotte Brontë, au risque du grisonnement', in E. Monti and P. Schnyder (eds), *Autour de la Retraduction: Perspectives Littéraires Européennes*, Paris: Orizons.

Bensimon, P. (1990), 'Présentation', *Palimpsestes*, 4: ix–xiii.

Berman, A. (1984), *L'épreuve de l'étranger*, Paris: Gallimard.

——. (1990), 'La retraduction comme espace de la traduction', *Palimpsestes*, 4: 1–7.

——. (1995), *Pour une critique des traductions: John Donne*, Paris: Gallimard.

——. (2000), 'Translation and the Trials of the Foreign', in L. Venuti (ed.), *The Translation Studies Reader*, London and New York: Routledge.

Bollack, J. (2010), 'Ouverture: Écriture et retraduction', in R. Kahn and C. Seth (eds), *La Retraduction*, Rouen and Le Havre: Publications des Universités de Rouen et du Havre.

Bopp, L. (1951), *Commentaire sur Madame Bovary*, Neuchâtel: Éditions de la Baconnière.

Bordas, É. (2006), 'Les histoires du terroir à propos des Légendes rustiques de George Sand', *Revue d'Histoire Littéraire de la France*, 106(1): 67–81.

Bosseaux, C. (2007), *How Does it Feel? Point of View in Translation*, Amsterdam and New York: Rodopi.

Bourdieu, P. (1977), *Outline of a Theory of Practice*, Cambridge: Cambridge University Press.

———. (1996), *The Rules of Art: Genesis and Structure of the Literary Field*, tr. S. Emanuel, Stanford: Stanford University Press.

Brisset, A. (2004), 'Retraduire ou le corps changeant de la connaissance sur l'historicité de la traduction', *Palimpsestes*, 15: 39–67.

Brooks, P. (1992), *Reading for the Plot: Design and Intention in Narrative*, Harvard: Harvard University Press.

Brown, A. (2005), 'Introduction', in G. Sand (ed.), *The Devil's Pool*, London: Hesperus Press.

Brownlie, S. (2006), 'Narrative Theory and Retranslation Theory', *Across Languages and Cultures*, 7(2): 145–70.

Burchfield, R.W. (ed.), (2004), *Fowler's Modern English Usage*, 3rd edition, New York: Oxford University Press.

Calvo, C. and Weber, J-J. (1998), *The Literature Workbook*, London: Routledge.

Canavaggio, J. (2010), 'Retraduire *Don Quichotte* pour la Pléiade', in R. Kahn and C. Seth (eds), *La Retraduction*, Rouen and Le Havre: Publications des Universités de Rouen et du Havre.

Carter, R. and Stockwell, P. (eds) (2008), *The Language and Literature Reader*, London: Routledge.

Casanova, P. (2002), 'Consécration et accumulation de capital littéraire: La traduction comme échange inégal', *Actes de la recherche en sciences sociales*, 1: 7–20.

———. (2004), *The World Republic of Letters*, tr. M. B. DeBevoise, Cambridge, MA: Harvard University Press.

Cellier, L. (1999), 'Préface and Dossier', in G. Sand (ed.), *La Mare au diable*, Paris: Gallimard.

Charles, M. (1995), *Introduction à l'étude des textes*, Paris: Éditions du Seuil.

Chatman, S. (1978), *Story and Discourse: Narrative Structure in Fiction and Film*, Ithaca: Cornell University Press.

Chesterman, A. (2000), 'A Causal Model for Translation Studies', in M. Olohan (ed.), *Intercultural Faultlines*, Manchester: St Jerome.

———. (2004), 'Hypotheses about Translation Universals', in G. Hansen, K. Malmkjaer and D. Gile (eds), *Claims, Changes and Challenges in Translation Studies*, Amsterdam: Benjamins.

———. (2006), 'Questions in the Sociology of Translation', in J. Ferreira Duarte, A. Assis Rosa and T.Seruya (eds), *Translation Studies at the Interface of Disciplines*, Amsterdam: Benjamins.

Chevrel, Y. (2010), 'Introduction: La retraduction – und kein Ende', in R. Kahn and C. Seth (eds), *La Retraduction*, Rouen and Le Havre: Publications des Universités de Rouen et du Havre.

Child, H.H. (1911), 'Everyman's Eleventh Fifty', *Times Literary Supplement*, September: 339.

Classe, O. (ed.), (2000), *The Encyclopedia of Literary Translation into English*, London: Fitzroy Dearborn Publishers.

Contat, M., Hollier, D., Neefs, J. and Waters, A. (1996), 'Editors' Preface', *Drafts: Yale French Studies*, 89: 1–5.

Cook, M.G. (1928), 'Little Fadette', *Times Literary Supplement*, November: 828.

Croker, J. (1836), 'French Novels', *Quarterly Review*, 56, April: 65–131.

Cronin, M. (1998) 'The Cracked Looking Glass of Servants: Translation and Minority Languages in a Global Age', *The Translator: Studies in Intercultural Communication*, 4(2): 145–62.

Crystal, D. (2005), *Dictionary of Linguistics and Phonetics*, 5th edition, Oxford: Blackwell Publishers.

Culler, J. (1974), *Flaubert: The Uses of Uncertainty*, London: Elek Books Ltd.

Deane-Cox, S. (2012), 'The Framing of a Belle Infidèle: Paratexts, retranslations and *Madame Bovary*', *Essays in French Literature and Culture*, 49: 79–96.

de Biasi, P.-M. (1996), 'What Is a Literary Draft? Toward a Functional Typology of Genetic Documentation', *Drafts: Yale French Studies*, 89: 26–58.

Defaye, T. (1998), *Gustave Flaubert, 'Madame Bovary'*, Rosny-sous-Bois: Bréal.

de Gaultier, J. (1921), *Le Bovarysme*, Paris: Mercure de France.

del Lungo, A. (2009), '*Seuils*, Vingt Ans Après: Quelques pistes pour l'étude du paratexte après Genette', *Littérature*, 155: 98–111.

Deppman, J., Ferrer, D. and Groden, M. (2004), *Genetic Criticism: Texts and Avant-Textes*, Philadelphia: University of Pennsylvania Press.

Desmidt, I. (2009), '(Re)translation Revisited', *Meta: journal des traducteurs / Meta: Translators' Journal*, 54(4): 669–83.

Didier, B. (1994), 'Société rurale, société urbaine chez George Sand', *Cahiers de l'Association internationale des études francaises*, 46: 69–92.

——. (1998), *George Sand écrivain: 'Un grand fleuve d'Amérique'*, Paris: Presses Universitaires de France.

Du-Nour, M. (1995), 'Retranslations of Children's Books as Evidence of Changes of Norms', *Target*, 7(2): 327–46.

Dutheil de la Rochère, M.H. (2011), 'Les métamorphoses de Cendrillon: Étude comparative de deux traductions anglaises du conte de Perrault', in E. Monti and P. Schnyder (eds), *Autour de la Retraduction: Perspectives Littéraires Européennes*, Paris: Orizons.

Eggins, S. (2004), *Introduction to Systemic Functional Linguistics*, 2nd edition, London & New York: Continuum.

Even-Zohar, I. (1990), 'Polysystem Theory', *Poetics Today*, 11(1): 9–26.

Ferrer, D. (1998), 'Le matériel et le virtuel: Du paradigme indiciaire à la logique de mondes possibles', in M. Contat and D. Ferrer (eds), *Pourquoi la critique génétique? Méthodes, théories*, Paris: CNRS Éditions.

Ferry, A. (2010), 'Quelle traduction française pour la *Penthésilée* de Kleist après Julien Gracq?' in R. Kahn and C. Seth (eds), *La Retraduction*, Rouen and Le Havre: Publications des Universités de Rouen et du Havre.

Flaubert, G. (1857/1971), *Madame Bovary*, Paris: Garnier Frères.

——. (1886), *Madame Bovary*, tr. Eleanor Marx-Aveling, London: Vizetelly & Co.

——. (1926a), *Correspondance, Nouvelle Édition Augmentée*, 1e série, Paris: Conard.

——. (1926b), *Correspondance, Nouvelle Édition Augmentée*, 2e série, Paris:Conard.

——. (1927a), *Correspondance, Nouvelle Édition Augmentée*, 3e série, Paris: Conard.

——. (1927b), *Correspondance, Nouvelle Édition Augmentée*, 4e série, Paris: Conard.

——. (1929), *Correspondance, Nouvelle Édition Augmentée*, 5e série, Paris: Conard.

——. (1930a), *Correspondance, Nouvelle Édition Augmentée*, 6e série, Paris: Conard.

——. (1930b), *Correspondance, Nouvelle Édition Augmentée*, 7e série, Paris: Conard.

——. (1905), *Madame Bovary*, tr. Henry Blanchamp, London: Greening & Co.

——. (1928), *Madame Bovary*, tr. J. Lewis May, London: J. Lane Bodley Head.

——. (1948), *Madame Bovary*, tr. Gerard Hopkins, London: Hamish Hamilton.

——. (1950), *Madame Bovary*, tr. Alan Russell, Harmondsworth: Penguin.

——. (1957), *Madame Bovary*, tr. Francis Steegmuller, New York: Modern Library.

——. (1959), *Madame Bovary*, tr. Gerard Hopkins, Oxford: Oxford University Press.

——. (1992), *Madame Bovary*, tr. Geoffrey Wall, Harmondsworth: Penguin.

——. (2007), *Madame Bovary*, tr. Margaret Mauldon, Oxford: Oxford University Press.

——. (2010), *Madame Bovary*, tr. Lydia Davis, New York: Viking Press.

——. (2011), *Madame Bovary*, tr. Adame Thorpe, London: Vintage.

Fludernik, M. (1994), 'Second-person Narrative as a Test Case for Narratology: The Limits of Realism', *Style*, 28(3): 445–77.

Fowler, R. (1996), *Linguistic Criticism*, Oxford: Oxford University Press.

France, P. (2006), 'French', in P. France and K. Haynes (eds), *The Oxford History of Literary Translation in English*, Oxford: Oxford University Press.

Frawley, W. (1984), 'Prolegomenon to a Theory of Translation', in W. Frawley (ed.), *Translation: Literary, Linguistic and Philosophical Perspectives*, Newark: University of Delaware Press.

Gambier, Y. (1994), 'La retraduction, retour et détour', *Meta: journal des traducteurs*, 39(3): 413–17.

Genette, G. (1966), *Figures I*, Paris: Éditions du Seuil.

——. (1980), *Narrative Discourse: An Essay in Method*, tr. J.E. Lewin, Ithaca: Cornell University Press.

——. (1987), *Seuils*, Paris: Éditions du Seuil.

——. (1997), *Paratexts: Thresholds of Interpretation*, tr. J.E. Lewin, Cambridge: Cambridge University Press.

Gentzler, E. (2001), *Contemporary Translation Theories*, 2nd edition, Clevedon: Multilingual Matters.

Glendinning, V. (2005), 'Foreword', in G. Sand, *The Devil's Pool*, London: Hesperus Press.

Goethe, J. W. von (1992), 'Translations', in R.Schulte and J. Biguenet (eds), *Theories of Translation: An Anthology of Essays from Dryden to Derrida*, Chicago: University of Chicago Press.

Godwin-Jones, R. (1979), 'The Representation of Economic Reality in George Sand's Rural Novels', *Studies in the Literary Imagination*, 12(2): 53–60.

Gouanvic, J-M. (1997), 'Translation and the Shape of Things to Come: The Emergence of American Science Fiction in Post-War France', *The Translator*, 3(2): 123–32.

——. (1999), *Sociologie de la traduction: La science fiction américaine dans l'espace culturel français des années 50*, Arras: Artois Université Presses.

——. (2002), 'The Stakes of Translation in Literary Fields', *Across Languages and Cultures*, 3(2): 159–168.

——. (2005), 'A Bourdieusian Theory of Translation, or the Coincidence of Practical Instances: Field, "Habitus", Capital and "Illusio"', *The Translator* 11(2): 147–66.

Gramley, S. and Pätzold, K.-M. (2004), *A Survey of Modern English*, 2nd edition, London: Routledge.

Haig, S. (1986), *Flaubert and the Gift of Speech*, Cambridge: Cambridge University Press.

Hale, T. (2006), 'Readers and Publishers of Translations in Britain', in P. France and K. Haynes (eds), *The Oxford History of Literary Translation in English*, Oxford: Oxford University Press.

Halliday, M.A.K. (1971), 'Linguistic Function and Literary Style: An Enquiry into the Language of William Golding's "The Inheritors"', in S. Chatman(ed.), *Literary Style: A Symposium*, New York: Oxford University Press.

——. (1994), *Introduction to Functional Grammar*, 2nd edition, London: Arnold.

—— and Matthiessen, C.M.I.M. (2004), *An Introduction to Functional Grammar*, 3rd edition, London: Arnold

Hamilton, J. F. (1978) 'From Art to Nature in George Sand's *La Mare au Diable*', in P. Crant (ed.), *French Literature and the Arts*, Columbia: University of South Carolina Press.

Hanna, S.F. (2005), 'Hamlet Lives Happily Ever After in Arabic: The Genesis of the Field of Drama Translation in Egypt', *The Translator*, 11(2): 167–92.

——. (2006), *Towards a Sociology of Drama Translation: a Bourdieusian Perspective on Translations of Shakespeare's Great Tragedies in Egypt*, Unpubl. PhD Diss., the University of Manchester.

Hatim, B. and I. Mason (1990), *Discourse and the Translator*, London and New York: Longman.

——. (1997), *The Translator as Communicator*, London and New York: Routledge.

Hays, M.M. (1847), 'Literary Notice', *Howitt's Journal of Literature and Popular Progress*, 2, July: 88.

Heath, S. (1992), *Gustave Flaubert, Madame Bovary*, Cambridge: Cambridge University Press.

Heilbron, J. and Sapiro, G. (2002), 'La traduction littéraire, un objet sociologique', *Actes de la recherche en sciences sociales*, 144: 3–5.

Hermans, T. (1996), 'The Translator's Voice in Translated Narrative', *Target*, 8(1): 23–48.

——. (1999a), 'Some Concluding Comments on the Debates and the Responses', in C. Schaeffner (ed.), *Translation and Norms*, Clevedon: Multilingual Matters.

——. (1999b), *Translation in Systems*, Manchester: St Jerome.

Herschberg-Pierrot, A. (1993), *Stylistique de la prose*, Paris: Belin.

Hewson, L. (2011), *An Approach to Translation Criticism:* Emma *and* Madame Bovary *in Translation*, Amsterdam and Philadelphia: John Benjamins.

Holbrook, J. (1928), 'Flaubert in English', *The Bookman*, 75(447), December: 202.

Hopkins, G. (1959), 'Foreword', in G. Flaubert (ed.), *Madame Bovary*, Oxford: Oxford University Press.

House, J. (1997), *Translation Quality Assessment. A Model Revisited.* Tübingen: Gunter Narr Verlag.

Huss, R. (1977), 'Some Anomalous Uses of the Imperfect and the Status of Action in Flaubert', *French Studies*, 31(2): 139–48.

Inghilleri, M. (2005), 'The Sociology of Bourdieu and the Construction of the "Object" in Translation and Interpreting Studies', *The Translator*, 11(2): 125–45.

Jahn, M. (2007), 'Focalization', in D. Herman (ed.), *The Cambridge Companion to Narrative*, Cambridge: Cambridge University Press.

Jakubowska-Cichon, J. (2011), 'Le portrait vocal de la mère dans les traductions polonaises de *L'Amant* de Marguerite Duras', in E. Monti and P. Schnyder (eds), *Autour de la Retraduction: Perspectives Littéraires Européennes*, Paris: Orizons.

James, C. (2004), 'No Way, Madame Bovary', *The Atlantic Monthly*, 294(3), October: 175–84.

Jaubert, A. (1990), *La Lecture pragmatique*, Paris: Hachette.

Jurgrau, T. (1991), 'Critical Introduction', in T. Jurgrau (ed.), *Story of My Life: The Autobiography of George Sand: A Group Translation*, Albany: State University of New York Press.

Kahn, R. (2010), 'Proust en allemande: « Noch einmal? » A propos d'une retraduction récente', in R. Kahn and C. Seth (eds), *La Retraduction*, Rouen and Le Havre: Publications des Universités de Rouen et du Havre.

—— and C. Seth (eds) (2010), *La Retraduction*, Rouen and Le Havre: Publications des Universités de Rouen et du Havre.

Kane, R. (2012), 'Book of a Lifetime: Madame Bovary, By Gustave Flaubert', *The Independent*, 28 April, Available at: http://www.independent.co.uk/arts-entertainment/books/reviews/book-of-a-lifetime-madame-bovary-by-gustave-flaubert-7682249.html [Accessed 04 June 2013].

Kapp, Y. (1976), *Eleanor Marx, Volume 2: The Crowded Years, 1884–1898*, London: Lawrence and Wishart.

Kennard, N.H. (1886), 'Gustave Flaubert and George Sand', *Nineteenth Century: A Monthly Review*, 20(117), November: 693–708.

Kerr, P. (2011), 'Scotsman Books of the Year', *The Scotsman*, 3 December, Available at: http://www.scotsman.com/the-scotsman/books/scotsman-books-of-the-year-recommendations-from-writers-including-val-mcdermid-ali-smith-and-alexander-mccall-smith-1-1990668 [Accessed 04 June 2013].

Kujamäki, P. (2001), 'Finnish Comet in German Skies: Translation, Retranslation and Norms', *Target*, 13(1): 43–71.

LaCapra, D. (1982), *Madame Bovary on Trial*, Ithaca, N.Y.: Cornell University Press.

Ladmiral, J.-R. (2011), 'Nous autres traductions, nous savons maintenant que nous sommes mortelles…', in E. Monti and P. Schnyder (eds), *Autour de la Retraduction: Perspectives Littéraires Européennes*, Paris: Orizons.

Lahire, B. (2003), 'From the Habitus to an Individual Heritage of Dispositions. Towards a Sociology at the Level of the Individual', *Poetics*, 31: 329–55.

Lane, B. (1988), 'Voyage et initiation dans La Mare au Diable', *Études françaises*, 24(1): 71–83.

Laurent, N. (2001), *Initiation à la stylistique*, Paris: Hachette.

Lefevere, A. (1998), 'Translation Practice(s) and the Circulation of Cultural Capital: Some Aeneids in English', in S. Bassnettand A. Lefevere (eds), *Constructing Cultures. Essays on Literary Translation*, Clevedon and Philadelphia: Multilingual Matters.

Le Hir, Y. (1965), *Analyses Stylistiques*, Paris: Armand Colin.

Leuven-Zwart, K.M. van. (1989), 'Translation and Original: Similarities and Dissimilarities, I', *Target*, 1(2): 151–81.

——. (1990), 'Translation and Original: Similarities and Dissimilarities, II', *Target*, 2(1): 69–95.

Levinson, S.C. (1983), *Pragmatics*, Cambridge: Cambridge University Press.

Lloyd, R. (1990), *Madame Bovary*, London: Unwin Hyman Ltd.

Lyons, J. (1977), 'Deixis, Space and Time', *Semantics*, 2: 636–742.

Marx-Aveling, E. (1886), 'Introduction', in G. Flaubert (ed.), *Madame Bovary*, London: Vizetelly & Co.

Massardier-Kenney, F. (2004), 'Traduire Valvèdre', *George Sand Studies*, 23: 70–7.

May, J.L. (1928), 'Introduction', in G. Flaubert (ed.), *Madame Bovary*, London: Bodley Head.

McDonald, P.D. (1997), *British Literary Culture and Publishing Practice, 1880–1914*, Cambridge: Cambridge University Press.

Miles, H. (1929), 'A Note on "The Devil's Pool"', in G.Sand (ed.), *The Devil's Pool*, London: Scholartis Press.

Monti, E. (2011), 'Introduction: La retraduction, un état des lieux', in E. Monti and P. Schnyder (eds), *Autour de la Retraduction: Perspectives Littéraires Européennes*, Paris: Orizons.

——— and Schnyder, P. (eds), (2011), *Autour de la Retraduction: Perspectives Littéraires Européennes*, Paris: Orizons.

Mortier, D. (2010), 'La retraduction du *Cercle de craie caucasien* de Brecht: Une entreprise mystérieuse', in R. Kahn and C. Seth (eds), *La Retraduction*, Rouen and Le Havre: Publications des Universités de Rouen et du Havre.

Mumby, F.A. (1974), *Publishing and Bookselling*, 5th edition, London: Cape.

Munday, J. (1998), 'A computer-assisted approach to the analysis of translation shifts', *Meta: journal des traducteurs / Meta: Translators' Journal*, 43(4): 542–56.

———. (2002), 'Systems in Translation: Systemic Model for Descriptive Translation Studies', in T. Hermans (ed.), *Crosscultural Transgressions: Research Models in Translation Studies II: Historical and Ideological Issues*, Manchester: St Jerome.

———. (2007), 'Translation and Ideology: A Textual Approach', *The Translator*, 13(2): 195–217.

———. (2008), *Style and Ideology in Translation: Latin American Writing in English*, New York: Routledge.

——— (ed.) (2009), *The Routledge Companion to Translation Studies*, London and New York: Routledge.

Naginski, I.H. (1991), *George Sand: Writing for Her Life*, New Brunswick and London: Rutgers University Press.

Nelles, W. (1990), 'Getting Focalization into Focus', *Poetics Today*, 11: 363–82.

Newman, E. (1895), 'Gustave Flaubert', *The Fortnightly Review*, 58(348), December: 813.

Nieragden, G. (2002), 'Focalization and Narration: Theoretical and Terminological Refinements', *Poetics Today*, 23(4): 685–97.

Nünning, A. (1990), '"Point of view" oder "focalization"? Über einige Grundlagen und Kategorien konkurrierender Modelle der erzählerischen Vermittlung', *Literature in Wissenschaft und Unterricht*, 23: 249–68.

O'Driscoll, K. (2011), *Retranslation through the Centuries: Jules Verne in English*, Oxford, Bern, Berlin, Bruxelles, Frankfurt am Main, New York, Wien: Peter Lang.

O'Neill, P. (1992), 'Points of Origin: On Focalization in Narrative', *Canadian Review of Comparative Literature/Revue Canadienne de Littérature Comparée*, 19: 331–50.

Ould, H. (1929), 'English Versions', *The Bookman*, 76(454), July: 222–3.

OUP (2013), Oxford University Press Catalogue, Madame Bovary: Provincial Manners, Available at: http://ukcatalogue.oup.com/product/9780199535651.do#.Ua4Jypzzm1k [Accessed 04 June 2013].

Paloposki, O. and Koskinen, K. (2004), 'A Thousand and One Translations: Revisiting Retranslation', in G. Hansen, K. Malmkjaer and D. Gile (eds), *Claims, Changes and Challenges in Translation Studies*, Amsterdam: Benjamins.

———. (2010), 'Reprocessing Texts: The Fine Line Between Retranslating and Revising', *Across Languages and Cultures*, 11(1): 29–49.

Pascal, Roy. (1977), *The Dual Voice: Free Indirect Speech and Its Functioning in the Nineteenth-century European Novel*, Manchester: Manchester University Press.

Perruchot, C. (1975), 'Le style indirect libre et la question du sujet dans "Madame Bovary"', in C. Gothot-Mersch (ed.), *La Production du sens chez Flaubert*, Colloque de Cérisy, Paris: Union Générale d'Editions.

Ponsonby, M.E. (1901), 'George Eliot and George Sand', *Nineteenth Century and After, a Monthly Review*, 50(296): 607–16.

Powell, D. (1990), *George Sand*, Boston: Twayne Publishers.

Price, G. (1998), *A Comprehensive French Grammar*, 4th edition, Oxford: Blackwell Publishers.

Proust, M. (1971), *Contre Sainte-Beuve*, Paris: Editions Gallimard.

Pym, A. (1998), *A Method for Translation History*, Manchester: St Jerome.

Rhys, E. (1911), 'Introduction', in G. Sand (ed.), *The Devil's Pool*, London: J.M. Dent.

Riffaterre, M. (1990), 'Fear of Theory', *New Literary History*, 21(4): 921–38.

Rimmon-Kenan, S. (2002), *Narrative Fiction: Contemporary Poetics*, London: Routledge.

Roberts, M. (2003), 'Preface', in G.Flaubert (ed.), *Madame Bovary*, tr. G. Wall, Harmondsworth: Penguin.

Saintsbury, G. (1878), 'Gustave Flaubert', *Fortnightly Review*, 23(136), April: 575–95.

——. (1891), *Essays on French Novelists*, London: Percival.

Samoyault, T. (2010), 'Retraduire Joyce', in R. Kahn and C. Seth (eds), *La Retraduction*, Rouen and Le Havre: Publications des Universités de Rouen et du Havre.

Sand, G. (1846/1999), *La Mare au diable*, Paris: Gallimard.

——. (1847a), *Marie*, tr. Anon, London: Chapman & Hall.

——. (1847b), *The Haunted Marsh*, tr. Anon, London & Belfast: Simms & McIntyre.

——. (1848), *The Devil's Pool*, tr. Francis G. Shaw, London: H.G. Clarke.

——. (1883–1884), *Correspondance: 1812–1876*, Paris: Calmann Lévy.

——. (1895), *The Devil's Pool*, tr. Jane M. & Ellery Sedgwick, London: J.M. Dent.

——. (1929), *The Devil's Pool*, tr. Hamish Miles, London: Scholartis Press.

——. (1966), *The Devil's Pool*, tr. Antonia Cowan, Glasgow: Blackie & Co.

——. (2005), *The Devil's Pool*, tr. Andrew Brown, London: Hesperus Press.

Schiavi, G. (1996), 'There Is Always a Teller in a Tale', *Target*, 8(1): 1–21.

Schor, N. (1980), 'Details and Decadence: End-Troping in Madame Bovary', *SubStance*, 9(26): 27–35.

——. (1993), *George Sand and Idealism*, New York: Columbia University Press.

Scott, C. (2006), 'Translating the Literary: Genetic Criticism, Text Theory and Poetry', in S. Bassnett and P. Bush (eds), *The Translator as a Writer*, London: Continuum.

Seth, C. (2010), 'Adam Smith retraduit par Sophie de Condorcet', in R. Kahn and C. Seth (eds), *La Retraduction*, Rouen and Le Havre: Publications des Universités de Rouen et du Havre.

Shaw, F.G. (1847), 'To the Editors of Howitt's Journal', *Howitt's Journal of Literature and Popular Progress*, 2, July: 318.

Simeoni, D. (1998), 'The Pivotal Status of the Translator's *Habitus*', *Target*, 10(1): 1–39.

Simpson, P. (1993), *Language, Ideology and Point of View*, London: Routledge.

Somers, M.R. and Gibson, G.D. (1994), 'Reclaiming the Epistemological "Other": Narrative and the Social Construction of Identity', in C. Calhoun (ed.), *Social Theory and the Politics of Identity*, Oxford, UK, and Cambridge, USA: Blackwell.

St André, J. (2003), 'Retranslation as Argument: Canon Formation, Professionalization, and Rivalry in 19th Century Sinological Translation', *Cadernos de Tradução*, 11(1): 59–93.

Steiner, G. (1998), *After Babel: Aspects of Language and Translation*, 3rd edition, Oxford: Oxford University Press.

Susam-Sarajeva, Ş. (2003), 'Multiple-entry Visa to Travelling Theory: Retranslations of Literary and Cultural Theories', *Target*, 15(1): 1–36.

———. (2009), 'The Case Study Research Method in Translation Studies', *The Interpreter and Translator Trainer*, 3(1): 37–56.

Tahir- Gürçağlar, Ş. (2002), 'What Texts Don't Tell: The Uses of Paratexts in Translation Research', in T. Hermans (ed.), *Crosscultural Transgressions*, Manchester: St Jerome.

Thomson, P. (1972), 'George Sand and English Reviewers: The First Twenty Years', *The Modern Language Review*, 6(3), July: 501–16.

———. (1977), *George Sand and the Victorians: Her Influence and Reputation in Nineteenth-century England*, London and Basinkstoke: The Macmillan Press Ltd.

Thorpe, A. (2011a), 'A Note on the Translation', in G. Flaubert (ed.), *Madame Bovary*, London: Vintage.

———. (2011b), 'Madame Bovary: The Everest of Translation', *The Guardian*, 21 October, Available at: http://www.guardian.co.uk/books/2011/oct/21/translating-madame-bovary-adam-thorpe [Accessed 04 June 2013].

———. (2013), 'My Nights with Emma B', *Cardiff University Distinguished Lecture Series*, Available at: http://www.cardiff.ac.uk/dls/lecturers/adam-thorpe.html [Accessed 08 April 2014].

———. (2014a), *Adam Thorpe*, Available at: http://www.adamthorpe.net/ [Accessed 08 April 2014].

———. (2014b), 'Adam Thorpe', *Facebook*, Available at: https://www.facebook.com/adamthorpe.author [Accessed 08 April 2014].

Toolan, M. (1988), *Narrative: A Critical Linguistic Introduction*, London and New York: Routledge.

———. (2006), 'The "Irresponsibility" of FID', in P. Tammi and H. Tommola (eds), *FREE Language, INDIRECT Translation, DISCOURSE Narratology: Linguistic, Translatological and Literary-Theoretical Encounters of FID*, Tampere: Tampere University Press.

Topia, A. (1990), 'Finnegan's Wake: La traduction parasitée', *Palimpsestes*, 4: 45–59.

Toury, G. (1995), *Descriptive Translation Studies and Beyond*, Amsterdam and Philadelphia: John Benjamins.

Uspensky, B. (1973), *A Poetics of Composition*, Berkeley: University of California Press.

Venuti, L. (1995), *The Translator's Invisibility: A History of Translation*, London and New York: Routledge.

——. (2004), 'Retranslations: The Creation of Value', in K.M. Faull (ed.), *Translation and Culture*, Lewisburg: Bucknell University Press.

——. (2013), *Translation Changes Everything: Theory and Practice*, London and New York: Routledge.

Vinay, J.P. and Darbelnet, J. (1958), *Stylistique Comparée du français et de l'anglais*, Paris: Didier-Harrap.

Vincent, L. (1916), *La langue et le style rustiques de George Sand dans les romans champêtres*, Paris: É. Champion.

Vizetelly, E.A. (1904), *Émile Zola: Novelist and Reformer*, London: John Lane.

Wall, G. (1992), 'A Note on the Translation', in G. Flaubert (ed.), *Madame Bovary*, Harmondsworth: Penguin.

——. (2004), 'Retranslating Madame Bovary', *Palimpsestes*, 4: 93–8.

Waugh, A. (1930), 'The First Three Years', *Fortnightly Review*, November: 715.

Whitebrook, M. (2001), *Identity, Narrative and Politics*, London and New York: Routledge.

Williams, D.A. (1978), 'Generalizations in "Madame Bovary"', *Neophilologus*, 62: 492–503.

Wolf, M. (2007), 'Introduction: The Emergence of a Sociology of Translation', in M. Wolf and A. Fukari (eds), *Constructing a Sociology of Translation*, Amsterdam and Philadelphia: John Benjamins.

——. (2011), 'Mapping the Field: Sociological Perspectives on Translation', *International Journal of the Sociology of Language*, 207: 1–28.

—— and Fukari, A. (eds) (2007), *Constructing a Sociology of Translation*, Amsterdam and Philadelphia: John Benjamins.

Index

www.ingramcontent.com/pod-product-compliance
Lightning Source LLC
Chambersburg PA
CBHW071400100726
47908CB00004B/1045

* 9 7 8 1 4 7 4 2 7 5 4 7 7 *